Public Policy Analysis:
A Political Economy
Approach

Public Policy Analysis:

A Political Economy Approach

Kenneth N. Bickers

INDIANA UNIVERSITY

John T. Williams

INDIANA UNIVERSITY

HOUGHTON MIFFLIN COMPANY   BOSTON   NEW YORK

Editor-in-Chief: *Jean Woy*
Sponsoring Editor: *Mary Dougherty*
Development Editor: *Katherine Meisenheimer*
Project Editor: *Florence Kilgo*
Editorial Assistant: *Cecilia Molinari*
Senior Production/Design Coordinator: *Sarah Ambrose*
Senior Manufacturing Coordinator: *Sally Culler*
Marketing Manager: *Jay Hu*

Cover design: Harold Burch, NYC
Cover image: Harold Burch, NYC

Printed in the U.S.A.

Library of Congress Catalog Number: 00-133857

ISBN: 0-395-85263-3

123456789-BBS-04 03 02 01 00

Contents

Preface

GOALS OF THE BOOK

In our teaching careers, we have taught dozens of courses and thousands of students, from first-year college students to advanced graduate students. Without a doubt, the subject area that we most enjoy teaching is American public policy. Part of the reason is that the subject matter is always changing, always fresh, and always close at hand. The main reason, however, is that students become enthusiastic about the learning process when they are able to see and feel the connections between their lives, the ideas that we as instructors are trying to convey, and the big, perennial issues that have animated the thinking of educated people for centuries.

Over the years, we have grown dissatisfied with the textbooks that were available for use in undergraduate public policy courses. We resorted to assigning a hodgepodge of book chapters, journal articles, and conference papers. Unfortunately, students too often found these readings to be abstract and inaccessible, because these readings assumed an advanced understanding of the subject area and required prior knowledge of sophisticated mathematical concepts.

This textbook is designed to introduce undergraduate students to public policy analysis utilizing the new political economy approach—the approach that has swept through graduate policy programs over the past couple of decades. The political economy approach to policy analysis asks how individual values and preferences get translated into collective processes and outcomes. This approach is thus directly related to debates about the meaning and operation of democratic systems; it is centrally concerned with how collective enterprises, from neighborhoods to nations, operate; and it treats the domain of government and the domain of markets as two sides of the same coin, inasmuch as both are instruments by which groups of individuals make collective choices.

Our goals in writing this textbook have been fourfold. First, we have sought to communicate the central insight of the political economy approach to public policy analysis. This insight, which we introduce in Chapter 1 and discuss at length in subsequent chapters, stems from the fundamental interplay between individual preferences and collective outcomes. In complex societies layers of interrelationships are at work, in which the efforts of individuals to achieve their goals often produce collective outcomes that are at odds with the preferences of those same individuals. This tension is inevitably at the heart of every policy debate. Indeed, for us the ongoing question of how to resolve this tension is a large part of what makes politics so interesting.

Second, we have tried to show how this tension between individual preferences and collective outcomes is tied to fundamental issues about democracy. The political economy approach is particularly useful in highlighting the trade-offs between different types of democratic institutions. Our argument is that the tension between the representation of individual preferences and the capacity of policymaking institutions to make and implement public policy choices is inherent to democracies. Chapters 2 and 3 are centrally concerned with these issues of democratic governance.

Third, one of our primary goals has been to describe the range of institutions that can be used for translating individual preferences into collective policy choices. For many people, the national government springs to mind first as the primary vehicle for implementing collective choices. But there are alternatives both within and beyond government. We look at the whole array of governments in the United States, which, in addition to the federal government, includes states, local governments, school districts, and special districts. Markets, too, serve as vehicles for aggregating individual preferences into collective outcomes, and thus are important instruments of collective choice in a democratic society. We spend a considerable portion of the text discussing the relative strengths and weaknesses of governments and markets as institutions of collective action. Chapter 4 introduces the major categories of collective action problems. Chapters 5 through 7 weigh the pathologies of different institutions and their capacities for solving these problems.

Our fourth goal in writing this book has been to utilize the political economy approach in the analysis of public policies in the context of the American political system. To borrow a phrase from Daniel J. Boorstin, the "genius of American politics" derives in part from the richness of institutional mechanisms for collective action that exist in this country. With the conceptual tools of policy analysis, students are able to see that this richness offers possibilities for implementing reasonably efficient policies by selecting and combining institutional mechanisms to take advantage of the strengths of each.

This is the theme that underlies Chapters 8 through 12. Chapter 8 discusses the mixture of top-down and bottom-up approaches to policymaking in America. Chapter 9 offers ways of thinking about the components of public policies and how these are related to the kinds of politics that often surround policy debates. Chapter 10 focuses on the role of bureaucracies in implementing policies and the possibilities of obtaining efficient bureaucratic implementation in the American context. Chapters 11 and 12 introduce techniques for evaluating and analyzing public policies and discuss how these are used in the day-to-day practice of policymaking in this country. Chapter 11 introduces techniques for analyzing policies that have been proposed for adoption. Chapter 12 introduces techniques that can be used to evaluate existing policies.

We finish the book with Chapter 13, which outlines some ideas about designing institutions to make sound public policies. We identify several sets of important criteria for designing institutions of public policy.

USES OF THIS TEXT

This book is designed for use as the primary textbook in undergraduate public policy courses. Instructors of such courses will find the frequent inclusion of case material in the inset boxes to be of use in stimulating discussion among students. The material in these boxes has been selected to highlight important concepts that are introduced in each chapter and to provide a starting point for discussing substantive policy issues.

Some instructors may wish to spend more time discussing specific policy topics. In those cases, a secondary textbook that deals with substantive policy cases may be assigned. Additionally, instructors may want to assign articles from local or national newspapers or weekly newsmagazines. This will help students tie the ideas presented in the text to perennial policy problems. We have found this combination of cases, topical articles, and the conceptual material in this textbook useful in helping students see the connections between abstract classroom discussions and the issues that come up in their daily lives.

Other instructors may choose to use this book in conjunction with a traditional stage-theory text. An instructor combining these approaches will want to concentrate on Chapter 3 when discussing policy agendas and agenda control. Section III of the book (i.e., Chapters 4–7) will be helpful for students when covering policy formulation. Policy implementation in the American context is a key theme that runs through Chapters 8–10. The uses of policy evaluation, along with examples, are the subject of Chapters 11 and 12.

Another way to use this book is in a course that focuses on a particular policy area. For example, it would work well in a course on American social welfare policy, regulatory policy, or economic policy. In these courses, an instructor would focus on Chapter 1, the chapters in Section III, and Chapters 8, 9, and 12. These chapters deal most directly with the tension between individual preferences and collective action and the relative strengths and weaknesses of markets and governments for addressing this tension. Similarly, the book could be used in a course that focuses on ethics and public policy. For this purpose, the chapters on democracy and the linkages between public policies and democratic governance would be of particular usefulness. These chapters include the ones contained in Sections I and II, along with Chapters 4, 6, 8, and 9.

In sum, we believe that this book can play an important role in a variety of courses. We hope that students and instructors will find it useful and enlightening.

ACKNOWLEDGMENTS

Several people have provided valuable advice and suggestions in the evolution of the text. We would like to acknowledge, in particular, all of the students, both graduate and undergraduate, in our public policy courses. They have served, sometimes unwittingly, as guinea pigs when we experimented with ideas that ended up on these pages, as well as with ideas that were abandoned along the way.

We would also like to thank the many people in and around the Workshop in Political Theory and Policy Analysis at Indiana University. The Workshop has provided a fertile environment for the writing of this book and has, through the years, hosted a number of colloquia devoted to stages of this project. Among the many people at these colloquia, we would like to especially thank Elinor and Vincent Ostrom, the co-founders of the workshop, as well as Mike McGinnis, Jimmy Walker, Virginia Hettinger, Larry Schroeder, Roger Parks, Susan Baer, Mike Craw, Ron Lake, and Bill Laverty for valuable comments and suggestions. We would also like to thank John Witte, Director of the LaFollette Institute at the University of Wisconsin, for moderating the final colloquium on the book project and for his careful reading of the manuscript.

Mike Wolf provided invaluable assistance in researching the material for most of the boxes that appear in the book.

Many reviewers provided helpful comments on the book at various stages in its evolution. These include Nathaniel Beck of the University of California-San Diego, William Bianco of Pennsylvania State University, James C. Clinger-mayer of Northern Kentucky University, Brian Collins of Oklahoma Christian University, James Granato of Michigan State University, Wendy L. Hansen of the University of New Mexico, David Martindale, Robert T. Nakamura of the State University of New York-Albany, Matt Potoski of Iowa State University, John T. Scholz of the State University of New York-Stony Brook, Edella Schlager of the University of Arizona, Robert M. Stein of Rice University, Paul Teske of the State University of New York-Stony Brook, David J. Webber of the University of Missouri, and Celeste Williams of the Fort Worth Star-Telegram.

Finally, we would like to acknowledge the able assistance and support that we have received from our editors at Houghton Mifflin, including Paul Smith and Melissa Mashburn, both of whom have now moved on to other publishing houses, as well as Katherine Meisenheimer, the editor with whom we have worked most closely throughout the project, and Florence Kilgo, the production editor for the manuscript. As is always the case, responsibility for any errors or flawed ideas is not the responsibility of any of these people, but is ours.

K.N.B
J.T.W.

I

Introduction

1

A Political Economy Approach to Public Policy Analysis

INTRODUCTION

The first indications of a problem appeared just a few days before Christmas 1999. Residents living near the White River in central Indiana began to report fish breaking the surface and swimming in a drunken fashion. Soon fish were dying by the tens of thousands. Their carcasses began collecting on the river's banks. Eventually, more than 80 tons of dead fish would be collected from the shores of the river, along with an undetermined number of mammals and birds that fed on the dead and dying fish. Thousands of people living in the White River watershed were afraid to drink the water for fear that they too would become ill—or worse.[1] The scope of the potential public health emergency could have been staggering. Only 40 miles downstream from the source of the problem lies Indianapolis, the twelfth largest city in the United States, which draws 60 percent of its drinking water from the White River.

What had gone so terribly wrong? To this day, the exact cause of this fish kill is in dispute. The state agency that is responsible for regulating water quality in Indiana has focused its investigation on an automotive parts plant located in Anderson, Indiana. This plant denies responsibility. What is known is that there was a massive release of contaminants into the river about a week before Christmas. Among the contaminants was ammonia, a byproduct of untreated sewage; this fact initially caused investigators to suspect the municipal wastewater treatment plants along the river. Soon, however, investigators began to suspect an industrial pollutant. Untreated sewage would have affected all fish, but only bottom-feeding fish were being exterminated. Clearly, some sort of dangerous substance had been released into the river. To date, evidence has centered on a chemical used in the production of auto parts.[2]

Fortunately, the toxin dissipated before it contaminated the Indianapolis water supply. But this incident is not the first for the White River—or for many American rivers. In the past two decades, there have been 274 spills into the White River, with 26 resulting in fish kills. The worst was in 1976, when sewage dumped from wastewater treatment plants in Indianapolis killed 5 million fish over a stretch of river reaching almost to Illinois. Indeed, the U.S. Geological Survey has found that the White River, like many others, contains a witches' brew of toxic and dangerous substances, including agricultural pesticides, nitrates, lead, mercury, polychlorinated biphenyls (PCBs), damium, chromium, selenium, and zinc.[3]

This episode is an example of a **negative externality.** Externalities are consequences of actions borne by third parties. Residents along the White River watershed, unsuspecting fish, and wild animals that eat fish were all put at risk by actions to which they had not given their consent. Externalities are an inevitable part of living in societies. All of us, every day of our lives, create consequences that affect other people, from the exhaust and noise of the cars we drive, to the carbon dioxide that we exhale as we breathe, to the aesthetic benefits that we provide to our neighbors by not allowing empty soda or beer cans and broken furniture to accumulate outside our homes. Unfortunately, some externalities (called negative externalities), such as the escape of pollutants into a watershed, can put others at substantial risk. Some externalities may actually be lethal. Must we simply accept negative externalities simply because externalities are an inevitable component of life in human societies? Or are there measures that we can adopt to mitigate negative externalities and to encourage positive externalities?

This question is at the heart of this book. At the most fundamental level, the question that we ask in this book is how people can solve problems that are created when they seek to live together in human societies. Our objective is to help you think more carefully and incisively about the kinds of problems that emerge whenever human beings interact with one another—in neighborhoods, communities, municipalities, states, or nations, as well as across nations. We want to provide you with tools for analyzing public problems. We want to help you and others think about the options that are available to people acting together and trying to overcome the problems that arise in human enterprises. This book explores many of the institutional solutions that can be, and have been, devised for problems often encountered as people seek to advance their common goals.

In essence, this book is about public problems and solutions to public problems. This book is thus intended to spur what, in the American political theory tradition, is often called **practical political reasoning.**[4] This type of reasoning takes the view that the activities of people in collective enterprises—such as churches, schools, business firms, markets, government agencies, political communities, and the like—exist to accomplish important individual and social purposes. The ways that people behave and interact within these enterprises reflect collective choices for accomplishing these purposes. Practical political reasoning is concerned with the effort to understand how institutions contribute to collective purposes and to find better ways to accomplish these purposes.

Practical political reasoning is thus the process of bringing intelligence and rationality to the task of trying to improve on the practice of collective enterprises. In short, it is policy analysis viewed in the broadest sense. It is the analysis of the institutional arrangements and practices that structure the actions of individuals as they seek to live their lives in human communities.

POLITICAL ECONOMY APPROACH

The approach to practical political reasoning that we explore throughout this book is known as the **political economy approach.** This approach to policy analysis is based on three key assumptions: (1) human behavior is purposive, (2) people's behavior is shaped by incentives and constraints, and (3) people are intelligent and creative.

Key Assumptions

The first assumption of the political economy approach is that human behavior is **purposive**—that people do things to advance their own goals and objectives. What this means is that people have **preferences** about what kinds of lives they want to live, what sorts of goals they want to accomplish, and what goods and services they want to enjoy. Preferences are the things or activities that each person favors or likes. They give pleasure or satisfaction. One person may want to be a doctor and another, a social worker. One person may derive pleasure from listening to classical music and another, from trading stocks and bonds. Individuals may have dozens of preferences, from the kinds of foods they like to eat at particular times of the day or seasons of the year, to the kinds of hobbies that give them pleasure, to the personal attributes that they look for when trying to find a husband or wife. Not all of these preferences can be met simultaneously. In fact, some preferences may have to be set aside in order for others to be met. For example, you may have enough money to eat out at a nice restaurant or to see a new movie, but not to do both. You'll have to decide which one is more important.

The multitude of preferences that individuals can hold creates sticky problems. Preferences of different people can conflict. For example, we all have been faced with the situation where we wanted to eat at one type of restaurant, but the people with us wanted to eat at a different type of restaurant. When faced with this situation, what were your options? **Persuasion** sometimes works. You may have been able to talk your friends into eating at the restaurant of your choice by giving them good reasons—the food would be better, the service quicker, the prices lower, or the location closer to your next destination. Other times **bargaining** may have worked. You may have agreed to go to the restaurant of their choosing next time, if they would agree to your choice this time. Perhaps you offered an incentive. You may have promised to buy their dinners or perhaps a round of drinks if they would go to the restaurant where you wanted to eat. Finally, sometimes **coercion** is used. Recall when you were a child. No doubt there were times when your family was going out to eat at a restaurant selected by your parents over your cries of protest. Perhaps you felt like a prisoner in the family automobile because your preferences were being ignored. Conflict among preferences means that sometimes we don't get our way.

The set of preferences held by an individual person can also have internal conflict. That is, as individuals we have to make tradeoffs among things that we value. You would like to obtain a college degree so that you can get a high-paying job after graduation, but you'd rather sleep in than go to class. You would like to go on a trip with friends during your spring break, but you need to work during the holiday to earn the money you need to pay your school expenses. Tradeoffs such as these are common. We make them daily when we make decisions about how to spend money. If you spend your money on a new pair of shoes, you no longer have it to spend on a new jacket. How you allocate your money among the various things that you want and need is one way to determine the strength of your preferences for different types of items. Problems occur, however, when some of the things for which you have a preference are unavailable because there are no properly functioning markets to provide you with the opportunity to purchase those things. You may have few options to make tradeoffs between eating at fast-food restaurants and eating herbicide-free foods at home, simply because it is difficult to ensure that the foods that you are buying are indeed herbicide-free. Likewise, you may have a preference for hiking and camping in unsoiled natural environments but be unable to realize that preference because you are unable to find parklands that are not overcrowded with hikers and campers. The problem, here, is not that you are unwilling to pay for the opportunity to enjoy herbicide-free foods or uncrowded parklands, but that these things are not being provided in sufficient quantities so that you can obtain them. Why some kinds of things that people value are underprovided is an important issue that we will look at later in this book.

The second assumption on which the political economy approach is based is that people's behavior is shaped by incentives and constraints. People generally prefer more of the things they value than less. Oftentimes incentives involve money, but they may involve other things, such as prestige, responsibility, or usefulness to society. At the same time, people cannot have everything they want, because they face constraints. Financial resources often are insufficient to permit buying the new car or the new clothes that a person has been eyeing. Talent to achieve excellence in basketball, piano playing, or the culinary arts may be woefully lacking. Training in a particular trade, such as law or medicine, may be costly and time consuming, and thus be beyond the reach of many who might want to have a career in that field.

From where do incentives and constraints come? **Incentives** are inducements. They are things that we want, either because they help us obtain other things that we want or because we value them for their own sake. A common incentive—though certainly not the only one—is money. Money allows us to purchase all sorts of things we want. The more money that we have, the more things we can purchase. Other incentives that operate like money are extra-credit points on exams, discounts on meals at restaurants, and rebates on clothing or other items after purchase at a department store. All these incentives help us obtain something that we value.

Some incentives are desired for their own sake. Such incentives, which typically are intangible, include recognition for accomplishments, prestige, and fame. One of the most powerful incentives in human history has been the promise of eternal salvation and its obverse, eternal damnation. Leaders who have been able to persuade their followers that they could determine what behaviors merited salvation or damnation have been able to mobilize powerful incentives to get people to make painful sacrifices.

Constraints are more complicated. Constraints are things that limit our ability to make the choices that we would like to make. Constraints include the difficulties associated with obtaining accurate information about the true quality and potential hazards of many of the choices that we make. These difficulties are often severe. Consider for a moment the problem of choosing what college to attend or what major to select. How can you be certain that you are making the right decision until years later, when it is much too late to choose an alternative path? Or consider the choice you make when you marry someone. How can you know that you made a good decision until you are already married, perhaps for a long time?

One of the most important kinds of constraints that we face is the one imposed by **rules**. Rules tell us what types of behaviors are permissible and what types are not, and also what penalties will be forthcoming if we violate the rules. Rules structure every aspect of our lives. Without rules, life would be chaos. From the beginning of recorded time, people have been devising rules to bring order, regularity, and predictability to human existence. Sometimes we tend to chafe at rules that seem unfair or arbitrary. After all, rules may inhibit our ability to do things that we would like very much to do. We usually follow rules not because we want to but because we are required to. We pay taxes, although we don't want to. Usually we remain stopped at red lights, even when there is no traffic nearby. Students must be at least twenty-one years of age to legally drink alcoholic beverages (a rule that would appear to be routinely broken on university campuses around the country).

If rules constrain us from doing what we would like, why do we have them? Why not repeal all laws and rules? The answer is that we need rules to allow us to obtain things that we need and want. For instance, consider the problems associated with taking a vacation to a distant place. What kind of trip would it be if you had placed a deposit on one kind of motel room, only to discover once you arrived that the motel was substantially worse than the one pictured in the marketing brochure? Would you still enjoy your vacation if your motel room were bug infested, the sheets and towels dirty, the paint peeling from the walls, and the air conditioner broken? If you thought it likely that you were going to find such atrocious conditions when you arrived at your motel, would you have ever even considered taking a vacation to that location? Or change the example and consider how you would react if, whenever you ordered a meal from a menu, you couldn't depend on being served. Fortunately, in this country such situations are rare; in the United States rules about false advertising are reasonably clear and, most of the time, effectively enforced. This country has a highly developed system of laws and rules about commercial transactions. American consumers and public officials alike play an active role in monitoring and ensuring compliance with rules of trade. In many other countries, the lack of effective monitoring and enforcement of rules poses a major constraint on the ability of people to express their true preferences.

The third assumption of the political economy approach to policy analysis is that people are intelligent and creative. They are inventive. They create new ideas, new rules, new institutions, new ways of doing things. Why is this assumption important? Because people aren't like lab mice in a maze, which have a preference for cheese but are constrained by walls and passages. When confronted with incentives and constraints, people often act on their preferences by devising new ways of doing things, creating new alternatives, changing the rules of the game, and (sometimes) finding ways to cheat. Through processes of rational discourse, individuals may choose to alter their preferences. Or they may decide to act collectively to overcome constraints by creating new rules or by establishing new institutions.

The predilection of people to be intelligent and creative is at the heart of this book. We have written this book with the hope that we can help you come up with new ways of solving policy problems using practical political reasoning. The book is organized around ways that groups of people have, from time to time, moved toward solutions to public problems. Often they have tried to design rules that do a better job of allowing people to attain a state of affairs where preferences are more closely met. We will look at a host of alternative ways of trying to structure behavior, from market competition, to community organizations, to centralized bureaucracies, and lots of things in between.

One of the thorniest issues we will face is how to minimize opportunities for **perverse behaviors.** Perverse behaviors are harmful to society but are consistent with the short-term self-interest of the people engaged in them. They include some of the oldest problems known to humans—cheating, criminality, and dishonesty. One of our main tasks will be to look at solutions to policy problems that involve trying to sort out and redirect incentives so that people will have a self-interest in doing things that are also good for others.

Individual Preferences Versus Collective Outcomes

The starting point of the political economy approach to policy analysis is the distinction between individual preferences and collective outcomes. The central tension of all social existence is that individual behavior often leads to collective outcomes that are not preferred by any individual. How is this possible? The answer lies in the fact that individual actions do not remain individualized. They combine with the actions of other people in ways that none of the individuals might have anticipated.

You desire, for example, a pair of the latest sports shoes. They are the current fashion, as demand for sports shoes is expanding throughout the industrialized nations. Because you try to find the best price possible for the shoes of your choice, as do other shoe buyers, a collective outcome is produced that neither you nor the others buying such shoes ever anticipated: To stay competitive, the manufacturers of sports shoes have been forced to seek out ever cheaper sources of labor to make the shoes. Shoe factories have sprung up across China, Vietnam, and other places where workers are paid pennies an hour to produce the shoes that you want to buy. How did this happen? No doubt you had no preference for the emergence of low-wage shoe factories in the Far East. You probably never considered that your desire for shoes was connected in any way with such a thing. You simply wanted a new pair of shoes, and you wanted to spend less, rather than more, money for them. So did lots of other people. Notice that the collective outcome turned out to be quite different from what you and others might have wanted.

The tension between collective outcomes and individual preferences is visible in every area of our daily lives. We want good roads, but we don't like it when too many other people choose to drive on the same section of good road on which we are driving. We like to visit national parks and wilderness areas, but we don't like it when wild animals become so dependent on eating garbage left behind by park visitors that the animals destroy campsites and make it unsafe for humans to camp in the wild. We want clean air, but we don't want to give up our automobiles or barbecue grills. Much of public policy is concerned with trying to find ways to resolve the tensions between individual preferences and collective outcomes.

One way of restating this issue is to draw a distinction between short-run and long-run preferences. In the short run, all of us would like to be able to obtain the goods and services for which we have preferences. In the long run, however, we have an interest in avoiding the perversities that our individual preferences can produce at the collective level. In the short run, we want affordable sports shoes; over the long run, we would like to prevent the emergence of sweatshops, at home or abroad. In the short run, we want to enjoy the wilderness; over the long run, we would like to minimize the exposure of wild animals to humans. In the short run, we want to keep driving our automobiles; over the long run, we would like to be able to breath clean air.

Smog in Los Angeles is the unintended consequence of a large number of individual actions, such as individuals choosing to drive cars rather than taking buses. *A. Ramey/Photo Edit.*

The problem is greater than just the distinction between short- and long-run calculations, however. The problem is that our individual actions, each perfectly consistent with our individual preferences, can and often do combine to produce collective outcomes that none of us would have chosen. Trying to be a good neighbor may mean taking good care of our lawns. But taking care of our lawns may involve the use of herbicides and pesticides that, when multiplied by every conscientious homeowner in the country, can do long-term damage to the environment and even to future generations of people. Even "green" lawn care practices that avoid herbicides, when practiced by everyone in a community, can reduce the habitat for some kinds of animals and plants and lead to a loss in diversity of species. We need not be evil or mean-spirited to produce collective outcomes that substantially harm one another.

This tension is at the heart of democratic politics. In a democracy, public policies are supposed to be governed by individual preferences, but often the public problems that we face are the product of the undesirable collective outcomes of individual preferences. So what are we to do? There are lots of answers to this question, but most of them involve trying to structure rules, incentives, and constraints to avoid undesirable collective outcomes while still permitting individual preferences to be expressed.

Major League Sports Example

To help clarify the tension between individual preferences and collective outcomes, consider a fairly commonplace situation. Let's say your favorite professional basketball team is the Chicago Bulls, the Boston Celtics, the Utah Jazz, the Orlando Magic, the Houston Rockets, the Los Angeles Lakers, the Miami Heat, or any one of the other National Basketball Association (NBA) teams. You want your team to have the best players in the league—players who deserve to be stars. You want a shrewd and savvy front office that can recruit and retain talent. You want a coaching staff that brings out the best of the team's potential. In short, you want your team to win. You want it to win the playoffs and be the champion. You want to be able to root for winners. That's what being a fan means.

Now consider what would happen if you got your wish—all the time, every year. Your team would win every game. No other team would be its match. The other teams might as well be playing Division III college ball. What would happen then? How much fun would you have as a fan? Where would be the suspense, the challenge, the contest? Fans would quit turning out for games. Television ratings would slide. Advertisers would begin to look for other venues to push their products. Revenues would fall. The league would wither and slowly die.

As a fan, your hope, at least in the short run, is that your team will win every game. Notice, however, that you also have an interest in the long-run viability of the game itself, which means that sometimes other teams should win. Other teams should have a shot at the championship. No dynasty should live forever—or even for more than a few years. In other words, you want the teams to be sufficiently close in talent and skill that games represent true contests. This is the major thesis of Box 1.1, which clearly shows what can happen when a league fails to ensure the competitiveness of its teams.

Therefore the NBA, like all professional sports leagues, has policies to try to ensure the competitiveness of its teams. There are league rules about drafting privileges, in order to ensure that the best new talent is distributed across all teams, especially weaker ones. There are rules that try to impose roughly equivalent salary levels across teams. There are rules about the distribution of TV revenues that are designed to keep some teams from being permanently advantaged and others disadvantaged. Teams, as well as individual players, are forever trying to get around these constraints as they pursue their short-run interests.

The ongoing problem for the NBA is thus to keep its rules from being evaded too often and too egregiously. It must try to protect the long-run interests of the sport as a whole. The rules of the NBA are not static or fixed. They have to be continually revised to cope with efforts by individual teams or players to get an advantage. The NBA adapts its rules to try to ensure, insofar as possible, that the sport, as a collectivity, will remain viable and competitive, and thus continue to attract the support of you and other fans. The NBA's

Box 1.1   *Athletic Competition and Fan Support*[1]

WHY ARE there so few fans of the Washington Generals or the New York Nationals? Washington Redskins supporters are fanatically devoted to their team. Don't tell New Yorkers that they support the Yankees, Rangers, or Giants any less than other fans support their teams. Why, then, don't the Washington Generals or the New York Nationals receive any support? Both these teams have had only one opponent throughout their history: the Harlem Globetrotters. While they trot around the globe with the world-beloved Globetrotters, these teams have accepted their roles as the noncompetitive stooges to the talented favorites from Harlem.

The Globetrotter dominance exemplifies a reality about sports: competition is vital for fan support. Cities love to think about their teams as possible dynasties, but they also cherish the chance to see their teams defeat bitter rivals. Rivalries arise through years of close competition. When the "Steel Curtain" defense of the Pittsburgh Steelers won a string of Superbowls in the 1970s and 1980, more than just the people of western Pennsylvania watched the games. One of the reasons was the intense competition in several Superbowls. Without viable competition, fans of winners tire of beating up on lesser opponents, while fans of losers tire of paying for tickets to see a team with few prospects.

The All America Football Conference (AAFC) provides an example of how the lack of competitiveness can lead to the failure of an entire sports league. The AAFC was dominated by the Cleveland Browns, who won every championship in the league's brief life between 1946 and 1949. In 1946, the upstart Browns had an average of 57,000 people attend their games, a number surpassed only by the New York Giants of the National Football League. In 1949, the dominant Browns were beating their competition so badly that fewer than 30,000 Clevelanders were coming to their games. Attendance at games of the other teams in the league was not even close to that. These numbers are remarkable, considering the support in the NFL today enjoyed by former AAFC teams, which include the San Francisco 49ers, the Buffalo Bills, the former Baltimore Colts, and the former Los Angeles Rams. These teams survived only because they were allowed into the NFL, a league that attempts to provide competitive parity among its teams.

The collapse of the AAFC shows that while Americans love a winner, they also love intense, and fair, competition. A victory over a rival in a key game is much more enjoyable than a series of blowouts over an overwhelmed opponent. Indeed, it would not have been a sad day in Mudville had mighty Casey not been batting for a win.

1. James Quirk and Rodney Fort, *Pay Dirt: The Business of Professional Team Sports* (Princeton, N.J.: Princeton University Press, 1997).

policymaking process expresses the tension between individual preferences and collective outcomes. The same is true when we turn to public policy-making.

CONCLUSION

The central actor in the political economy approach to policy analysis is the individual—for two reasons. First, individuals and their actions are what lead to collective problems. Second, and more important, individuals, when armed with the conceptual tools of political economy become instruments for understanding and reforming collective practices. Individuals can and should master the tools and concepts of policy analysis so that each individual can better understand how collective enterprises operate the way they do, why they sometimes exhibit failures, and what options may be available for improving policy performance. Hence, the political economy approach gives us a new and more interesting way to see individuals and the communities in which they live. This approach to policy analysis has much to reveal about modern complex societies.

Key Terms

negative externality *p. 4*
practical political reasoning *p. 4*
political economy approach *p. 5*
purposive *p. 5*
preference *p. 5*
persuasion *p. 5*

bargaining *p. 6*
coercion *p. 6*
incentive *p. 7*
constraint *p. 7*
rule *p. 7*
perverse behavior *p. 8*

Notes

1. Kyle Niederpruem and Bonnie Harris, "First Response to Big Fish Kill Found Deficient," *Indianapolis Star* (January 16, 2000).

2. Tina King, "Substance Killing Fish in White River," *Indianapolis Star* (January 16, 2000).

3. David Rohn, "Problems Lurk Just Below the Surface," *Indianapolis Star* (January 26, 2000).

4. Charles W. Anderson, *Pragmatic Liberalism* (Chicago: University of Chicago Press, 1990).

II

Democracy and Governance

2

Democratic Governance and Public Policy

INTRODUCTION

Since the rise of the modern nation-state about five hundred years ago, governments have often been viewed as a tool to make groups of individuals better off than they would be in some conjectured state of nature. Governments are instruments for collective action. They mobilize individual resources, including money, energy, and labor. Governments permit the application of those resources on a scale that far exceeds the capabilities of any individual. This capability is a two-edged sword. On the one hand, modern governments can provide benefits to citizens and enhance the quality of life in societies in ways not even imaginable a century or two ago. On the other hand, modern governments can do enormous harm, trampling on the personal liberties of their own citizens and endangering the citizens of other countries.

Consider the problem of crime. In your local newspaper within the past few weeks, or even in this morning's edition, you can no doubt find an article describing the violent death of someone in your community. Maybe you knew the person who was killed; more likely, you did not. Perhaps the person was murdered by a family member, or perhaps by a total stranger. Or perhaps the person was the victim of a car accident in which the one at fault was intoxicated. It seems as if every day there are newspaper articles describing violent crimes: robberies, arsons, rapes, carjackings, assaults, and on and on.

Crime is a terrible thing. It robs people of a sense of well-being. It makes them fearful not just for themselves but for their children, their loved ones, and their friends. It turns simple errands into occasions for apprehension. People may begin to feel a sense of dread, or even panic, when confronted with the need to make a trip to the grocery store, the laundry, or the video store late in the evening. Ordinary citizens may begin to feel that they, rather than the criminals responsible for committing the crimes, are the ones behind bars, entrapped in their homes.

Crime is also a difficult public policy issue. Indeed, it raises some of the most fundamental problems that confront governments and citizens. Implicated in this issue is the question of what sorts of behaviors should be defined as criminal and who should be able to make this determination. Should majorities of citizens be able to decide that gun possession is a crime, because guns are often the instruments of violence? Should majorities be able to decide that those who are most likely to engage in crimes—for example, young adult males—can be subjected to extra police surveillance and preemptive arrests? Should majorities be able to tell teenagers that regardless of their individual behaviors, they should be liable to arrest for violating curfew laws?

Notice that for the most part we have been considering the possibility of violent crimes. Let us also consider the more mundane behaviors that society finds problematic: for example, the failure of fathers to provide child support payments to the mothers of their children, the seeking by teenage girls of abortions to terminate unplanned pregnancies, the failure of some parents to ensure that their children receive schooling, or the panhandling by homeless people for money on downtown sidewalks. In every case, law and order always comes at the expense of someone's freedom.

The problem is more difficult than this, however. The question of how to cope with crime raises fundamental questions of what it means to have governments. Endowing government agencies with sufficient powers to fight crime means that those powers can be used for evil, as well as good. Governments with the authority to detain and question suspected wrongdoers may do the same to citizens they find troublesome. This problem is not limited to authoritarian regimes, such as the Chinese government that so violently suppressed the college students in Tiananmen Square in 1989. Even in democratic countries such as the United States, innocent people have sometimes been faced with strong-arm government tactics simply for having the wrong skin color or an accent associated with a different country.

How, then, should we think about governments and the policies they pursue? The first rule is that we need to avoid gross distinctions about whether governments are inherently saintly or evil. If governments are always good, why are checks and balances needed to keep government officials from exploiting their offices at public expense? And if governments are always evil, why do they seem so necessary? We shall find that there are no easy answers about what the government should and should not do, or about how effective the government can be in solving public problems. We will also see why the role of government and its usefulness, effectiveness, and motivations are themselves sources of intense political debate in modern societies.

Before endeavoring to tackle such enduring questions about government, we must first understand the nature of public problems, the public that defines such problems, and the theoretical underpinnings of various approaches to governance. We cannot evaluate what the government can do and should do without first understanding the connection between the government and the public. If we can better understand the nature of the public, we can begin to think about how to evaluate a government's performance and thus how to design governance institutions so as to improve the degree to which government is democratically responsive. In doing so, we can learn to think about public policy in terms of how governments serve different publics.

DEMOCRATIC THEORY: HOBBES, LOCKE, ROUSSEAU, AND RAWLS

One of the great turning points in human history was the development of a line of thinking that is known as the **social contract tradition.** The social contractarians, beginning with Thomas Hobbes (1588–1679), turned traditional ways of thinking about politics and government upside down. Until the social contractarians came on the scene during the seventeenth century, most people saw politics and government in terms of highly constrained, hierarchical systems of social relations into which all humans were born and stayed throughout their entire lives.

The burning questions of politics, for people operating under this older way of thinking, typically involved disputes over which leaders in society could rightfully claim authority to rule. Authority to rule, it was claimed, came from God, so disputes were as often ecclesiastical as political, involving conflicts among and between kings, popes, bishops, and feudal lords. The separation of church and state, a concept familiar to all Americans today, would have seemed absurd to people in this earlier period. The role of the public in deciding questions of government was largely irrelevant, except as pawns in the often lethal games played out by those who claimed authority to rule over them.

The social contractarians rejected the entire hierarchical premise on which this older view of government was based. They placed the public at the center of their theory of government. By doing so, they provided the theoretical underpinnings for democracy as a system of governance. According to the social contractarians, government should be founded upon the choices and consent of the people. This was a revolutionary idea. The social contractarians argued that government, as well as other social institutions, was devised by people to help them overcome the dangers and inconveniences that exist in the absence of such institutions.[1] Thomas Hobbes, the first of the social contract theorists, argued that the kind of government necessary to ensure peace is an overawing absolute dictator, which he called **Leviathan.** His argument was that people would so greatly fear the chaos that would exist in the absence of social institutions that they would invite in an absolute dictator to impose order and peace upon their society. The flaw in Hobbes's argument is that people would then be exposed to the capriciousness and unchecked power of the dictator.

One need only consider Adolf Hitler's Germany or Pol Pot's Cambodia to recognize that governments, with their ability to engage in organized terror, can be far more dangerous than any single individual.

Later social contractarians, such as John Locke (1632–1704), identified a major problem in Hobbes's thought. Locke said, "Absolute Monarchy [is] . . . inconsistent with Civil Society, and so can be no Form of Civil Government at all." For Locke, the only legitimate form of government is established when people, through their **individual consent,** "put on the bonds of Civil Society" and thereby form a political community. For Locke, this meant that people voluntarily chose to establish governments. Subsequent social contractarians have followed Locke's emphasis on free consent and the need, in a free society, to maintain limitations on government power. The central idea, to all social contractarians, is that people form governments to remedy the social ills confronting them. Government action is legitimate only when the public consents to it. In this way, government power is yoked to the needs and preferences of individuals, regardless of their wealth, social status, or title. This idea was revolutionary when it swept across the monarchical kingdoms of Europe three hundred years ago.

Jean-Jacques Rousseau (1712–1778), who was at once one of the purist proponents of the social contract and one of its sharpest critics, identified a quandary in social contract theory that we will confront repeatedly in this book. He realized that there are times when the public, or at least significant factions within the public, holds preferences for government action that are reprehensible. The list of such occasions in U.S. history is uncomfortably long; it includes the treatment of American Indians throughout much of U.S. history, Jim Crow laws in the South that discriminated against African Americans until not too many years ago, the confinement of Japanese Americans during the Second World War, discrimination against women in the workplace, antipathy toward immigrants even today, and school policies until a few years ago that forced left-handed children to write with their right hands. You can probably add examples of your own.

When government authority is to be mobilized whenever a majority of the public demands action, serious inequities can be perpetrated on minorities (groups of individuals who are different in some respect). Here is the problem: If government action is to be a product of individual preferences, which are sometimes repugnant, how can we be certain that government actions are ever justified?

Rousseau posed this problem in terms of a great paradox: "The general will is always right, but the judgment that guides it is not always enlightened."[2] Rousseau was saying that people's preferences are sometimes suspect, and consequently people do not always choose what they ought to choose. But how can we tell when preferences are acceptable and when they are not? And who will get to decide what people ought to choose? Rousseau never came up with a fully satisfactory solution to this problem. At one point, he proposed that a society founded upon a social contract required first a great legislator to give people the institutions that they ought to have and to teach people what they ought to want. The catch was that the legislator was to be constrained from employing force or superior reason, because citizens must still freely consent to government institutions if those institutions are to be obligatory. At another point, Rousseau argued that society must be based upon an extensive program of private education that will produce fully self-reliant citizens, free of all social prejudices. At other points, Rousseau advocated an education in nationalistic and patriotic symbols to forge a common identity for all citizens and thereby build a unified nation-state. Underlying all these ideas in Rousseau's writings was the theme that education is needed to fashion citizens who would be capable of giving their consent to a properly ordered society.

The problem that Rousseau identified is a thorny one. Democratic theory presumes that preferences should determine public policies. Therefore, we must accept, at least provisionally, the idea that preferences are generally socially acceptable, not socially repugnant. We believe that preferences usually—but not always—should be treated as acceptable. We need some way to differentiate between acceptable and repugnant preferences. How can we do this? There is no simple answer to this question. Sometimes things that have been viewed as acceptable in the past are later rejected as unacceptable. Sometimes the reverse has occurred. The question is, How can one tell which preferences should be viewed as acceptable bases for determining public policy and which preferences should be ignored?

A modern social contractarian, John Rawls, has proposed a method that many thinkers find useful in trying to distinguish between acceptable and unacceptable policy preferences. Rawls argues that the source of the illegitimacy of many preferences is that people often desire policies that advantage themselves to the detriment of others. The desire for such policies is sometimes intentional—for example, when a corporation lobbies for special tax benefits or barriers to keep other companies out of its line of business. Sometimes the desire for obtaining an advantage over others is almost completely irrational, as is the case when people discriminate on the basis of race, religion, or sexual orientation.

Rawls proposes a method that he calls the **veil of ignorance**. He asks us to imagine putting ourselves behind a veil so that we do not know anything at all about our personal characteristics, attributes, or possessions. Rawls tells us to consider a proposed policy or government action from this position of ignorance. In other words, we do not know if, when we emerge from behind this veil, we will be male or female, old or young, black or white, rich or poor, right-handed or left-handed, talented or just average. If a policy still seems acceptable, even without our knowing the specifics of our own situation, then the policy preference can be presumed to be legitimate and acceptable.

Try a mental experiment using this veil of ignorance. Consider, for example, the arguments by white supremacist groups that African Americans, Jewish people, homosexuals, and other minorities should be banished from the United States. Such a policy preference would clearly be rejected as illegitimate, because a person holding this preference would not know whether he or she might actually be African American, Jewish, homosexual, or a member of some other minority group. The Rawlsian veil-of-ignorance test demonstrates that the arguments by white supremacists are self-serving and offensive.

Now try a harder case. Consider the argument that government funding for the student loan program should be continued or even expanded. Behind the veil of ignorance, you cannot tell whether or not you are a college student. But you might believe that expanding college opportunities is something that benefits not only potential college students but also society as a whole due to the resulting increase in productive capacity, knowledge, and skills. The question becomes whether or not the student loan program has positive spillover effects (a concept we will return to in a later chapter) that benefit more than just the minority of young people who might qualify for the program itself. If so, a preference for continuing or expanding government funding of the student loan program would be defensible. If the program merely transfers wealth from the rest of society to a small number of people without any positive benefits to anyone else, however, then a preference to fund the program would not pass the Rawlsian veil-of-ignorance test.

DELIMITING THE PUBLIC

Democratic governance links the purpose of government to the **public** and its preferences. But the question of who constitutes the public is not as simple as it first might seem. Who is the public? Is it everyone in your neighborhood? Everyone in your town or city? Your state? How about everyone in the country or the North American continent? The world? We need to be able to know what delimits the public to know whose preferences should be considered in devising public policies. How can we do this? In trying to define *public,* it is useful to think not in terms of a single public that exists in a society but in terms of multiple, overlapping publics. A useful definition of a *public* is the set of individuals who are likely to be affected by the consequences of a particular problem. Obviously, problems can vary enormously in the scope of their consequences.

This way of thinking about publics has a long history in American democratic theory. Writing almost three-quarters of a century ago, John Dewey wrote that the source of a public is "the perception of consequences which are projected in important ways beyond the persons and associations directly concerned in them."[3] What this means is that a public is a group of people whose common bond is that they are affected by the consequences, directly or indirectly, of some activity. Following Dewey, we define publics in terms of groups of people who are potentially affected by the consequences of an activity or problem. This means that a public is not simply those upon whom a problem has a direct impact. It also includes people for whom the consequences are indirect.

For example, acquired immune deficiency syndrome (AIDS) in the United States started out as a problem that most directly affected homosexuals and intravenous drug users. As time went on, it became clear that the public affected by AIDS included a much larger population than just those persons infected with the virus. The affected public includes those who are human immunodeficiency virus (HIV) positive, public health officials, families and friends of AIDS victims, and everyone whose lifestyle is altered due to the possibility of infection with the virus that causes AIDS.

In other cases, the public is much narrower. For example, the problem of automobiles speeding through a neighborhood creates a public made up mainly of residents and visitors in the neighborhood. They are the people who are affected by the possible consequences of the speeding. Those who live elsewhere are unaffected and are thus not members of the particular public that exists around this speeding issue. Note that our definition of a *public* excludes those who are not affected by the consequences of an activity or problem. To be a member of a public requires that you, as well as others, are in a position to perceive direct or indirect consequences of a set of actions.

Why do we define *public* in this way? First, it focuses attention on the problems that governments are called upon to try to fix. Second, it leads us to search for ways of matching policies to particular publics. One of the situations that often leads to conflict in a society is when policies benefit a small number of individuals at the expense of everyone else. Small groups of people benefiting from a policy is not in and of itself a bad thing. However, if the policy does not address a problem that conceivably could be encountered by a substantial part of a public, then the policy will inevitably lead to pockets of the public benefiting at the expense of a large majority of the public.

Thus, we need to understand and define the affected public to understand the best approach to making effective public policy. If we do not do so, we increase the likelihood of conflict; after all, people do not like paying for a policy from which they do not benefit. Given enough policies of this type, the only way to govern is to trade off votes across coalitions, creating a political landscape in which governing is replaced by **quid pro quo bargains**, that is, bargains of the type, "you scratch my back, I'll scratch your back." When these bargains predominate, policy debates are about who wins and loses, and not about whether real public problems are solved by policy. Democratic politics degenerates to a process of slicing the pie so that everyone gets something, without regard to whether public problems are solved.

This political condition has become one of the major policy dilemmas at the federal level in the United States. In response to national crises, such as the Great Depression, World War II, the Cold War, and the denial of civil rights to African Americans in the southern states, the federal government was called upon to assume responsibility over many issues that have separate (though partially overlapping) publics. Unfortunately, it is difficult to have truly democratic policymaking when so few people, in relative terms, are directly affected by many of the policies of the federal government.

It is not surprising that one of the biggest issues cited by individuals time and again is the size of the federal tax bill. Such controversy is to be expected;

when a large government like that in the United States tries to accomplish so many tasks, individuals invariably see only a proportion of the benefits from their taxes, even if they are satisfied when they do reap some benefits and want the government to continue providing them. This dilemma is fueled by having one government govern over so many different publics.

There is an immense array of choices in the United States as to the level and composition of governments that may be used to address problems faced by publics. Whereas most people think first about the federal government for solutions to policy problems large and small, there is a great deal of vitality at the state and local levels, with a rich array of options for finding solutions to problems. Box 2.1 provides an example that illustrates this point.

WHAT IS GOVERNMENT?

Before we focus on how governments can help solve problems, we first must ask what government is. At one level, the answer to this question is straightforward: governments are instruments through which people engage in collective action. Governments are able to compel people to behave in ways that improve the well-being of everyone in society. Why are they able to motivate people in such a way? To answer this question, we must first ask, what is government? **Government** can be defined as an organization that possesses the legitimate means of coercion in a society. Let's consider all three parts of this definition: organization, legitimacy, and coercion.

Organization

Saying that a government is an **organization** means that the government possesses an institutional structure in which the persons carrying out official tasks hold positions that are formally defined with respect to their responsibilities. These positions are independent of the particular people who happen to hold them. Governments can take many organizational forms.

The U.S. government, for instance, is divided into three branches of officeholders who have separate, but overlapping, powers to make, execute, and adjudicate public policies. It also includes a very large set of bureaucracies that are designed to carry out scores of policy activities, as well support functions for the government itself. The mechanisms by which individuals are selected to hold government positions vary. Members of Congress hold two- or six-year terms, depending upon whether they are in the House of Representatives or the Senate. House members represent essentially equal numbers of constituents, whereas senators represent whole states, regardless of how many people happen to live in each state. Presidents serve four-year terms and must be elected by a plurality of the voters in states that together make up a major-

Box 2.1   Lake Lemon Conservation District

SOME YEARS ago in Monroe County, Indiana, a group of individuals organized themselves into an effective public for the purpose of solving a water recreation problem surrounding Lake Lemon, a reservoir created to serve the county and the city of Bloomington. The lake is now too small to serve such an important purpose, but it is still important as a local recreation area. Individuals living in the area around the lake had become increasingly concerned that the lake had a host of unaddressed problems, most notably increased vegetation that could render it useless for recreational purposes.

A petition was circulated to create a conservation district that would tax area residents to service the lake. These residents, many of whom would doubtless respond to surveys that taxes, especially at the national level, were too high, signed enough petitions to create this district. The Lake Lemon Conservation District would have the power to coerce individuals in the district—namely, the residents who signed the petition—to pay for conservation efforts. People had direct involvement, and they overwhelmingly decided and acted on a solution. That is, this district matches the affected public to the problem. Those people who pay also benefit from the policy and vice versa.

Some political scientists have been skeptical of **special districts** because they appear, based on criteria they often use to evaluate public policy, to be insulated from normal democratic processes. These are governments that exist to provide a simple type of service, such as education, electricity, or drinking water. Nancy Burns, for example, argues that the recent proliferation of special districts was actually an attempt by elites to create autonomous policymaking institutions insulated from public input.[1] Is this the case with the Lake Lemon Conservation District? It does not appear to be. Whereas many special districts perhaps are without some of the conventional attributes of democratic governance, such as voting, they have other properties that are quite appealing: most notably the fact that the affected public, and only the affected public, pays for the services.

No doubt if Lake Lemon becomes overgrown by vegetation after the Conservation District is supposed to be managing the lake, many individuals paying for the service will find ways to address their grievances. Democratic pressure will be visible precisely when it needs to be. Why? Individuals will be able to identify precisely who is responsible for any failures in solving the underlying lake-related problems. But the opposite is also true. Individuals tend to stay out of the process if a problem doesn't exist. The creation of this special district provides an incentive for the responsible policymakers not to be rascals. Officials in the Lake Lemon Conservation District will hear from residents if lake-related problems reappear. These officials may face calls for the abolishment of the Conservation District or demands that the state initiate an investigation of how tax revenues have been spent. They have strong incentives not to shirk the responsibilities of the district.

1. Nancy Burns, *The Formation of American Local Governments* (New York: Oxford University Press, 1994).

ity of the country's population. Judges, by contrast, serve for life and are selected not by popular election but by presidential nomination and confirmation by a majority of the U.S. Senate. The personnel that staff bureaucracies are selected according to a variety of rules, but most are hired on the basis of exams, educational and professional credentials, or appointment by the president.

Even the town or city where you live has a government that is, among other things, an organization consisting of positions that are formally defined. Although far less complex than the U.S. government, every municipality, county government, school district, water district, or state government is an organization. Mayor, city council, police officer, city planner, garbage collector, dog catcher—each of these is a formally defined position that exists independent of the particular occupant of the position. In every case, the people filling jobs in government, from mayor to mail clerk, operate in organizations that specify how each of the positions will be filled, how long and under what circumstances the holders of the positions can continue to occupy them, and what the holder of each position is expected to do.

Legitimacy

Most governments, most of the time, seek to be viewed as legitimate in the eyes of their citizens. When a government has **legitimacy,** it means that its citizens are predisposed to accept the actions of the government, not just when they happen to agree with those actions but also when they disagree. Legitimacy is more than a sense of resignation that the government can do whatever it wants. It is a sense that the actions of the government, at least most of the time, serve the public interest.

To be sure, governments can survive without legitimacy, at least for a while, but only through the widespread exercise of repression and terror. Where governments lack legitimacy, leaders live in fear of their populations. Thus, governments that lack legitimacy tend to crumble when they are no longer able to keep their citizens acquiescent through the application of fear. This tendency was a major factor in the disintegration of the Soviet Union; the rejection of communist leaders in Poland and the other countries in Eastern Europe; the upheavals in Nicaragua, Guatemala, and South Africa; and the rejection of military dictatorships in Argentina, Chile, Korea, and Uganda. It will be a key element in how events unfold in China, Cuba, Bosnia, and Indonesia.

How do governments acquire legitimacy? Historically, it was common for a government to garner legitimacy by claiming that its actions were divinely decreed. When citizens are inclined to believe that their leaders have special knowledge of God's will and are divinely inspired, a government can rely on an enormous reservoir of support. In such countries, symbols and rituals have been used to suggest that the leaders were selected by God and that their actions were mandated by divine will. The monarchies of medieval Europe gained their legitimacy on this basis. Even today there are countries where legitimacy is derived, at least in part, from claims that the country's rulers are divinely inspired—for example, Iran and Algeria.

Today most governments derive their legitimacy from democracy. Democratic processes allow citizens to express their agreement or disagreement with government leaders and their actions. The most visible mechanism of democracy is voting. By going to the polls, people are able to express their assent or dissent, to say yes or no. The opportunity to vote reinforces the belief that government actions are an extension of what the public, or at least a majority of the public, wants.

It is not surprising, then, that some of the most contentious struggles in American history have been over the extension of the franchise (that is, the right to vote). The Civil War, among other things, was about the legal status of African Americans. Should all Americans, regardless of skin color or place of origin, be granted legal rights to fully participate in American economic and political life, with the right to vote, own property, move freely about the country, and enjoy the full range of benefits of American citizenship?

The Civil War did not fully resolve this issue; the country has continued to grapple with issues of race, prejudice, and discrimination for a long time since the end of that war. In similar fashion, the suffrage movement, which began long before the Civil War and continued long after it, was about the extension of the franchise to women—a right not granted until ratification of the Nineteenth Amendment to the U.S. Constitution in 1920. Most recently, the so-called youth revolution, with close ties to both the civil rights and antiwar protests of the 1960s, culminated in the ratification of the Twenty-Sixth Amendment in 1971. This amendment extended the right to vote to Americans between the ages of eighteen and twenty-one.

The key to democracy is that citizens can express approval or disapproval of government actions and thereby influence those actions. Voting is one method of expression, but voting occurs only on an episodic basis and is a rather crude way of trying to express specific opinions on complicated issues. Consequently, vibrant democracies are characterized by a political climate that is open to the expression of ideas, the articulation of a wide variety of opinions, and vigorous debate. This climate typically flourishes where there are legal protections for freedom of speech and assembly and a free press that is able to challenge government policies and actions. The word used to describe this aspect of democracy is **voice**.

The expression of opinions and ideas—voice—is a means by which democratic systems allow for the identification of policy problems and for the articulation and consideration of alternative policies. Moreover, the very fact that debate has occurred tends to legitimize whatever policies are ultimately selected, because people have had an opportunity to be heard and participate in the formulation of the policies.

In many democracies, citizens also have an additional—and quite powerful—way to express their approval or disapproval of government policies.

Government policies are often complex undertakings involving political officials and citizens. *Spencer Grant/Photo Edit.*

Where the costs of moving are relatively low and where there are lots of distinct government jurisdictions, citizens who are dissatisfied with the mix of public policies in a particular local jurisdiction can relocate to another jurisdiction that offers a mix of public policies more in line with their preferences. They can move. This aspect of democracy is termed **exit**, also often called *voting with your feet*, because preferences are expressed through mobility decisions. Thus, where mobility is a potential threat, governments must be much more keenly attuned to preferences of citizens, because people have the option of leaving. We will consider this type of democratic process below. Here, it is important simply to notice that in some countries, but not all, the overall structure of government permits individuals to express their preferences not merely at the ballot box or through assembly and speech but also through the choices they make when relocating.

One last point about legitimacy of governments and its connection to democracy is important to note. Democracies allow citizens to vote out a set of government leaders without causing the system of government to fall apart. There is a separation between the leadership and the system of government. A group of leaders may be found to be inadequate. Voters can "throw out the bums." The system of government, however, can continue to be viewed as legitimate. Indeed, the legitimacy of the system of government may, in fact, be enhanced by the periodic removal of the government's leaders, because the removal demonstrates that the public, in the end, continues to hold the upper hand. It shows that citizens are sovereign. The same is not true in most non-democratic types of government. In such governments, the ouster of a set of government leaders often brings about the collapse of the whole structure of government and initiates a period of chaos and crisis.

Coercion

The third component of government is coercion. More than anything else, coercion is what separates government organizations from nongovernment organizations. Governments impose taxes and fines; take property; arrest, detain, and imprison; impanel juries; execute criminals; draft young people into armies; and wage war. Modern governments can mobilize coercion on a truly terrifying scale: nuclear weapons, chemical weapons, bombs, missiles, mortars, grenades, and bullets; armadas of submarines, destroyers, cruisers, battleships, and aircraft carriers; hordes of warships, fighters, bombers, and attack planes; swarms of attack helicopters and transports; massive columns of tanks, troop carriers, mobile missile launchers, artillery, radar jammers, assault troops, and infantry—the list goes on and on.

Coercion and the threat of coercion is the stock-in-trade of government. It is a primary instrument available to governments that permits them to accomplish tasks that private individuals and organizations can perform poorly, if at all. Consider the relatively mundane problem of building a highway. Government coercion is not required for the actual tasks of grading the terrain, preparing the underlying soil, pouring concrete, and building retaining walls and bridges. Indeed, these tasks can be accomplished quite easily by private construction companies. But to be useful, a highway has to provide travelers with the ability to go all the way from one community to another. This means that a continuous right-of-way must be acquired for the highway. A single landowner that refuses to sell a strip of land for the highway right-of-way can potentially wreck the entire highway project, cutting off access between two communities. Governments, therefore, have the power, known as **eminent domain,** to define rights-of-way and acquire property for roads, as well as for other public purposes. Eminent domain is the legal procurement, with compensation to the owner, of property that is needed by government to further the public good. When a government exercises its right of eminent domain, certain legal proceedings must be followed, and landowners must be compensated for land that is acquired; ultimately, though, landowners have no choice as to whether the government will take part or all of their property through coercion.

As in the case of a highway linking two communities that otherwise would be cut off from one another, government coercion may be in the interest of the public as a whole, and thus be justifiable. But coercion can also be used in ways that are detrimental to particular individuals or groups. The fact that government can compel individuals to do things (such as sell their property) to accomplish public purposes is what makes government such a useful instrument. Nonetheless, this same power is why it is important to consider ways to keep government from becoming predatory. How to obtain the benefits from the ability of government to exercise coercive power while still maintaining government's legitimacy is the central riddle of constitutional design. This perennial problem is the dilemma that we explore in the next section.

DEMOCRATIC GOVERNANCE

In all societies, **governance** is ubiquitous. In its barest form, governance is simply the process of translating individual preferences into policies. Governance is ongoing at all levels and facets of society.

As an illustration of this fact, remember the last time you were in a student organization that was trying to decide its goals and methods. You were directly engaged in governance. Or consider anticrime policies and the importance of governance efforts at every level of government. In addition to national anticrime policy and the policies of states and local governments is the sum total of all local neighborhoods' efforts to monitor and alert police to the possibility of crimes. The effort on the part of such neighborhoods is itself an act of governance. This governance is as real, and often as important, as the latest policy debate in Congress about lengthening penalties for some set of crimes.

It is essential, if we are to understand this complex process called governance, that we be vigilant in avoiding the fallacy that the only governance that takes place, or at least that is important enough for our interest, is at some large, centralized level. If we make this mistake, we inevitably are going to misunderstand the role and importance of government and governance in society. Governance exists at all levels of society.

The view of governance presented in this text, like that of the social contractarians, is that governance should be about the demands and desires of the public to find solutions to the problems confronting the public. This is not the only way to view the process of governance. Here, we present two caricatures about governance. Some prefer to think that governance is about power relationships: Who gets what, and how? Others, including us, focus on how governments solve public problems and how publics are made better off. Let's call the former governments Type A governments, and the latter, Type B.

Proponents of the Type A model need only point at the endless historical role of governments in redistributing resources from losers to winners.[4] To these scholars, governments are centers of power for distributing resources to supporters and members of the government. In this model of government, politics is genuinely, and probably inherently, about **distributional conflict.** It is about who should benefit and who should bear the costs of government. Type A governments solve problems as an afterthought or, if at all, as an unintended consequence of these distributional activities.

The Type B model conceptualizes governance primarily in terms of attempts to solve public problems. In this view, distributional conflicts are unintended consequences of trying to determine how best to solve problems. Scholars of the Type B model emphasize the functional role of government. Governments solve problems, sometimes imperfectly, but they are capable of more than serving simply as resource distribution centers.

These two models are not antithetical. They emphasize two different conceptions of the ways in which government authority can be used. It is interesting to note, however, the extent to which the framers of the U.S. Constitution saw these two purposes as needing to be carefully reconciled. In designing a constitution for the United States, one of the primary goals of the framers was to establish a system of government that could be effective in thwarting threats to national security and could build and maintain prosperous domestic commerce. At the same time, a way had to be found to curb the possibilities that such a government could itself become a danger to citizens. In defense of the proposed constitution, the writers of the Federalist papers argued that the best way to realize the effectiveness of a strong national government that could address pressing public needs, while at the same time avoiding the effects of factions of people trying to bias government policies to benefit themselves at the expense of others in society, was to have a large, territorially expansive government that incorporated checks and balances both between the branches of government and between a central government and the states. James Madison, one of the principal writers of the Federalist papers, saw the problem this way:

> The great security against a gradual concentration of the several powers in the same department, consists in giving to those who administer each department the necessary constitutional means and personal motives to resist encroachments of the others. The provision for defense must in this, as in all other cases, be made commensurate to the danger of attack. Ambition must be made to counteract ambition. The interest of the man must be connected with the constitutional rights of the place. It may be a reflection on human nature, that such devices should be necessary to control the abuses of government. But what is government itself, but the greatest of all reflections on human nature? If men were angels, no government would be necessary. If angels were to govern men, neither external nor internal controls on government would be necessary. In framing a government which is to be administered by men over men, the great difficulty lies in this: you must first enable the government to control the governed; and in the next place oblige it to control itself, to which our inquiries are directed.[5]

It should be emphasized that modern democratic governments are a combination of both Type A and Type B governments. Governments gain legitimacy from solving public problems, but democratic politics ensures that distributional consequences of public policies persist. Distributional consequences are not in themselves indicators of bad public policies. All public policies have some distributional consequences. However, policies are not legitimate simply because someone, somewhere, voted for them. Legitimate public policies attempt to solve public problems. Distributional consequences may result, but they should not be the primary goal of public policies.

Most policies have sufficient distributional consequences to fuel political battles; these battles are inevitable. It is impossible to design political institutions that eliminate the possibility of distributional consequences. Thus the goal should be to design institutions so that distributional forces can be accommodated at the same time that government actions can be focused in a manner that leads to policies that adequately address public problems. The question of how to design government institutions in that way is tackled in the next chapter.

CONCLUSION

There is a tendency among many policy analysts to think primarily about the national government. This tendency is unfortunate. There should be no a priori preference for a particular level of government. Instead, efforts should be made to create governance institutions that match policies to affected publics. Those individuals governed by the institution then have an incentive to address that governance when it fails. Local issues that are governed by national policies hardly allow that possibility. Not all issues are local, however, and thus there is a place for policy at higher levels of government. Some policies should be made within local neighborhoods, others by local governments, still others by states or the federal government, and indeed, some policies should be made by international organizations like the United Nations. Democracy flourishes best when policies are produced by governments at the same level as the consequences of the problems that are being addressed.

In summary, we should not choose just one "proper" level of government— whether it be the national government or some neighborhood association—for solving problems. We need to prescribe governance institutions that are at whatever level of government allows the preferences of affected publics to be considered in the design of policy solutions. We cannot abolish the fact that some nonpublics will sometimes pay for benefits to others, but we can understand that when this situation occurs too often it leads to pathological politics and a loss of democracy. The question is how to focus the power of government in a manner that resolves problems faced by publics. In essence, we want to know how to design appropriate public policies.

Our position, at least as a starting point, is that a government is pursuing an appropriate public policy when the policy makes the public better off than if no policy had existed. In other words, the test of public policy is in terms of the impact on members of the public. This thesis will occupy much of our attention throughout this book, and the complexity of this simple assertion will soon become apparent. This chapter has begun to explore the assertion's complexity by discussing the meaning of governance and identifying the governed.

Key Terms

social contract tradition *p. 19*

Leviathan *p. 19*

individual consent *p. 20*

veil of ignorance *p. 21*

public *p. 22*

quid pro quo bargain *p. 23*

government *p. 24*

organization *p. 24*

special district *p. 25*

legitimacy *p. 26*

voice *p. 27*

exit *p. 28*

eminent domain *p. 29*

governance *p. 30*

distributional conflict *p. 30*

Suggested Readings

Dawson, Christopher. 1948. *Religion and Culture*. New York: Meridian Books.

Dewey, John. 1946. *The Public and Its Problems*. Chicago: Gateway Books. Originally published by Henry Holt, 1927.

Hobbes, Thomas. 1968. *Leviathan*. Edited with an introduction by C. B. MacPherson. Baltimore: Penguin Books.

Locke, John. 1960. *Two Treatises of Government*. Edited by Peter Laslett. Cambridge, England: Cambridge University Press.

Mansfield, H. C., Jr. 1978. *The Spirit of Liberalism*. Cambridge, Mass.: Harvard University Press.

Mill, John Stuart. 1956. *On Liberty*. Indianapolis: Bobbs-Merrill.

Niebuhr, Reinhold. 1932. *Moral Man and Immoral Society*. New York: Charles Scribner's.

Rawls, John. 1971. *A Theory of Justice*. Cambridge, Mass.: Belknap Press of Harvard University Press.

Riley, Patrick. 1982. *Will and Political Legitimacy*. Cambridge, Mass.: Harvard University Press.

Rousseau, Jean Jacques. 1967. *Social Contract*. Edited with an introduction by Lester G. Crocker. New York: Pocket Books.

Notes

1. The social contractarians arrived at this revolutionary principle by first imagining what is often referred to as a state of nature. The state of nature is not necessarily a situation that actually existed in some historical sense. It was used by the social contractarians as a device for considering a world in which governments do not yet exist; a world in which social institutions have not yet been invented; a world populated by people living without the benefit of rules, customs, and social norms. For the social contractarians, the state of nature implied that there was a fundamental sense in which all people are equal—an equality derived from, if nothing else, the ability of the weakest person to kill the strongest while asleep. In the absence of government and other

social institutions, the people would find their lives, at best, filled with inconveniences and at worst, a miserable existence. In the dark, foreboding words of Thomas Hobbes, the state of nature is akin to a state of war in which "the life of man [is] solitary, poor, nasty, brutish, and short" (Thomas Hobbes, *Leviathan*, intro. and ed. by C. B. Mac-Pherson (Baltimore: Penguin Books, 1968, Part I, ch. xiii, p. 186).

John Locke, writing half a century later, saw the state of nature as being sometimes idyllic but potentially as terrifying and dangerous as the state of war described by Hobbes. The danger in the state of nature, according to Locke, stems from the absence of a common authority that can arbitrate disagreements, settle disputes, and mete out appropriate punishments for transgressions.

2. Jean Jacques Rousseau, *Social Contract,* ed. Lester G. Crocker (New York: Pocket Books, 1967), p. 41.

3. John Dewey, *The Public and Its Problems* (Chicago: Gateway Books, 1946; originally published by Henry Holt, 1927), p. 39.

4. Jack Knight, *Institutions and Social Conflict* (New York: Cambridge University Press, 1992).

5. Federalist paper no. 51.

3

Forms of Democracy and Implications for Public Policy

INTRODUCTION

Democracy is not easily defined. The roots of the word come from ancient Greece and mean "people" and "governance." Most simply, democracy is any system of government where people govern themselves, as opposed to **autocracy** or aristocracy, where one person or a small group of individuals, respectively, governs everyone. Thus, democratic institutions can be very diverse, including a number of mechanisms that enable, to a greater or lesser extent, individuals to govern themselves. Democracy is used to describe governing schemes that use direct techniques for allowing people to decide policies, legislatures and representatives, or even self-governance, the latter probably being the democratic mechanism most consistent with the Greek roots of the word democracy.

In modern societies, democracies are made up of complex sets of decision rules that make use of a mix of different institutions. For example, in California, people elect a mayor, council, legislature, and governor (among others) to represent them. However, it is very easy to place on statewide ballots **initiatives,** which are policy proposals to be voted on directly by individuals in **referendums.** These referendums are policy proposals that, if they receive a majority of affirmative votes, become law. Also, self-governance and other forms of democracy are used to make policy. Most state and local governments make use of initiatives and referendums. Thus, **direct democracy** has an important place in American politics, though the national government does not use this mechanism. We typically refer to American democracy as representative, because localities, states, and the national government use representatives to make policy. **Representative democracy** is a government where individuals choose agents (usually by voting), such as legislators, and an executive to make governmental decisions.

Political institutions not only provide a set of rules by which political actors must abide but also structure democratic policymaking. We will see that these institutions in part limit the fairness of democratic decisions so that governance has some level of coherence. In doing so, the choice of institutions becomes a major element for ensuring sound governance.

Representation is a method of democracy in which publics delegate responsibility for governing to a president, governor, mayor, legislature or legislatures, council, or a combination of these. How well this works is hotly contested. We introduce direct democracy first so that we understand its limitations. These limitations in fact help us understand why representative government is difficult to evaluate in terms of how well people are represented. We also consider problems encountered when the majority rule mechanism is used to choose policies or leaders. Majority rule is not well equipped to represent permanent minorities, and we use the problem of race in the United States to illustrate this problem.

DIRECT DEMOCRACY

The easiest way to think about how popular sentiments are aggregated into group or public choices is to consider direct democracy. With direct democracy, we want to map the preferences of individuals into a single preference or sentiment for society. As we will see below, this is easier said than done.

We will use an abstract and simple example to show the limitations of voting as a democratic mechanism of policy choice. Consider three people, Gus, Sharon, and Gladys, who must decide collectively among three policies. They can choose to build a road (R), build a bridge (B), or do nothing (S, for "status quo"). The preference profiles are as follows:

Gus: BpRpS
Sharon: RpSpB
Gladys: SpBpR

Here, p is an operator denoting "preferred to." Thus, for Gus, the bridge is preferred to the road, which is preferred to the status quo.

We say that these preference orderings are transitive. **Transitivity** is a logical condition. We would think Gus illogical if he somehow preferred the status quo over the bridge. Transitivity means that if we have a preference ordering, we know the preference of the individual for any paired alternatives. That is, if Sharon prefers the road to the status quo and the status quo to the bridge, if her preferences are transitive she must prefer the road to the bridge. Now suppose these individuals choose to vote to determine which project, if any, will be constructed. There are many methods of voting, but let us suppose that they use majority rule in which two alternatives are compared, with the first-round winner being compared with the third alternative. The winner of the second round is the overall winner and is the democratic choice for the group. The ordering of the votes constitutes one **agenda** for decision. An agenda is a list of decisions that are to be made in a specified order.

In our example, suppose Agenda 1 calls for the following voting order:

Agenda 1

Vote 1: Bridge versus road: Bridge wins.
Vote 2: Bridge versus status quo: Status quo wins.

The status quo wins for Agenda 1 because Gus and Gladys prefer the bridge to the road in Round 1 and vote for it, and Sharon and Gladys prefer the status quo to the bridge in Round 2 and vote that way.

Two remaining potential agendas could be used. Agenda 2 pits the bridge and the status quo in Round 1:

Agenda 2

Vote 1: Bridge versus status quo: Status quo wins.
Vote 2: Status quo versus road: Road wins.

For this agenda, the road wins because the bridge is defeated in Round 1, and Gus and Sharon prefer the road to the status quo and vote for it. The democratic choice for this voting mechanism depends on the way the agenda is designed.

Indeed, Agenda 3 provides the final piece of the puzzle:

Agenda 3

Vote 1: Road versus status quo: Road wins.
Vote 2: Road versus bridge: Bridge wins.

Here, the bridge wins because Gus and Sharon vote for the road in the initial round, and the bridge beats the road in the second round because Gus and Gladys prefer it and vote for it.

This example shows that depending on the agenda, any of the alternatives could win majority approval. This means that directly voting on a policy does not ensure that the policy chosen is the will of the people. It is important to note that this is representative of a quality of all voting systems, although depending on the system, the arbitrariness may take different forms. We use this simple example because it illustrates this problem in the clearest possible fashion. It is also important to note that this and other voting systems do not always fail. If Gus preferred the road to the bridge, the road would be the clear majority winner, no matter what the agenda.

This example does more than show that voting systems sometimes fail to produce clear democratic winners. If a voting system fails, the winner will be chosen in either an arbitrary or a nondemocratic fashion. Furthermore, when voting systems fail, we usually do not know it. Thus, there is an inherent limitation to making group choices that are a function of individual desires, and this makes choosing public policies for society difficult.

ARROW'S POSSIBILITY THEOREM

The problem with democratic choice is even more fundamental than the problems associated with voting. Nobel Prize–winning economist Kenneth Arrow unexpectedly found that there exists no mechanism, in theory or practice, that aggregates individual preferences into a group preference ordering without violating certain principles of fairness and logicality.[1] By this we mean that for a group to have a preference ordering like that of Gus, Gladys, and Sharon, there is no way to guarantee that the resulting preference ordering will be logical (based on the preferences of the individuals in the group) or fair (based on democratic principles). Arrow's contribution resulted in the birth of a field of study called **social choice theory,** where students of voting try to find voting systems that best reflect preferences in society. In this section, we present Arrow's conditions and describe the implications of Arrow's theorem.

Arrow's general possibility theorem set out to show that, given a small number of requirements, a rational group preference ordering can be produced by some, or any, method of aggregating individual preferences. His methods were designed to produce a logical ordering of group preferences from an ordering of individual preferences. He declared several different conditions that would be democratic and logical. If it were possible to design a system of aggregation consistent with these conditions, then treating the group as a rational or coherent entity would make sense.

Arrow's conditions were very technical and allowed him to use basic, though abstract, mathematics to find out if a democratic correspondence between individual and group was possible. The conditions are meant to encompass the meaning of democratic choice. We list and describe the following six conditions.[2]

- *Universal Admissibility of Individual Preference Orderings* The condition of universal admissibility of individual preference orderings provides for any preference of any member of society to be admissible. The condition is a requirement of populist democracy. If someone holds an opinion, it should be heard. A democracy should not arbitrarily ignore certain individuals by ignoring their preferences.
- *Monotonicity* If a mechanism is used that generates a winning alternative, that alternative should not change if a person changes his or her mind in the direction of the winning alternative. For example, suppose that Alternative A wins and Alternative B comes in second. The monotonicity rule requires that if A wins and someone changes his or her preference from B to A, A should continue to win. This condition requires the social choice mechanism to be logical.

- *Citizens' Sovereignty* The citizens' sovereignty requirement means that people matter, so the preferences of people should matter. If some action is always chosen, no matter what the preferences of individuals, then the group choice can hardly be called democratic. This is a very simple concept. If a group is democratic, then citizens of that group should have an impact on the preferences of the group.
- *Unanimity* The unanimity requirement makes sure that a non-unanimous group choice is not preferred to a choice that has unanimous approval. If A is preferred to B by everyone, and the social choice mechanism chooses B, then this violates the unanimity condition. Unanimity is clearly a democratic or fairness condition.
- *Independence of Irrelevant Alternatives* The condition of independence of irrelevant alternatives requires any paired comparison between two alternatives by the group to be unaffected by any other alternatives of the group choice. Suppose that a society is trying to decide between spending additional money on defense and providing a new recreational park. The independence of irrelevant alternatives postulate requires that if a third option is introduced, such as providing a subsidy for home ownership, this introduction of a third alternative does not change the relationship between defense and providing a new recreational park. This condition, related to transitivity for individuals, is a clear requirement for logicality. It would not be rational for a person to change his or her preference between beef and chicken once mutton were introduced as an alternative, so it would not be desirable for the group ordering to change in a similar way.
- *Nondictatorship* Nondictatorship is a democratic requirement that for any group larger than two individuals, one single person should not be able to determine the social choice. This requirement is clearly one that must be consistent with democratic choice. Thus, it promotes fairness.

Implications of Arrow's Theorem

Arrow showed that it is impossible to produce a social choice mechanism, usually thought of as a voting system, that does not violate one of these six conditions. The consequences of Arrow's theorem are huge. No voting system can guarantee a logical and fair (democratic) choice. The theorem is startling; it has received an enormous amount of attention since it was introduced, because scholars have been very interested in trying to find methods of voting that lessen the sting of the theorem.

What does all this mean for public policy? Rather than being an abstraction away from reality, the theorem has been shown to imply enormous consequences for public policy. Most important, there exists no mechanism to determine, without doubt, what policies people want. This complicates cost-benefit analysis (see Chapter 11), as well as less formalized ways of determining what the public wants. Arrow's theorem indicates that it is problematic to use public opinion polls or surveys for understanding public preferences, as well as other mechanisms meant to measure public opinion. Indeed, the efforts of policymakers to make government policies consistent with public preferences are made problematic. How do we know what the public wants? Arrow tells us that there will always be uncertainty about this.

These implications of Arrow's theorem help us understand the nature of policy analysis: policy analysts can often be portrayed as elitists. Policy analysts typically try to figure out what is good for society apart from visible expressions of societal interests, because the interests of society, as conveyed through democratic mechanisms, can easily be dismissed as error-prone. This analysis is done in part because individuals are thought to be ignorant of what is good for society. But more important, policy analysts (at least) implicitly understand the problem of group choice. The potential for group choice to be illogical gives elites additional ammunition for arguing they should make policy, perhaps within broad guidelines of what the public wants.

Implications for Politics of Arrow's Theorem: Riker's Strategic Politician

William Riker, an influential social choice theorist, argued that Arrow's theorem has a fundamental consequence for democratic policymaking.[3] Social intransitives, as conveyed in the voting example above, suggest that clever politicians can take advantage of the fact that no pure general will of the people can be determined.

In the case where Gus, Gladys, and Sharon were trying to decide on transportation improvements, one smart politician in control of the agenda, known as **Riker's strategic politician,** could determine the social choice. Suppose Sharon controls the order of the voting; that is, Sharon controls the agenda. Clearly, Sharon would prefer to pit the bridge versus the status quo, a pairing in which the status quo would win. In the second round, the road would then meet the status quo, and the road would win. By being a clever agenda setter, Sharon turns out to be a dictator.

Riker's democracy is one where clever politicians win such policy battles, often changing the landscape of the American party system. He argues that the Civil War was produced by cleavages in the American electorate that were cleverly, but tragically, exploited by politicians. Likewise, Edward Carmines and James Stimson make an argument that the party structure in the United States in the 1950s was systematically transformed due to the issue of race that became a major focus of party politics after the 1950s.[4] Race drove a wedge in the past way of doing politics, and the nature of policy debates was changed forever. The implication of Riker's and Carmines and Stimson's arguments is that the democratic will of the people is manipulable, to some extent, by politicians who have some control over the agenda of policy. While race is obviously a very important political issue, it entered the agenda of American politics only after strategic politicians realized that race could change the political landscape. In essence, the introduction of race was a new alternative that changed the equilibrium of American politics. As Arrow proposed, new alternatives will often change democratic outcomes.

Thus, agenda setting becomes very important to understanding politics. Direct democracy, in a pure form, cannot exist. Controlling the agenda is a source of power. Thus, elites have more power than typical citizens. Elites who can mobilize the people will have distinct advantages. Thus are the vagaries of democracy. Those elites who can use the preferences of the people to change the direction of policy will hold a strong advantage. The fact that there is no single democratic will of the people allows this.

Hence public opinion is important, but its impact on policies is filtered through the strategic use of power by elites. The ability to control the agenda is an important source of elite power. Even if technology allowed every individual to voice a preference on public policy, there would be no obvious way to use this information in such a way that we could say that every social decision was democratic. However, we rarely depend only on direct democracy.

THE ROLE OF INSTITUTIONS

Note that in the discussion about the problems of direct democracy, there is little role for political institutions. **Institutions** are the rules that govern political decisions. These rules include how votes are taken and counted, who has the power to make public policy, and other rules of the game. Institutions may appear as constitutional, statutory, and judicial rules of action. Until now, we have observed few institutions in our discussion of direct democracy. Indeed, the institutions implied in Arrow's theorem are very sparse. However, Arrow's theorem does suggest how institutions will work in a real-world political system. Institutions structure outcomes, limiting the nature and scope of political actions and choices.

Recall that Arrow's system of preference aggregation has two values, logicality and democratic fairness. No system of preference aggregation can satisfy completely both values. One way to think about democratic institutions is that they limit democratic fairness to achieve some level of logicality. That is, institutions place limitations on the fairness of outcomes in order for these outcomes to have some coherent meaning.

Consider a typical legislature. Are all individual members of a legislature treated equally? When voting on a bill, each vote counts the same. However, the agenda is controlled in a way that gives some members more power than others. The bill that the legislature votes on has been shaped by many institutions and individuals that are given different agenda powers. A bill must be reported by a committee, so members of the committee have more power than members on the floor. The chair of the committee will often have more power than members; he or she may have the power to table, or kill, a bill before the committee is allowed to vote on reporting the bill to the floor. Usually an agent, such as the speaker of the House, will have power over chairs of the committees. Is this system a bastion of democracy? It is not, if you have different beliefs than the speaker and the majority party.

Historically, there have been several periods in which reformers tried to make the U.S. Congress more democratic. Most recently, this happened in 1974. Primarily, committees, and especially committee chairs, were made much less powerful. If sufficient numbers of committee members or members on the floor favor a bill, it can be reported to the floor over the objections of the committee chair. Before 1974, the chair had the power to table any bill. Many people believe that these reforms went too far and resulted in a Congress that was much less effective at solving the problems in the country.

By now you are beginning to understand the role and nature of political institutions. The types of political institutions are too numerous to list. However, we have identified a nonexhaustive and sometimes overlapping typology of institutions:

Constitutional A constitution places limits on the actions a government may take, as well as outlines the broad rules that enable actions by political actors. However, constitutions do just about anything, and many of the kinds of institutions listed below are often defined in a constitution.

Electoral Electoral institutions define how elections will be used to determine who sits in a legislature, who is going to be in the executive and other offices, and how policies might be adopted through direct democracy procedures. Electoral institutions vary tremendously throughout the world.

Administrative No executive or legislature can determine all public policies. Some power must be delegated to administrative institutions, or bureaucracies (see Chapter 10). The role of nonelected bureaucracies is an important element of the institutional structure.

Legislative Legislative institutions determine how individuals are represented and how legislation is made. Important in legislative institutions is how agendas are set before votes are taken. Most legislatures are set up so that committees specialize to better use information about various policy areas.

Executive Almost all countries have an executive, although in parliamentary systems executive authority arises from the legislature. Executives have powers that legislatures are too clumsy to handle. In the United States, a predominate power of the president is the making of foreign policy.

Judicial In the United States, the judiciary is one of the three branches of government. The function of the courts is to interpret laws and the Constitution, as well as to try criminal and civil conflicts. Judicial institutions also vary tremendously throughout the world; often, the judiciary is not a separate branch of government but part of the executive branch or the legislature.

Statutory The laws passed by legislatures, signed by executives, and interpreted by courts also constitute important political institutions. Laws are a byproduct of other institutions, but they lie at the core of how political systems try to shape individual behavior to better society. Included in these statutes are regulations, criminal laws, civil laws, and property rights.

Obviously, political institutions are ubiquitous. However, some institutions are better than others. Given the role of institutions—bringing coherence to democratic political decisions—there exist some basic rules about the way institutions should be developed and used. We highlight three of these.

First, statutory institutions should change more often than other institutions. If, say, legislative institutions can be changed as easily as statutes, then battles over particular legislation may result in battles over institutions. If non-statutory institutions can be changed as easily as statutory institutions, then logicality or coherence will suffer. This happens because the limitations of majority rule apply to institutions as well, and institutions would fail to function as a means for achieving coherent governance.

Second, strong institutions should be designed so that they instill public trust. In 1936, when an intransigent Supreme Court continually found New Deal policies unconstitutional, President Franklin D. Roosevelt tried to increase the size of the court to offset conservative justices. Public opinion was strongly against this move, and the initiative failed. Thus, the idea that there would be nine members of the court was a resilient institution, one not changed easily for political reasons.

Third, institutions should result in coherent political decisions with as little reduction in fairness as possible. The balance between fairness and logicality is not well understood. There is no secret formula for obtaining the perfect balance. However, there are clearly situations where there is too little coherence or too little fairness. For example, authoritarian political regimes clearly have too little democracy. Likewise, at least to most outside observers, California's heavy use of direct democracy provides too little coherence.

REPRESENTATIVE DEMOCRACY

In this section, we describe some concepts of representation that will help us further understand the complexity of real-world governance. Most democratic theorists presuppose that for most social decisions, some representative (such as a president) or some representative body (such as a legislature) will design statutes. Of course, some bureaucracy will administer such laws, and often a judiciary will interpret them. In the United States, we typically use representation based on geographic location (**geographic representation**). This choice is common among many nation-states, but it is not the only way people can be represented.

Hanna Pitkin argued that conceptions of representation take on very different forms.[5] Geographic representation, as practiced in the United States, is just one of several forms of representation. For example, **descriptive representation** is a form that attempts to create a representative body that looks like the populous. If 24 percent of the population is a certain ethnic group, then descriptive representation calls for approximately 24 percent of representatives to be the same ethnic group. By contrast, **substantive representation** calls for people with a certain policy preference to be represented at the appropriate rate. The use of representation and the types of representation depend on constitutional orders, which may or may not be appropriate for a given populous.

Any form of representation will emphasize one attribute that some people share and suppress other attributes. Consider the consequences of the geographic representation in the United States. What do you have in common with other people who live in your general area? Many people in your area may have similar incomes and social status. In other geographic districts, religion or ethnicity may be shared. But, of course, you differ in many different ways from your neighbors. Often, individuals have little in common with the majority in their voting district. If you are young and live in Florida, you may find that more people in your district are octogenarians than twenty-somethings. If you are heterosexual and live in the Castro district in San Francisco, you may find that more gay men or lesbians than heterosexuals live in your district. If you are white and live in East Los Angeles, you may find more minorities than whites in your district. In short, geographic distribution hardly guarantees that you will be substantively or descriptively represented.

An emphasis on a single representational attribute can lead to a cleavage in the larger society along that dimension. Geographic representation contributed to the Civil War. In the South, the concentration of a plantation-style economic system, slavery, and a commodity-exporting economy contrasted greatly with the northern economy. In the North, the economy was based on manufacturing and exporting of finished goods. This distinction led to political and military conflict. Representation based on ethnicity and religion is an important ingredient in the ongoing instability in the Balkans. In fact, ethnicity is a very important factor for understanding why democracies fail to quell internal conflicts. Box 3.1 provides a graphic example of how different democracies have tried to cope with this problem.

Thus, geographic representation, because it is familiar, might appear to work reasonably well, except when some other problem lines up along geographic lines (for example, the oil crises of the 1970s). However, geographic representation is susceptible to a more subtle but expensive tendency of democratic failure than are other forms of representation.

Representatives often favor distributive policies over more broad-based considerations. **Distributive policies** produce goods and services that are enjoyed by only a fraction of the overall population, usually based on geography. Concentrated benefits are provided to a particular locale, and constituencies that elect a representative want the benefits from these programs. However, everyone pays for distributive policies, regardless of where they live. For example, improvement of airport and harbor facilities, renovation of polluted industrial facilities, expansion of roads, reclamation of deforested green areas,

Calvin and Hobbes

by Bill Watterson

and creation of rails-to-trails bicycle projects all benefit local constituents, with few, if any, benefits for the rest of the polity. The problem is not that these programs have no merit. Rather, the question is, Which programs should be funded, and by whom?

What is the impact of this tendency to pursue distributive policies? One important fact is that the costs of these projects are disconnected from the benefits flowing from them. If the city of Peoria, Illinois, seeks federal funding for road improvements, will the citizens of Peoria support funding of this project? One would hope that citizen support would depend on the benefit flows from the project relative to the costs. Indeed, we will see in Chapter 11 that the ideal project will maximize the ratio of benefits to costs.

Unfortunately, Peoria's choice about whether to support this project depends on the ratio of benefits, almost all to Peoria's populace, to the costs to residents of Peoria. With geographic representation, Peoria will pay only a very small portion of the real costs of the project if the federal government is funding the project. Residents of New York, California, Texas, and California will pay for much of the project, and most of these people will never set foot in Peoria. This changes only a little if Peoria pays 10 percent and the nation as a whole 90 percent, which is currently the way many public works projects from the federal government operate. The citizens of Peoria may want the road project even if the costs exceed the benefits, since most of the costs are borne by taxpayers living elsewhere. Residents would never want to fund such a project if they had to pay for the entire thing.

Now, you may say that such a system could work if other cities also got their fair share. The problem is that what is fair is not very smart. Fort Wayne, Bakersfield, Boise, and Omaha all want a piece of the action. What results is a phenomenon called **universalism.** Because of the distributive pressures of a legislature's representing geographic districts, there exists a severe problem of how to allocate distributive policies. Universalism is a norm that says everyone

Box 3.1 Consociationalism in Yugoslavia and Lebanon

IN THE United States, social divisions are complex and overlapping. While people may have different ethnic or racial ties, they often share religious allegiances or economic concerns. Conversely, they may have different religious backgrounds but share allegiances to the same professional sports teams or political parties. Our social characteristics tend to be crosscutting, preventing group divisions from becoming fixed and permanently opposed. This is not always the case. In Switzerland, for example, French speakers live in a particular canton (state) and German speakers in another, while Italian speakers live in another separate canton. The ethnic, cultural, and linguistic differences separate people; they do not crosscut, as in the United States.

Democratic countries with such a situation often choose a form of democracy that political scientist Arend Lijphart has named **consociational democracy**.[1] Instead of one president or prime minister winning an election and governing alone, these nations choose a coalition of leaders that represent different social groups. Instead of elections meaning winning everything or losing everything, this coalition attempts to moderate differences and build consensus among different social groups. Each significant sector of society can veto any legislation that it opposes, and the nation's civil service typically ensures that public works and programs are distributed evenly. Finally, each sector typically dominates one particular area, and each is given some localized governmental rule over its area. This form of government has been a profound success in diverse European societies, such as Belgium, the Netherlands, and Switzerland. Unfortunately, this consociational system of democracy failed in two countries: Yugoslavia and Lebanon.

Yugoslavia had always been a powder keg for ethnic division and violence. With three major religions, linguistic differences, six national republics, and long histories of bellicosity between groups, it is amazing that Yugoslavia held together as long as it did. Following World War II, the charismatic leader Marshal Tito kept the communist country unified and independent of both the Soviets and the West. Following his death in 1980, the constitution established collegial executives—with rotating Communist Party leadership and also a rotating presidency. This ensured a consociational system where each particular group would be assured of executive control of the Communist Party and the state executive office.

1. Arend Lijphart, "Typologies of Democratic Systems," *Comparative Political Studies* (April 1968), pp. 3–44.

gets something; relatively equal numbers of goodies are distributed to every district. This results in a very expensive outcome. Projects are funded due to norms rather than their benefits relative to costs. In fact, what can result is a sum total, across the entire country, of projects whose benefits are less than their costs. This situation may or may not occur. However, it is almost a sure thing that the cost-benefit ratios for these projects will be lower than if the beneficiaries of the projects bore the costs of the projects. Box 3.2 offers an example of how this issue plays out in the reelection strategies of members of Congress.

Two things began to erode the smooth working of consociationalism. First, some republics began to call for a multiple-party system rather than only the Communist Party, and some noncommunists began to win elections within these republics. Second, the Croatian, Slovenian, and Macedonian republics declared themselves fully sovereign within Yugoslavia. Serbian republic leaders introduced a new constitution that stripped other regions of autonomy and, in effect, stripped their elected officials of power. When the economically prosperous Slovenian and Croatian republics declared their independence, it triggered a civil war between Serbs and Slovenes that eventually spread to war between Croats and Serbs. The multiethnic republics of Bosnia and Kosovo became battlegrounds for warring ethnic groups in ensuing years. Consociationalism failed because the institutional mechanisms could not restrain the ethnic, religious, and linguistic differences that divided Yugoslavia.

Lebanese consociationalism failed for other reasons. Lebanon has four major religious groups: Maronite Christians, Druse (a sect split from Islam), Sunni Muslims, and Shi'ite Muslims. During the period of French imperial control, Lebanese parliamentary seats were distributed evenly among the larger Christian and Muslim populations, with seats given to Druse reflecting their proportion of the population. After independence, each different group was to have a share of parliamentary seats and control over cabinet positions: Maronites as president, Sunni Muslims as prime minister, Shi'ite Muslims as president of the Chamber of Deputies, and Druse leaders as head of defense. As consociationalism prescribes, each group had a say in the governing coalition.

Two enormous changes led to the disintegration of the smooth-running consociationalism. First, the charismatic Egyptian leader Gamal Abdul Nasser created a unifying pan-Arab identity for Muslim Arabs. Muslim Lebanese began to identify with other Middle Eastern Arabs more than they did with fellow Lebanese citizens of different religions. Second, the Muslim population grew faster than the Christian and Druse populations, and the influx of Palestinian refugees displaced by Israel further heightened the population disparity. Thus, the once-even split of seats in the parliament and positions in the cabinet no longer fit the actual distribution of groups in Lebanese society. This situation called into question the efficacy of consociationalism—it no longer served its original purpose of giving each group a proportional allocation of governmental representation. Following internal political violence and fueled by ties between internal groups and different external nations such as Israel, Iran, and the United States, the situation in Lebanon disintegrated into a terrible civil war in 1976 that lasted for more than a decade.

Since resources are limited, the overprovision of distributive projects and policies will almost surely lead to some neglect of broader, national social problems. Problems such as health care, air traffic control, coastal water quality, and management of fisheries all must compete with distributive policies for scarce resources. Of course, if such policies can be turned into distributive ones, then these problems may be dealt with, and this is one way the federal government approaches these types of problems. Education becomes a national issue, and the federal government provides money to schools for extra teachers. Or crime becomes a national issue, and the federal government provides funding

Box 3.2   *The Congressional Pork Barrel*

Why does **pork barrel** spending, which is the funding of projects whose costs exceed their benefits, continue if American citizens wish to end what they often see as wasteful spending? Are our leaders merely gluttonous spenders? Political scientist John Ferejohn concentrated on river and harbor improvement legislation and highlighted three main reasons why pork barrel projects continue: geographic congressional representation, majority rule, and the congressional committee system.[1]

As stated in the text, the costs of public works projects are spread across the whole country, while the benefits accrue to the specific geographic area in which the project is located. Elected officials understand this and do what they can to ensure that they provide these benefits to their districts. For many incumbents, this is a great advantage in fending off challengers at reelection time. Former senator Alfonse D'Amato was often jokingly called "Senator Pothole" for his public works efforts in New York. D'Amato did not mind this, however, because to him it signified the hard work he did on behalf of his constituents.

The second cause of pork barrel spending, majority rule, stems from elected officials' logrolling. **Logrolling** refers to one member of Congress supporting another member's pet project in order to receive support on her own pet project. One of the first things representatives or senators learn is that they must "go along to get along." If a member tries to block projects proposed for other districts, that member is very likely to find that he is unable later to gain support on issues of importance in his district. Thus, it makes no sense to rock the boat.

Finally, the congressional committee system places certain members on appropriations committees, which decide whether to spend money on projects. Both the House and Senate appropriations committees have subcommittees that deal with public works. The districts represented by members on these subcommittees often receive a disproportionate amount of public works dollars. Some members of these subcommittees become pork barrel barons. The current chair of the House Transportation and Infrastructure Subcommittee (the name was changed from Public Works to avoid the negative association with pork barrel projects), Republican congressman Bud Shuster of Pennsylvania, has directed enormous amounts of federal dollars to projects in his district. Indeed, to get to the heart of his district from the Pennsylvania Turnpike, one has to take the Bud Shuster Highway.

Not all public works programs are wasteful; the nation's infrastructure needs to be attended to. The issue is the projects for which the costs outweigh the benefits. In the 1994 midterm elections, Republican candidates for Congress tapped into a growing public dissatisfaction for wasteful congressional spending by painting incumbent Democrats as pork barrel spendthrifts. While the Republicans decried such programs, studies have shown that the now-incumbent Republican revolutionaries have developed pet projects at levels similar to their Democratic counterparts.[2] This gives further credence to Ferejohn's notion that the mixture of geographic representation, majority rule, and the committee system, rather than party or ideology, is primarily responsible for pork barrel projects.

1. John Ferejohn, *Pork Barrel Politics* (Stanford, Calif.: Stanford University Press, 1974).

2. Kenneth N. Bickers and Robert M. Stein, "The Pork Barrel in a Republican Era," paper presented at the annual meeting of the Midwest Political Science Association, Chicago (April 17–20, 1999); and Andrew Taylor, "GOP's War on Pet Projects Bogs Down in Temptation," *Congressional Quarterly Weekly* (August 22, 1998), pp. 2264–2269.

for extra police officers. In this way, many problems are addressed, but how well and how efficiently are very difficult to know. And there are always true national problems that will continue to be shortchanged by the politics of distributive policy.

PRINCIPALS AND AGENTS

Representative democracies elect delegates, or **agents,** who are supposed to represent constituencies. There are various notions of what representation entails. Representation is sometimes understood to be the communication of constituent preferences with as little alteration as possible. Sometimes representation is understood to mean that the representative, having been duly elected, should use his or her own judgment as to what is in the best long-term interests of constituents, even if the constituents themselves do not agree with that judgment. Still other times, representation is understood as being the correspondence between characteristics of constituents, such as race, ethnicity, or religion, and the characteristics of the elected representative. Consequently, it is possible for legislators from the same state to act in very different ways, even when they are all trying faithfully to represent their constituents.

From the implications of Arrow's theorem we know that elites, including elected representatives, who are able to exercise control over the choices presented to the public possess the ability to manipulate outcomes. Representative democracy, however, poses a second dilemma. A pervasive problem with representative democracies, of all types and flavors, is the problem of monitoring the behavior of the elected representatives. Monitoring is required to ensure that the representatives are doing what constituents expect of them, regardless of the type of representative government that is used. Monitoring of elected officials is a difficult and costly task for constituents, and this gives representatives the opportunity to pursue goals other than those favored by their constituents.

Representatives are agents. We refer to publics as **principals.** We will use the same terminology in Chapter 10, and we use this more abstract formulation to draw an analogy to other principal-agent relationships. If you work for Quicky Mart, you are an agent of the owner of that convenience store. And if you work at the dorm cafeteria, you are an agent for the university. If you are the president of the United States, you are an agent of the nation's people. If you are the secretary of agriculture, you are the agent of the president of the United States and thus indirectly an agent of the people of the United States.

Principals want to control agents. In fact, the ideal world for a principal would be for agents to do exactly what the principal wants. Unfortunately, this is not feasible. Agents want to do other things, too, in large part because no individuals want to do just someone else's bidding if they are free to act in their own interest. The Quicky Mart clerk may not really want to treat customers the way the owner wants them treated. Furthermore, the clerk may want to steal, read when she is supposed to be mopping, and generally goof off. We refer to this behavior as **shirking,** which is any activity that satisfies the agent at the principal's expense. Most students and professors should have little difficulty understanding this concept. Students often try to find quick and easy ways to satisfy requirements without doing the work. Unfortunately, as much as faculty members bemoan this problem, they themselves sometimes try to find ways to minimize the effort that goes into preparation for a class.

Principals devise a wide-ranging set of strategies to control agents. These strategies fall into two categories. First, principals try to create incentives to keep agents from shirking. These incentives may be positive, such as profit sharing, or negative, such as using drug testing and lie detector tests. Second, principals may try to create team players through psychological motivation. They try to make the agent feel bad about shirking. Doing this is trickier than using incentives, but some evidence shows that psychological methods are necessary, just as incentives are, to control agents.

When applied to representatives in government, we see that these measures are hardly available to citizens. About the most a citizen can do to control a representative, other than voting, is responding effectively to opinion polls. Of course, other mechanisms may be available, such as litigation, but any extraordinary monitoring and sanctioning would be very difficult. The reason we elect political officials in the first place is that we want them to do the work. We are too busy to run government. We have little incentive to monitor the day-to-day activities of elected representatives. Thus, the principal-agent problem in representative government is potentially huge.

Of course, the principal-agent problem is only a problem if elected agents have reason to shirk, but they almost always have a reason. There are two major incentives for elected representatives to shirk. First, they may be **ideological shirkers;** that is, they may want to pursue ideological agendas that are at odds with the ideological preferences of the majority of their constituents. Second, they may respond to **rent seekers,** groups that want policies to benefit themselves at the expense of the public at large. Other forms of shirking also exist, but these two types have the most important impact on representative government.

As you may guess, ideological shirking occurs when representatives have a different ideological makeup than their constituencies. When representatives think the public is not paying much attention to what they are doing, they may vote for legislation that their constituents would never support. Ideological shirking is often identified by constituents if representatives are not careful. Thus, representatives who want to vote differently from their districts may often do so. Note also that the implications of Arrow's theorem will make ideological shirking easier than it otherwise would be.

Ideological shirking is probably a relatively low cost behavior. The policy consequences of rent seeking are similar to those of ideological shirking: the public gets policies it does not want. But there is a difference. With ideological shirking, the representative has different policy positions than her constituency and votes on legislation accordingly. With rent seeking, the representative attempts to influence policy in order to seek some reward from the rent-seeking group. In the most virulent form of rent seeking, political officials seek bribes or, more quaintly, tribute for producing policies favorable to some group. Bribery is illegal, but in many democracies bribery is the typical way much business gets done. In advanced democracies, bribery is less of a problem. However, it still happens, and leaders are sometimes caught.

A more subtle form of bribery occurs when political officials make policies to encourage political campaign contributions. Organized interest groups try to rent seek, whereby they provide campaign contributions in exchange for influence on policy. Of course, overt influence peddling is illegal. Thus, any direct connection between campaign contributions and public policy outputs is illegal. However, such influence is difficult to enforce. Did an official make a policy in response to a campaign contribution, or did the representative support the policy because he believed the policy was good for the constituency or the country? To prove that an official broke a law, a clear connection between the contribution and the policy must be substantiated. Thus, laws fail to provide incentives that abolish rent seeking by interest groups. Rather, laws make political officials careful in the methods they use to support interest groups that give monetary support to their candidacies.

Of course, these difficult-to-enforce laws about influence peddling make monitoring by the electorate particularly difficult. Watchdog groups, such as Ralph Nader's Common Cause, help. But attention to such secondary sources of information is not steadfast among most Americans, so the typical citizen is privy to only the most flagrant of violations of influence-peddling laws. American citizens occasionally have been motivated to punish these offenses, but such offenses are difficult to substantiate.

Rent seeking by organized interests often results in policies that the public would not want. This happens because representatives are able to take advantage of people's inability to monitor representatives' actions. Compounding this problem is the fact that representatives may be able take advantage of our inability to monitor and thus become relatively immune to our ability to turn them out of office at election time. That is, representative democracy can create a new social class in society—what columnist George Will has called the *political class*.[6] This class of government representatives and employees has in its interest to pursue policies that perpetuate itself. Special interests can provide the resources necessary to keep bureaucracies strong by supporting incumbent politicians who support those bureaucracies.

How do interest groups provide the resources to perpetuate the political class? Rent seeking by interest groups has two important effects. First, it can supply elected officials with campaign coffers that are flush with money. With these funds, an incumbent running for reelection can so outspend any challenger that the challenger never has a fighting chance of winning. Second, organized groups that stand to benefit most from the incumbent's staying in office may actively seek to keep strong potential challengers from entering a race against the incumbent. They can do so by signaling potential challengers that campaign dollars will not be forthcoming and by persuading potential challengers not to enter the race. The result is an electoral system in which many incumbents face little or no opposition. If this happens, real democracy no longer exists.

Of course, many recent calls for reform of the political system are focused on reducing the importance of interest groups in electoral and bureaucratic politics. The calls for term limits of representatives to Congress were an effort to weaken the importance of incumbency in congressional elections. In 1994, many candidates for Congress, mostly Republicans, vowed to stay in office only a short period once elected. It is interesting that some of these members of Congress now have vowed to run after their self-imposed limit expired.

Calls for campaign finance reform are another attempt to make money less important in elections. One of the most innovative ideas for diminishing rent seeking is to require that all campaign contributions be put into a blind account so that candidates would be unable to determine the source or amount of any particular contributions to their campaigns. This would be analogous to the so-called Australian ballot. This voting system originated in Australia. It allows voters to cast their ballots in private. It was adopted in the United States in the 1900s to ensure that votes cast by the public are insulated from the prying eyes of candidates and party bosses. The Australian ballot helped eliminate much of the corruption that once surrounded the voting process. The "Australian" fund-raising accounts would likewise make it impossible for elected officials to know from whom contributions were collected, and thus whose rent-seeking efforts should be rewarded. From the perspective of potential campaign contributors, the value of campaign contributions would be greatly diminished. Contributors would know that the amounts and sources of their contributions would be shielded from the elected representatives and thus would be of little use in currying favor for their causes. Unfortunately, to this date, the focus on term limits and campaign finance reform has had little impact on the rent-seeking behavior of interest groups, members of Congress, or the bureaucracy.

PERMANENT MINORITIES

One of the most difficult problems associated with democracy as a mechanism for making collective choices is the potential for some group of people to become a permanent minority. The legitimacy of democratic processes derives in part from the expectation that although policy outcomes might not match our preferences on some issues, outcomes will match our preferences on some of the issues that are important to us. When one group of people is relegated permanently to the minority, losing on issue after issue, the legitimacy of the democratic process becomes suspect. That is, democracy should not have systematic biases that lead to a stable majority-minority situation.

The most egregious case of a permanent minority in American history was the treatment of black people by white people in the southern states from the earliest days of European colonization of North America until the 1960s. African Americans in southern states were enslaved during much of this period, but even after the formal end of slavery at the end of the Civil War, they continued to be systematically stripped of civil rights, denied the right to vote, and reduced to the status of servitude. Skin color provided a public cue as to the identity of African Americans and made it easy for the majority to exclude this minority from equal participation in society. Indeed, even in places where African Americans constituted a majority of the population, they continued to be subjected to inferior treatment, because the rules of the game (that is, state constitutions, statutes, and local ordinances) had been previously designed by white majorities to ensure that blacks would continue to be denied the political, economic, and social rights enjoyed by whites.

The treatment of African Americans is the most glaring, but not the only, case of a racial group that has found its interests repeatedly and systematically ignored or denigrated by the majority of citizens. Asian immigrants from the middle of the nineteenth century until after World War II were another group of people who were systematically discriminated against. Asian men were induced to come to the United States with offers of high-paying employment. Once here, however, they found themselves facing systematic discrimination and terrible working conditions. Many of the men were forced to join work crews constructing rail beds and tunnels for railroad companies, hazardous work even without the extremes of heat and cold in the mountains and deserts of the American West. For much of this period, women from Asian countries were denied the right to immigrate to the United States. Until well into the twentieth century, most Asian immigrants were prohibited from becoming naturalized citizens. They were forbidden from owning property. They could not marry Caucasians. During World War II thousands of Japanese Americans, most of whom were U.S. citizens, were forcibly uprooted from their homes and placed in internment camps that were little more than prisons.

In both the African American and Asian American cases, the groups targeted for discrimination had little recourse. They were denied formal rights to participate in the political process, and thus they had little legal leverage to change the laws that assigned to them second-class citizenship or any citizenship at all.

Consider, for comparative purposes, the case of gay men and lesbians in American society. The proportion of gay men and lesbians in the population appears to be somewhere in the range of 5 to 10 percent (though determining the exact proportion has always proved difficult), and it has apparently been fairly stable over time. There are no visible cues, such as skin color or eye shape, differentiating homosexuals from the rest of the population. Yet laws in every American state prevent homosexual persons from enjoying the same rights and privileges as heterosexuals. Why? The answer is that homosexual persons constitute a permanent minority. On issues directly affecting the rights of homosexuals, heterosexuals are in the majority. To the extent that issues are framed as rights for homosexuals, it has proved nearly impossible for homosexuals to forge coalitions with sufficient numbers of heterosexuals to win legislative changes. Whereas African Americans and Asian Americans were denied entry to the voting booth to try to obtain more equal treatment, homosexuals have been able to use their votes, but they have still regularly and repeatedly lost.

What is the recourse for groups that have become permanent minorities? Sometimes, unfortunately, there is little recourse. This is why the emergence of a permanent majority-minority cleavage is so pernicious in a democracy.

Sometimes, however, measures are available to minority groups. Leadership within the minority group can try to redefine the issues that affect the group in ways that build common ground with members of the majority. The plight of African Americans was helped immeasurably by the active, and often heroic, participation of black servicemen in World War II. This participation allowed blacks to ask why their brothers, fathers, and sons were fighting and dying in Europe and the Pacific to overturn racist regimes, only to be relegated to second-class status because of their race when they returned home to the United States. This was a valid question and one that resonated with many whites. It went far toward the development of coalitions between whites in the northern states and blacks in the South and near South to overthrow the Jim Crow laws that maintained the system of segregation in the South.

The other strategy that sometimes works is for members of the minority group to seek recourse through the judicial system, rather than the electoral or legislative systems. By slowly and painstakingly bringing before the courts cases that build a body of precedents, it is sometimes possible to chip away at, and eventually overturn, discriminatory laws.

This method was a key strategy of African American civil rights advocates. The landmark case, *Brown v. Board of Education* (1954, 1955), which led the way to the desegregation of public schools, was the product of a strategy engineered by the Legal Defense and Educational Fund of the National Association for the Advancement of Colored People (NAACP), under the leadership of Thurgood Marshall (who would later be named the first black man to the U.S. Supreme Court). The first series of cases brought by Marshall attacked the "separate but equal" doctrine that had evolved in the wake of the Supreme Court's *Plessy v. Ferguson* decision in 1896. This doctrine had resulted in two separate societies in the United States—one for whites and one for nonwhites—with dramatic disparities in the quality of the public facilities for each group.

Over a twenty-year period, the NAACP used the courts to try to force southern states to make public facilities, especially schools, that were designated for African Americans to be equal in fact, and not merely in name, to the facilities available to whites. The goal of this legal campaign was to build the groundwork for an assault on the inherent inequality of separate facilities by demonstrating that schools and other public places could never provide truly equal opportunities so long as they kept black and white people separated. It was this that the *Brown v. Board of Education* case put to an end. The ruling held that separate educational facilities were inherently unequal and could never be made equal so long as separation was allowed to persist.

Note that this strategy of utilizing the courts can be very slow in redressing the injustices suffered by permanent minorities. The situation of African Americans has improved dramatically over the past generation, but there continue to be differences in the treatment of whites and blacks. Asian Americans have benefited greatly by the gains of blacks, because many of the legal changes won by African Americans were extended to Asian Americans. Gains for homosexuals have been slower—continuing testimony to the difficulties faced by minority groups in overcoming legal and cultural impediments that keep them in permanent minority status.

CONCLUSION

In this chapter, we confronted the strengths and the many unfortunate difficulties in trying to rely on democratic choice as a means for making sound collective decisions. Democracy can take many forms. It can be direct or representative, and representative democracy can be based on geography or shared interests. Unfortunately, every form of democracy turns out to be susceptible to one or more types of failures. In real life, there is no perfect system for making collective choices.

In summary, the problems associated with democracy include the following:

1. The manipulation of outcomes through control of the order in which choices are presented to the public.
2. The over-emphasis in representative democracies on one particular attribute of constituents to the detriment of other potentially important attributes.
3. The difficulties faced by the public in trying to oversee the job performance of representatives.
4. The opportunities for representatives to service the needs of well-organized groups at the expense of the general public.
5. The potential for democracies to have within them permanent minorities that may be systematically harmed by majorities over long periods of time.

Key Terms

democracy *p. 35*
autocracy *p. 35*
initiative *p. 35*
referendum *p. 35*

direct democracy *p. 35*
representative democracy *p. 35*
transitivity *p. 36*
agenda *p. 37*

Suggested Readings

Abrams, Robert. 1980. *Foundations of Political Analysis: An Introduction to the Theory of Collective Choice.* New York: Columbia University Press.

Buchanan, James, and Gordon Tullock. 1962. *The Calculus of Consent.* Ann Arbor: University of Michigan Press.

Burke, Edmund. 1961. *Selected Writings and Speeches.* Edited by Peter Stanslis. Garden City, N.Y.: Doubleday.

Dahl, Robert. 1956. *A Preface to Democratic Theory.* Chicago: University of Chicago Press.

Etzioni, Amitai. 1975. *A Comparative Analysis of Complex Organizations: On Power, Involvement, and Their Correlates.* Rev. and enlarged ed. New York: Free Press.

McPherson, C. B. 1973. *Democratic Theory.* Oxford: Oxford University Press.

Miller, Warren, and Donald Stokes. 1963. "Constituency Influence in Congress." *American Political Science Review* 57: 45–56.

Ordeshook, Peter. 1992. *A Political Theory Primer.* New York: Routledge.

Rhoades, Steven. 1985. *The Economists View of the World.* Cambridge, England: Cambridge University Press.

Riker, William. 1986. *The Art of Political Manipulation.* New Haven, Conn.: Yale University Press.

Riker, William, and Peter Ordeshook. 1973. *An Introduction to Political Theory.* Englewood Cliffs, N.J.: Prentice-Hall.

Sears, David, and Jack Citrin. 1982. *Tax Revolt.* Cambridge, Mass.: Harvard University Press.

Notes

1. Kenneth Arrow, *Social Choice and Individual Values,* 2nd ed. (New Haven, Conn.: Yale University Press, 1963).

2. William Riker, *Liberalism Against Populism* (San Francisco: W. H. Freeman, 1982).

3. *Ibid.*

4. Edward Carmines and James Stimson, *Issue Evolution: Race and the Transformation of American Politics* (Princeton, N.J.: Princeton University Press, 1989).

5. Hanna Pitkin, *The Concept of Representation* (Berkeley: University of California Press, 1967).

6. George Will, *Restoration: Congress, Term Limits and the Recovery of Deliberative Democracy* (New York: Free Press, 1992).

III

Collective Action and
Democratic Governance

4

The Problem of
Collective Action

INTRODUCTION

Societal problems are all around us. Typically, the natural response to these problems, such as pollution or war, is to say, "Why can't people just do the right thing and not pollute or not fight wars?" Many would often refer to such problems as stemming from the irrationality of individuals and society as a whole. This is the easy interpretation, but one that fails to show adequate understanding of the underlying causes of social problems, and one that in fact impedes solutions to what are referred to as **collective action problems.** These types of problems result when individually rational actions produce outcomes at the group level that do not appear to be very rational.

Individual actions aggregated to the group level often have unintended consequences for society, or what we will more commonly refer to as a group, the aggregation of individuals. These consequences can result even when individuals act rationally. While rationality is a contested concept that we will define below, the idea is simple. Individuals acting in a very intelligent manner may, in the aggregate, lead to problems for the group. Understanding why this happens is the key to unlocking solutions to group problems. Ignoring this process actually becomes self-defeating, because asking individuals to do what is good for a group is often a hollow and futile exercise.

Solutions to problems a group encounters often revolve around providing incentives to individuals to act differently than they would otherwise act if no solution were proposed. Solving problems at the group level, then, depends on policies that change incentives so that individuals, when acting in their own interest, will also be acting in the group's interest. This requires solving collective action problems, because these arise when individual interests are at odds with the interests of the group as a whole.

Not all unintended consequences of individual action cause collective action problems. For example, sometimes individuals acting according to their own desires leads to a more prosperous group. The classic market of Adam Smith is such an example, in which the aggregation of individual actions makes the group better off. This is why the choice of policy for most liberal countries, where individuals have certain rights and liberties, includes a choice for when government should and should not limit or regulate individual behavior.

Thus, collective action problems arise when individual actions are predominantly and consistently not in the interests of the group. We present in this chapter the basic logic of this problem. Collective action problems are sometimes solved by individuals alone, by coercive action by governments or others, and by a plethora of other institutions that have evolved over millennia of human history. Matching the solution to the problem is an incredible challenge for policy analysts.

INDIVIDUAL FOUNDATIONS
OF COLLECTIVE ACTION

Social scientists sometimes use baseline models to understand social process. A baseline model oversimplifies the world but is useful because it allows analysts to obtain a reasonable, if imperfect, understanding of the incentives facing individuals. We use a baseline model to see how individuals and groups face policy problems. Thus, the models of collective action problems are conceptual tools that analysts use to try to understand why individual actions are sometimes inconsistent with group goals. But before we are able to present this problem, we must first provide an explanation for the way typical individuals behave.

Rationality assumes that individuals are capable of choosing the best alternative they see available to them. Rational individuals therefore are capable individuals. This does not mean they choose behaviors that comport with any one specific world view. Rational individuals may choose many different actions, and it is often difficult to determine whether they are indeed rational. The rationality assumption does not give us enough to understand human behavior.

Social scientists gain much leverage by adding an additional assumption to rationality so that they can make predictions about human behavior that are ultimately capable of helping policy analysts. This assumption is that individuals have **self-interest**. Together with the rationality postulate, this means people will choose what is best for them. This assumption will become a very powerful tool in predicting what individuals will do in reaction to public policy, primarily because it helps us understand collective action problems and potentially solve them through action designed to change the interests—sometimes called **preferences**—of individual actors. Thus, altruism or good intentions are not the foundation of solving group problems, although some policies do try to change individual preferences rather than altering incentives.

Rationality is a formal concept that is handy for predicting the behavior of individuals. We assume that individuals make decisions, and these decisions lead to actions that result in consequences for the individuals. Aggregating actions across all individuals in a group allows us to understand the consequences of individual actions for the behavior of the group. Without some basis for understanding and predicting individual actions, we would have little guidance for understanding the consequences of individual behavior for group outcomes, because we could not predict the behavior of individuals in the first place. Less formal reliance on other motivations and actions occasionally may reap benefits to the policy analyst, but we believe a more ad hoc approach to individual behavior is more counterproductive than helpful.

Ad hoc policy analyses—policy analyses not based on general principles—are less likely to produce innovative policy proposals, because such analyses are less likely to produce insightful predictions about group outcomes from individual behavior. There is a tendency to confuse group outcomes with individual motives. For example, the failure of a community to pay for adequate crime protection may be perceived to be caused by the failure of individuals to care about the crime problem. Resulting public policies might try to change people's opinion of crime.

Understanding that collective action problems occur because individual incentives are inconsistent with group well-being is thus fundamental. Assuming that individuals are rational and self-interested allows us more power to understand these problems.

Rationality implies that individuals know what they want, even though they may have some uncertainty about their preferences, and also that they choose accordingly. For purposes of policy analysis we must make assumptions about what these preferences may be. We also will assume that individuals are self-interested, meaning that they will make decisions aimed at making themselves better off than they would otherwise be.

This assumption is somewhat controversial, because humans are more complex animals than mere selfish actors seeking immediate gratification. We do not disagree. But self-interested does not mean selfish; humans possess individual positive motivations toward other members of family and group that are self-interested in the sense that individuals are social animals who realize that enlightened self-interest rarely means selfishness. We will be able to work with this idea once we introduce the idea that certain social institutions lead individuals to respect and act on the preferences of others.

THE LOGIC OF COLLECTIVE ACTION

Economist Mancur Olson, early in his career, wrote a book entitled *The Logic of Collective Action* that has had an enormous impact on the disciplines of political science, policy studies, and sociology.[1] In it, Olson used economic analysis to understand why individuals are not likely to voluntarily try, against their interests, to make their group better off. Countless examples include voluntary contributions to union dues, charities, and public interests. The key behind Olson's motivation was to explain why voluntary compliance to rules that make the group better off, as well as voluntary contributions to causes that do the same, falls immensely short of the amounts one would expect if there were no collective action problem. That is, while individuals may think helping the poor is a worthy goal and would make society better off, voluntary provisions for doing so fall far, far below what we would expect. This is a collective action problem.

One small example can aid in our understanding. Local public television stations are in part funded by the Public Broadcasting System; other funding comes from voluntary contributions from individuals. Public television has a tremendous number of viewers who do not regularly, if ever, contribute. This is a collective action problem, though it is one that has been partially solved. For every problem that is solved, there are many latent ones that are not.

To foreshadow our discussion of solutions to the collective action problem before we more fully describe the problem, let's discuss how public television solves the collective action problem. Through coercion? No, jackbooted thugs don't go from door to door, looking for nonproviders to make them pay their fair share. Instead, the federal government requires individuals to pay taxes, and a small part of these taxes are used to fund national and local public television. However, this subsidy is not enough to produce the quality of programming and broadcasting local providers deem necessary. A second method, of which we all are so aware, is appeals for direct donations from individuals. Box 4.1 describes an alternative way that has been devised to accumulate revenues to pay for television programming.

Collective action theory predicts that usually most, if not all, individuals will refrain from voluntarily contributing to group efforts, which is what many do. Olson cleverly realized that when providers seeking funding for public projects do not have power of coercion, then **selective incentives** will be used to try to induce more contributions. Selective incentives are the tangible items of value offered only to contributors. We all know about the tote bags, *Sesame Street* paraphernalia, and Grateful Dead CDs that local public television pledge drives make available, and these items often provide enough individual benefits for additional people to contribute. Furthermore, the types of goods provided by the local public television stations often identify the contributor as a contributor; this fact increases incentives for contributions, because then individuals can show neighbors, friends, and family that they are selfless providers.

Box 4.1   Television Licensing in the United Kingdom

AMERICANS CONSTANTLY complain about television commercials. While some commercials are amusing, many irritate us. In the United Kingdom, the British Broadcasting Corporation (BBC) does not use advertising to fund its broadcasts. Like the Public Broadcasting System (PBS) in the United States, the BBC is partially funded by the government. Unlike PBS, however, the BBC does not raise funds from the public. Individuals in the United Kingdom are required to pay for the right to own a television set. This money goes to the BBC. There are also three privately owned commercial television networks.

Programming on the BBC is often very bad by American standards. On the BBC, viewers come to expect garden shows in prime time, bishop-to-bishop coverage of chess tournaments, and soap operas that make *Days of Our Lives* look like a Stephen Spielberg production. It is interesting to note that many Americans believe that television in the United Kingdom is high in quality. In fact, the few shows that are imported to the United States are very high in quality. This constitutes a selection bias. Most British shows are not rebroadcast in the United States.

How exactly does the United Kingdom fund television? Rather than simply taxing all individuals to provide television, the United Kingdom uses a television-licensing scheme that is supposed to work like a user fee. Those with television sets are supposed to buy licenses from TV Licensing, an arm of the British Post Office. A license for any color television set that an individual owns costs about $150 a year. For a black-and-white TV, the cost is only about $50.

Of course, people have an incentive to free ride. Many British citizens know that this TV-licensing scheme is very difficult to enforce. The maximum penalty for using a television without a license is about $1,500. That is steep, but the chances of getting caught are slight. Thus, many people avoid paying the TV tax and watch the BBC without a TV license. If it were cable, these folks would not buy it. This is exactly what we expect people to do when appropriate incentives to provide for the collective good are not in place. In this case, free riding may have become socially acceptable, as 75 percent of all individuals think that the BBC does not provide programming worth the money.

Box 4.2 shows how the United States Golf Association (USGA) uses selective incentives to attract members. Modest provisions for collective goods, such as those employed by the USGA, should be contrasted with other situations that surely would draw little voluntary compliance. Suppose a group, thinking that watching public television will make better citizens of everyone and thus make the group better off, decides to make television sets available to all members of the community. Suppose also that no coercion is involved and that individuals need only drop by a television distribution center and pick up a television. At this spot, voluntary contributions are requested, and if an individual makes a contribution equal to the cost of the television, they receive a

Box 4.2 *The USGA and Selective Incentives*

THE UNITED States Golf Association (USGA) is a voluntary association. Neither its leaders nor its members think of it as a political organization. It is true that it is not primarily a political organization. Its main purpose is to administer (in conjunction with the Royal and Ancient Golf Club of St. Andrew's, Scotland) the rules of golf and hold competitions. However, in recent years it has also been involved in funding research on turf and the environmental impact of golf courses. This latter function provides the potential for the USGA to become more political, because environmental groups have become increasingly hostile to the development of new golf courses. The number of individuals playing golf has skyrocketed, so a scarcity of golf courses may at some point result in the political system pitting golfers against environmentalists.

For the USGA to serve any of the above functions, it must have dues-paying members. However, the functions of the USGA produce collective goods—that is, benefits that go to all golfers, whether or not they are members of the USGA. The USGA does make money on three of the most important golf tournaments it sponsors, but it could not exist without member contributions. How does the USGA get members to voluntarily provide for the collective good?

It provides selective incentives, goods and services that individuals would not be able to enjoy without being a member. That is, to provide the collective goods that the USGA wants to provide, it makes private goods available to individuals who join. In essence, the profits the USGA enjoys from providing these private goods fund the collective goods, as well as the salaries of the administrators.

What selective incentives does the USGA provide? First, it gives members the first shot at buying tickets to the events it sponsors. This is not very important in regard to the U.S. Mid-Amateur, but it is a huge benefit for the U.S. Open. These tickets often are sold months in advance of the event. A magazine, *Golf Journal,* is unavailable to nonmembers but free to members. Members receive the latest rules of golf free of charge. USGA merchandise can also be purchased at a discount. And if this is not enough, some merchandise is labeled "members only," meaning that it cannot be bought by nonmembers. This incentive, along with an official-looking "bag-tag" that identifies individuals as members of the USGA, gives members a way of identifying themselves as members. This identification provides a way of telling the world that the member is a citizen of golf in good standing. For the $25 membership fee, this is not a bad group of benefits.

Of course, other voluntary associations and interest groups use selective incentives. In fact, every group that needs a large number of individuals to function uses selective incentives. Group life insurance programs, rental car rate reductions, and hotel rate reductions are among common incentives. The Sierra Club offers a magazine and product discounts that potential members are likely to enjoy. These selective incentives are provided so that a potential member will be persuaded to join because the benefits are close to or greater than the price of membership. Millions of people join voluntary associations each year, in part due to the selective incentives that accompany membership in the associations.

tote bag that announces, if they carry it, that they provided this support. Would individuals contribute the necessary funds to pay for the televisions? Not many people would. This is why we rarely witness expensive goods being provided via voluntary contributions.

One classic example of a collective action problem is national defense. What if the Defense Department, like public television, asked for donations so that the country could be secure from invasion? Would you pay? Another classic example is jury duty. If jury duty were subject to only voluntary participation, relatively few people would choose to participate on juries. Worse, the people who would choose to serve on juries might have tastes and preferences that would make them very much unlike a jury of "peers." To solve these problems, public policy analysts often prescribe coercion. People must be on juries if called. People who refuse to serve can be arrested and prosecuted.

But we are getting ahead of ourselves; we have already mentioned various solutions to collective action problems that will be described in detail below, and we have mentioned the role of markets that we have not yet introduced. We now turn to more fully explaining the collective action problem.

The collective action problem centers around the concepts of **free riders** and **public goods.** Public goods are goods from which all members of a group benefit, if any one member of the group receives the benefit. If anyone receives a benefit, everyone receives the benefit. If these goods are provided to the group,

OLIPHANT © 2000 UNIVERSAL PRESS SYNDICATE. Reprinted with permission. All rights reserved.

which as a whole will have access to them, there are likely to be free riders, who obtain benefits without paying for these goods. Because individuals are (usually) rational and (often) self-interested, they have an incentive to allow others to pay for the goods so that they can be free riders. The logic of collective action, then, provides the explanation for why these goods will not be provided. Everyone will wait around to free ride, no one will pay for the good, and these collective goods will not be provided. Hence, individual action, which is fully consistent with individual interests, will lead to the group's being worse off than if the goods were provided. This is the classic collective action problem.

This description is the worst-case scenario, and policy analysts have endeavored to clarify the nature of goods so that we better understand collective action problems. Thus, to understand these problems, policy analysts conceptualize, in very simple terms, different dimensions of any good. This will be done in a later chapter. By a good, we mean any thing from which individuals may potentially derive satisfaction or pain.

GENERIC SOLUTIONS TO COLLECTIVE ACTION PROBLEMS

Throughout the remainder of this text we consider how institutions should be structured to best provide for the collective good. Typically, solving collective action problems is a complex enterprise, and in any particular circumstance solutions can never follow a simple blueprint. Blueprint thinking is the enemy of clever, imaginative, and successful policy analysts.

Because generalizing from simple blueprints is not enough, it is useful at this stage of our thinking to describe generic solutions—ways that collective action problems can be solved without regard to the intricacies of a particular problem. Generic solutions only suggest certain types of solutions in real-world situations. We can think of them as academic, but we hope to show you later in this text that they are more than that.

Repeated Interaction Among Individuals

Robert Axelrod refined an idea that had been brewing for over a decade.[2] In the early 1980s, he showed that in certain circumstances, individuals who repeatedly interact have an incentive to cooperate with one another. This means that individuals will cooperate even though it is in their short-term interests to do otherwise. They will cooperate because the gains from cooperation over time outweigh the loss in short-term benefits of not doing so.

To understand this better, Axelrod used a game to show the potential benefits of cooperation. A game is a matrix that shows outcomes from two or more
actions taken by individuals. Collective action problems result from the fact
that outcomes are determined by all individuals in society. One person,
through individual actions, cannot determine outcomes. Thus, a matrix that
shows what will happen with combinations of outcomes can be very useful.
Collective action problems can be represented as **prisoner's dilemma** games,
that is, situations where the players in a game would be better off if they co-
operated, but because of their inability to trust one another, fail to cooperate.

Why noncooperative action is the typical prediction from such a game can
be easily understood by looking at the following matrix:

Column Player

	Cooperate	Defect
Cooperate	3,3	0,5
Defect	5,0	1,1

Row Player

The way to read this matrix is as follows. Each player plays the game at the
same time as the other player. We call the player choosing the row the row
player and the other the column player. The row outcome, provided as a number with higher being better for the player, is the first number in the cell. The
second number is the payoff for the column player. For example, when the row
player plays cooperate and the column player chooses defect, the payoff for
the row player is 0, and that of the column player is 5.

Each player can choose to cooperate or defect, but notice that neither
player can determine the actual outcome. The row player can determine *row*
and the column player can determine column, but neither can do more. Thus,
the outcome depends on the action of both players. Now if you were either
player (we have made the game symmetric, meaning both players face the exact same situation), what would you choose to do if you were trying to maximize the payoff, or your value of the outcome of the end result of the game?
Assume for the moment that you cannot influence the other player in any way.

The prisoner's dilemma game, as reported in Box 4.3, has a single predicted
outcome. Neither player, acting by herself, would choose to cooperate, because the defect option always provides the highest value. This is one way to

---

Box 4.3   *The Origin of the Prisoner's Dilemma*

THE PRISONER'S dilemma is such a common representation of the failure of self-interested individuals to cooperate that it has taken on epic proportions in social science. Two individuals who have common interests, given the strategic nature of their interaction, will fail to cooperate because each individual's interests make it difficult to trust the other person.

The term prisoner's dilemma comes from the following story. The police capture two suspects, who they believe should be charged with conspiring to commit a crime. The police, however, lack the evidence to win a conviction against the duo, so it is in the police department's interest to obtain confessions from one or both. Of course, if the suspects can cooperate with one another rather than the police, then the police, at best, will be able to obtain only slight penalties against the perpetrators.

Thus, the police want the suspects to talk. Each suspect wants the other to be quiet. Understanding this situation, the police interrogate each suspect separately from the other. The police will offer a better deal to the suspect who snitches on the partner. If both suspects snitch, they are in bad shape, because evidence is strong they committed the crime. If both stonewall, then evidence is thin, and both get a minimal sentence. But when one snitches and the other stonewalls, then the snitch gets by with a minor sentence (in return for turning state's evidence), and the stonewaller is clobbered with a strong sentence. Therefore, the suspects have an incentive, in the absence of some trust or binding contract with one another, to snitch on one another. However, if both follow this strategy it will result in severe penalties against each, because the state then will have the strongest evidence against each.

If the prisoner's dilemma story is accurate, then how do suspected criminals ever coordinate their actions? There are many ways, but the most obvious story is that associated with the way organized crime solves this dilemma. If a member of organized crime snitches, what happens? It is usually worse than the sentence that would result if the suspect snitched on the accomplice. Suppose a suspect could obtain a one-year sentence from snitching, but the consequences would be an organized crime hit (death sentence) for snitching. The suspect obviously has an incentive to stonewall. Thus, the penchant for stonewalling by members of the Mob and other crime syndicates has an origin in solving the prisoner's dilemma.

---

represent a collective action problem, although collective action problems can be represented as different game structures as well. However, this is the most difficult collective action problem to solve, because both players have an obvious strategy to play defect. If some way were found to solve this collective action problem, then other collective action problems could also be solved based on the same logic.

Axelrod's approach suggests a very important solution. Axelrod's **prisoner's dilemma experiments** showed that if individuals are repeatedly playing the same game, and if they care about future outcomes instead of only current outcomes, the best way to play the game involves a strategy called **tit for tat.** This strategy, which makes sense only in repeated play, calls for players to cooperate initially and then do whatever the other player did in the previous round.

As you will see in Box 4.4, Axelrod happened upon this novel solution by having social scientists and computer enthusiasts supply him with computer programs with long-term strategies. He then held a tournament in which he allowed these programs to play each other in a series of long-term interactions. The tit-for-tat strategy won over the long haul, even thought it never did well in any particular face-to-face interaction. The tit-for-tat strategy has several characteristics that make it ideal for use when one faces a prisoner's dilemma game over repeated plays with the same individual.

It is highly unlikely that players find themselves in a situation where they cooperate only because Axelrod's stringent conditions hold. However, the importance of Axelrod's analysis is that it is very possible that institutions can be constructed so that individuals are more likely to play a tit-for-tat type of strategy. We would want people facing a prisoner's dilemma or collective action problem to know one another. Thus, we would want to scale actions and potential solutions to the smallest common denominator. This suggests that it is not an accident that people are nicer in Indianola, Iowa, than in New York City. However, even collective action problems, such as neighborhood crime, can be addressed at a local level if neighbors work to monitor streets. The implication of Axelrod's solution to collective action problems is that voluntary compliance in such situations is more likely if the scale is small (for example, neighborhoods versus boroughs).

A related important component of cooperation is the repetition of play and the shadow of the future. Of course, this component is more common in situations where individuals are likely to confront one another over time, which will happen in situations of small scale. A small scale makes it likely that there will be a shadow of the future.

Voluntary Cooperation Versus Coercion

Public policy analysts often emphasize the failure of voluntary cooperation when trying to solve collective action problems. However, things are more complex than simple theory predicts. Sometimes individuals do provide for the collective good. This section gets into the sticky territory where simple theories do not explain individual actions very well.

Public policy analysts need to understand when individuals will provide resources for solving collective action problems. In a social vacuum, people usually will not cooperate in the resolution of collective action problems. But people are not in social vacuums. Why would they cooperate in a social environment? Robert Putnam introduced the concept of **social capital.** Although

Box 4.4   *Axelrod's Prisoner's Dilemma Experiments*

ROBERT AXELROD set out to find the best way for someone to overcome the inevitability of the prisoner's dilemma.[1] He chose to perform a novel experiment. He asked a number of academics to tell him, using computer programs, how they would play this game, if faced with it over and over. Academics from a variety of disciplines, including economics, political science, and biology, were asked to submit their strategies for playing this game many times over a period of time.

Axelrod performed the experiment a second time and asked computer enthusiasts to enter the fray and design computer programs with long-term strategies to win. His goal was to find out if any one program performed better than others. The outcome was a surprise to the entrants of the tournaments. A simple four-line program written by psychologist Anatol Rappaport won each time. The winner was determined based on the outcome of the prisoner's dilemma game over many plays.

Why did Rappaport succeed? He used a program called Tit-for-tat. This program is very simple. It returns a cooperate for any other cooperate it encounters, and it returns a defect for any other defect it encounters. Axelrod calls this a "nice" strategy. It is nice to other nice strategies, and it punishes "non-nice" strategies. This strategy is also hard to take advantage of, because aggressive strategies will gain very little by trying to use the tit-for-tat strategy.

After the computer experiments were performed, Axelrod went on to show that a number of applications of this principle appear to operate in the real world. These include such a diverse set of cases as a live-and-let-live system in trench warfare in World War I and the success of animals employing a tit-for-tat strategy when placed in prisoner's dilemma situations.

An interesting property of the tit-for-tat strategy is that it cannot beat any other single strategy in a one-to-one encounter. It wins in a society at large because it never loses badly because of its nice strategy. This might seem counterintuitive, but in a world where individuals employ many different strategies, few will beat tit for tat in the long run. In short, it works well against other nice strategies, and it never works very poorly against non-nice strategies.

1. Robert Axelrod, *The Evolution of Cooperation* (New York: Basic Books, 1984).

this concept does not explain all social cooperation, it is probably the best way to understand why there exists voluntary compliance in the face of collective action problems.[3] Social capital is the accumulation of social relations capable of providing individuals incentives to take part in collective action. Social capital is that which prevents society from being a set of individuals acting as if they are in a social vacuum.

Social capital is probably easier to describe by example than by definition. Suppose you greet people you see everyday with a smile. You do this because you know that this facilitates communication with people, and communication can give you all kinds of advantages in solving problems over time. Furthermore, you know that the smile indicates you are a nice person. Contrast your niceness with a grump who never smiles and usually snarls when communicating. The grump will have more problems communicating with people over time, and this will be costly. Acting nice, then, is a way to produce long-term social benefits that will ultimately pay off for you. It is in your long-term interests to be nice.

This last example is not a particularly substantive one. Consider a neighborhood of middle-class homes. It is well known that the value of any one house in the neighborhood depends on the values of others. Furthermore, the condition of the exteriors of homes, as well as lawns and landscaping, also affects the value of all homes in the neighborhood. This is a classic collective action problem, because no one homeowner can really influence the value of the neighborhood, and it is costly to keep the exteriors and yards of homes nice.

What makes people keep up the external appearances of their homes? Some people simply care and get value from this. Other people, who do not care as much, do realize that neighbors may be unhappy if they let their lawn and bushes go, do not paint the house, and so on. By making the exterior of a house attractive, homeowners are building social capital with neighbors. This capital can be important at unpredictable times in the future. By building goodwill—that is, social capital—with your neighbors, it is easier to obtain assistance in lots of little and big ways, such as collecting your mail or picking up your newspapers while you are out of town, bringing you food when you are sick, or perhaps helping you clear tree branches off your lawn after a windstorm or ice storm. In these ways, social capital leads to what most people think of as neighborliness.

Social capital can be an elusive concept. This is perhaps the most important lesson about the rise in people bowling alone, as shown in Box 4.5. Social capital is produced in an almost infinite number of ways and affects social relations in as many ways. Axelrod's ideas about reciprocity help us understand why social capital can be important in explaining how individuals in societies cooperate with one another when simple theories assume they will not.

This much said, it is important to understand the historic evidence that tells us that social capital stocks have rarely been high enough to solve every collective action problem individuals face. We still do not understand very well how to design societies to increase social capital. Even successful self-governing societies throughout the world not only endure but actually allow shirking (an individual's doing something against the group's interest). It is probably true that any successful community that solves many problems because of vast reserves of social capital will be hard to duplicate in another community.

Thus, policy analysts have typically not spent much effort in trying to solve societal problems by making more successful efforts to produce voluntary compliance. Instead, policy analysts usually focus on coercive means for the solution of problems. Indeed, many public policy analysis textbooks focus on little else. We learn about governments that have a legitimate capacity to use force to ensure that individuals do not shirk in their responsibility to society.

Box 4.5   *Bowling Alone*

A RECENT STUDY by Robert Putnam makes the case that there is deterioration of social capital in the United States. Putnam finds the root of this problem in declining group associations. Besides noting that membership in churches, unions, and fraternal organizations is decreasing, Putnam uses bowling league membership as a yardstick of how social capital has receded. Between 1980 and 1994, the number of bowlers increased by 10 percent, but participation in bowling leagues had dropped by 40 percent, a phenomenon Putnam called bowling alone. Thus, Putnam titled his piece "Bowling Alone: America's Declining Social Capital."

Is bowling trivial? It is not if one considers that as many people bowl in a year as attend church, and a third more people bowled than voted in the 1994 congressional elections.[1] Further, Putnam highlights the importance of league bowlers passing time together and talking among themselves. Talk could cover the latest football score but could also cover the latest school board policy, local zoning issues, or other subjects that might get people involved in politics and public policy. Hearing that a bowling buddy plans on attending a meeting at her child's school covering school safety might impel a bowler to go as well. Each incremental step tends to lower the disincentives to collective action.

Putnam also discusses the important two-way relationship between public policy and social capital. As noted, social capital can promote political participation. Listening to bowling partners over beer and pizza may make fellow bowlers aware of issues that would never have crossed their radar had they been home watching television.

But public policy can also influence social capital. As author Jane Jacobs warned approximately forty years ago, before the construction of massive high-rise government housing for those in poverty, the displacement of settled communities with established communication and economic patterns can extinguish the communities' needed social capital.[2] How can collective action problems be solved without the norms of a community to persuade members to do so? It is difficult to argue that ruining communities' social capital by constructing highways through neighborhoods and by gutting the neighborhoods in which low-income families lived to build shiny new high-rise urban renewal projects strips the "inducement" for individuals to help solve collective action problems. Putnam correctly points out the importance of integrating social capital into discussions of public policy formation.

1. Robert Putnam, "Bowling Alone: America's Declining Social Capital," *Journal of Democracy* 6, no. 1 (1995): pp. 65–78.
2. Jane Jacobs, *The Death and Life of Great American Cities* (New York: Random House, 1961).

Governments use two basic mechanisms to ensure individual compliance for collective action. Governments tax people to create the resources needed to provide collective goods for society. This coercion focuses on the resources needed for government. Governments also regulate individual behavior so that people do not behave in a way that hurts society.

One interesting conjecture is that coercion is never enough to satisfactorily change the incentives of individuals so that they never shirk. In fact, it would probably be too expensive to do so. One scholar of incentives and organizations found that it was impossible to create an affordable incentive structure so that members of a production team would not have an incentive to shirk.[4] This suggests the rationale for government's use of coercion in society: it would probably be too expensive to reduce shirking to zero.

To illustrate this conjecture, let's consider the problem of crime control. If we simply use coercive means to try to control crime, the costs can be very staggering. The United States, over the last decade and a half, has pursued an increasingly costly attempt to reduce crime at the national, state, and local levels. There has been a tremendous increase in the number of prisons, the imprisonment of offenders, and expenditures on enforcement. Yet crime levels remain high.

Public policy analysts understand that means other than coercion are also necessary for preventing crime, a particularly extreme form of shirking. Neighborhoods that have active crime watchers have lower levels of violence and burglaries than do neighborhoods that do not have this mechanism. High-crime areas are inevitably those that have low social capital. More police and harsher punishment can change people's incentives, but they do so at very high costs. At some point the high costs become counterproductive.

An antidote to the problem of shirking behavior may lie in organizational design involving a mix of coercive and noncoercive measures. An interesting finding in the academic literature is that shirking behavior can be controlled by leadership that orients organizational processes toward the production of what is basically social capital.[5] Coercion supplemented with designs that produce social capital is superior to incentive systems alone. Public policy analysts are coming to understand that coercion, while important, cannot do everything. These analysts understand that policies should help foster social control of collective action problems rather than transcending them. Coercion alone cannot suffice.

INSTITUTIONS FOR SOLVING COLLECTIVE ACTION PROBLEMS

In one of the most important books published to date on collective action, Elinor Ostrom shows that an immense number of institutions for solving collective action problems exist.[6] Many of these institutions do not require a powerful government to coerce individuals, but they also do not simply presume that individuals somehow cooperate to solve problems. Using many examples throughout the world, Ostrom shows that communities can successfully govern themselves through a variety of monitoring and sanctioning mechanisms designed over time to solve collective action problems.

Ostrom's primary argument is that public policy analysis has largely focused on coercive solutions because of the belief that individuals cannot overcome collective action problems themselves without resorting to an overpowering state. Ostrom points out that there is a large middle ground between **laissez-faire policies,** which leave things alone, and policies that require the formation of a government to coerce individuals through taxation and regulations. Indeed, policies should help individuals, whenever possible, in the policymaking process. One way for this to occur is through **co-production,** which is the idea that government and individuals, working together, produce policy outputs. For example, rather than thinking that it is up to schools alone to educate children, co-production forces us to realize that it is up to both schools and families.

Once we understand this middle ground, many alternative policies are admitted to our tool bag. Furthermore, and just as important, it is dangerous to ignore the fact that individuals do solve some collective action problems as well as co-produce. Ostrom finds that when governments make top-down policies as if individuals are helpless, these policies have the potential of breaking up existing self-governing institutions. A village without a full-time professional police force must think about how to limit problems of crime. All too common is the higher-level government provision that creates a situation where individuals act as if the problem is no longer theirs. Rather than using traditional institutional arrangements to solve problems, these individuals may instead look to the central government for more and more help.

This is not to say there is little place for government coercion in public policy. Rather, it is to warn us that the existence of a potential collective action problem is not grounds, in and of itself, for government action. A good policy analyst will ask the following questions before pursuing such intervention:

1. *Is there evidence that the collective action problem actually exists?* We may think that just because there is no overt policy being administered by a government agency, there is a problem. It may be that local communities have found a solution to the problem without resorting to government to solve the problem for them.
2. *If there is evidence that a collective action problem is not being addressed by the individuals themselves, what are the potential solutions?* How heavily we depend on the government relative to individuals to solve the problem will depend on the nature of social capital and other potential self-governing institutions in the community.
3. *Will intervention by higher levels of government hurt existing institutional structures?* The costs of coercion should be weighed against the benefits that the coercion is meant to produce.
4. *How do we evaluate whether the solution is working?* There needs to be additional means for allowing the individuals being governed to evaluate the effectiveness of policies. An old saying about democracy is that the one who wears the shoe best knows if it fits. The best democratic policy allows for the individuals being governed to play key roles at each point in the process.

CONCLUSION

In high school civics classes and college-level introductions to political science, we learn about how people should and do go about addressing government for societal problems. Indeed, much of the time is spent on voting, being a member of an interest group, and working for a political party. These teachings obscure the fact that people also can solve their own problems. It would be difficult for U.S. citizens to provide for national defense, but at one time in the United States, militias played a major role in doing this. It is quaint to think about those days today, because national defense is clearly too large and sophisticated to be provided through self-governance. But other issues and problems are not too big to be solved by people themselves.

Contemporary civics training also focuses on large national governments and much less on state and local governments. Again, this focus trains people to make problems national issues when in some ways they are not. Since the latter half of the twentieth century we have been in a period in which policy has been nationalized. Good things have resulted, such as increased civil rights and liberties, but there also have been costs. These costs include an erosion in the ability of communities to govern themselves. There are major controversies about what different levels of government should and should not do. A useful discussion of policy alternatives must also include the costs and benefits of intervention by government at any level, because coercion alone cannot solve collective action problems. We have argued that defining the nature of the public is particularly important in policy analysis. If we do not do this, we cannot know how we might understand the institutional structures that already exist.

Key Terms

collective action problem *p. 61*
rationality *p. 62*
self-interest *p. 62*
preferences *p. 63*
selective incentive *p. 64*
free rider *p. 67*
public good *p. 67*

prisoner's dilemma *p. 69*
prisoner's dilemma experiments *p. 70*
tit for tat *p. 71*
social capital *p. 71*
laissez-faire policy *p. 76*
co-production *p. 76*

Suggested Readings

Banfield, Edward. 1958. *The Moral Basis of a Backward Society.* New York: Free Press.

Crawford, Sue, and Elinor Ostrom. 1995. "A Grammar of Institutions." *American Political Science Review* 89(3): 582–600.

Hardin, Russell. 1982. *Collective Action*. Baltimore: Johns Hopkins University Press.

Lichbach, Mark. 1996. *The Cooperator's Dilemma*. Ann Arbor: University of Michigan Press.

Moe, Terry. 1980. *The Organization of Interests*. Chicago: University of Chicago Press.

Mueller, Dennis. 1989. *Public Choice II*. Cambridge, England: University of Cambridge Press.

Ostrom, Elinor. 1990. *Governing the Commons: The Evolution of Institutions for Collective Action*. New York: Cambridge University Press.

Taylor, Michael. 1987. *The Possibility of Cooperation*. Cambridge, England: University of Cambridge Press.

Notes

1. Mancur Olson, *The Logic of Collective Action* (Cambridge, Mass.: Harvard University Press, 1965). It is interesting that this book was a published version of Olson's doctoral dissertation.

2. Robert Axelrod, *The Evolution of Cooperation* (New York: Basic Books, 1984).

3. James Coleman, *Foundations of Social Theory* (Cambridge, Mass.: Harvard University Press, 1990). For a path-breaking application to politics, see Robert Putnam, *Making Democracy Work: Civic Traditions in Modern Italy* (Princeton, N.J.: Princeton University Press, 1993).

4. Bengt Holmstrom, "Moral Hazard in Teams," *Bell Journal of Economics* 13 (1982): 324–340.

5. Gary Miller, *Managerial Dilemmas: The Political Economy of Hierarchy* (New York: Cambridge University Press, 1992).

6. Elinor Ostrom, *Governing the Commons: The Evolution of Institutions for Collective Action* (New York: Cambridge University Press, 1990).

5

Government and Collective Action Problems

INTRODUCTION

Government is a key instrument by which groups of people solve collective action problems. The reason is simple. Governments have at their disposal a variety of mechanisms by which they can compel people to act in particular ways. This characteristic is what makes governments powerful instruments in overcoming collective action problems. It is also what makes governments so potentially dangerous. In this chapter, we discuss what government is and how governments utilize the threat of coercion in addressing collective action problems. Then we turn to the question of how governments should be structured so that on the one hand they have the necessary resources and capacities to solve the problems that they are expected to solve, and on the other hand they are prevented from using their powers for illegitimate purposes. Historically, several ways of structuring the governance of societies have been devised. We consider the Leviathan state, federalism, and self-governance and compare these structures with a structure of governance known as polycentrism.

GOVERNMENT AND THE COLLECTIVE ACTION PROBLEM

What makes governments such useful instruments for solving collective action problems? The answer to this question lies in the fact that governments combine processes that engender legitimacy with the capacity to organize and exercise coercion. Different governments vary greatly in the degree to which they can combine these things. In general, however, governments are able to utilize the processes from which they derive legitimacy to adopt policies to inhibit the tendency of individuals to free ride, hold out against collective action, or both. We look at how this works in the context of a couple of illustrations.

Let us consider again the public policy problems associated with trying to build a highway between two communities. As we saw in Chapter 2, governments frequently exercise coercion in the form of **eminent domain** to force landowners to sell their land so that government can build roadways. To be of any use, a highway must be a continuous ribbon of pavement between two end points. The ability of any particular landowner along the proposed right-of-way to hold out against selling a strip of property for the project is a type of collective action problem. By holding out, a landowner can undermine the whole highway project. Knowing that his or her willingness to sell is pivotal to the whole project, the holdout landowner has a strong incentive to charge an extortionate price for the strip of property—and the backers of the highway project will have little choice but to pay. But notice that every landowner along the proposed right-of-way has exactly the same incentive. Each and every one of them will want to hold out in order to charge a price for their property that is far in excess of what they could get for it in the open market.

This highway example, however, gets even more complicated. A related problem occurs with regard to the people who will be asked to pay for the highway project. Each potential user of the highway will benefit if the highway is completed but will be better off individually if able to avoid paying for the costs of constructing and maintaining the road. All potential users would like to use the road but let others pay for it. That is to say, they have an incentive to free ride. This incentive is the same for all potential users of the highway, and thus, in the absence of some intervention, no money will be contributed by anyone toward its construction.

So how can any road be built? Landowners will demand a king's ransom for each acre of right-of-way; potential users will all seek to free ride and avoid paying for it. The answer to the question of how any road can be built is that a government intervenes to ensure that landowners cannot take undue advantage of the need for a continuous right-of-way and that free riding does not undermine the financing of the highway. The government exercises the right of eminent domain and forces landowners along the proposed right-of-way to sell their property to the government.

Why is a government able to do this? Eminent domain is a legal process by which the government demonstrates that its acquisition of the landowners' property is in the public interest. The process culminates in the government's making a payment for the land based upon an assessment of the "fair market value" of the land (that is, a price that the landowner would be able to obtain were the land sold to someone else to be used for its current purpose). What makes this process legitimate? Certainly there is something suspect about a government's taking people's property against their wishes. But the answer to what makes it legitimate lies in the application of procedures that are designed to ensure that property is taken only when the purpose to which the property is to be put is demonstrably in the public interest and the owners have been fairly compensated for their losses.

A similar principle underlies the ability of governments to ensure that potential users of the highway don't free ride with regard to paying a share of the costs of the highway project. Governments avoid free riding by levying taxes or fees across entire categories of citizens. A government can tax its citizens, which avoids the free rider problem, at least with regard to the potential users of the highway that lies within its jurisdiction. Alternatively, a government can levy fees on fuel so that all purchasers of fuel within the government's area of jurisdiction contribute to the costs of building the new highway. A government also can charge tolls to all users of the new highway itself. However, this mechanism requires that the actual costs of construction be financed with government bonds, which must be guaranteed by the taxpayers of the government should the tolls prove insufficient to pay off the costs of constructing the highway. Regardless of the particular financing mechanism adopted, the government will use its power to ensure that no one who owes payment to the government escapes paying. People who try to avoid payment can be fined, their wages garnished, and their property repossessed. Indeed, just the threat of a government's collection powers induces most people "voluntarily" to pay what they owe.

What makes the taxes and fees levied by a government legitimate? Again, the answer lies in the application of procedures designed to ensure that the taxes and fees are to be used for public purposes and that the distribution of the burden is arguably fair. The specific procedures by which governments arrive at their tax levies vary. Whatever the procedures are, two things matter: (1) that the procedures used by a particular government are viewed by most of the public as leading to policies that are in the public interest and (2) that the procedures are actually followed.

Legitimacy of government procedures, and by extension the policies that flow from those procedures, can be fairly fragile. When a government is perceived to misuse its coercive powers, it is often not long before belief in the legitimacy of government institutions comes into question. This is one reason why governments often try to use their coercive powers sparingly, preferring instead to offer inducements or rewards for people to act in desired ways. Tax subsidies and grant payments are used to induce behaviors. These policy instruments utilize positive incentives to get people to do things. Sometimes, however, positive incentives fail to produce behaviors. Negative incentives, such as the threat of fines, incarceration, or worse, may have to be employed.

Consider, as an illustration, the problem that countries face in recruiting soldiers to fight in their armed forces. This is not a trivial collective action problem. It may make the difference between survival and defeat for a country. While in times of great national crisis everyone's interest is served by having the country defended by a well-armed, fully manned military, it is in each person's narrow self-interest not to be put at great personal risk by enlisting in the armed services. It is rational, from a purely self-interested level, to free ride and let others volunteer to go off to war. How, then, can the military obtain sufficient numbers of soldiers?

In the case of "popular" wars—that is, wars that have broad public support—patriotism, love of country, and the prospect of glory and adventure may be adequate to compel young men and women to volunteer for military service. Typically, however, even when wars are popular, countries resort to both carrots and sticks to induce people to serve in the military.

The carrots for voluntarily enlisting often include a choice of assignments while in the military, generous postservice educational grants, subsidies to decrease the costs of purchasing a home, discounted food and health care prices, preferential treatment in hiring and promotion, and many other things.

The stick most often takes the form of the draft. The draft usually incorporates a process to exempt young people who have legitimate reasons not to serve in the military, such as a physical or psychological impairment. Sometimes, however, exemptions have been allowed for those enrolled in college; married men; those with children; and at least during the American Civil War, those who could afford to pay a substitute to enter the military for them. Generally, being drafted has been made a significantly less attractive option than enlisting. Being drafted often has meant a lack of choice over assignments, a higher probability of seeing combat, a lower pay scale, limited opportunities to advance in rank, and fewer postservice benefits. Moreover, a person who tries to evade the draft may be sentenced to prison, assigned dangerous domestic duties (for example, parachute jumps into forest fires), or in some countries, executed.

In the case of "unpopular" wars, the carrots described above often prove woefully inadequate to entice people to enlist. Despite the best efforts of government leaders to glorify the cause, it is sometimes difficult for governments to persuade families to send off their young people to fight for an abstract cause or against an unfamiliar enemy. Under these circumstances, the government may have to organize coercion on a massive scale simply to force its population to contribute resources for the war effort and to draft sufficient numbers of people into the military. In Vietnam, armed bands of government agents were employed to dragoon young Vietnamese men and even teenagers into military service.

The result can be ugly, with the government waging a battle against its own population—a population that has become increasingly unsupportive of the war effort. Punishments against people who try to evade draft efforts may become severe. Suspected draft evaders and deserters may be summarily executed. Groups of people at the local level may begin quietly to hide young people from government draft agencies. Tax evasion may escalate. Protests and even riots may occur. There may even be cases of sabotage against government facilities and military operations. Indeed, popular opposition to war may eventually undermine the ability of the government to continue its war efforts.

Burning draft cards during the Vietnam War was one way individuals showed their disagreement with the military policies of the U.S. Government. *Archive Photos.*

The point here is that the efficacy of coercive powers to solve collective action problems can be ruined by a loss of popular legitimacy. Belief in the legitimacy of government policies is not automatic. One component of a government's ability to use coercion, while maintaining its legitimacy, is careful following of established procedures that are designed to ensure that a particular application of coercion addresses a public problem. This was the point of the highway construction example discussed above. The second, and ultimately more important, component of the ability to use coercion is ensuring that the policy objective that the coercion is intended to serve is something that, at some fundamental level, is supported by the public.

The problems that national governments—including the American government during the war in Vietnam—have faced when trying to utilize the draft indicate clearly that without underlying public support, the specific procedures that a government follows are ultimately irrelevant. Once significant numbers of the public turn their backs on the government's policy, the continued application of coercion to pursue that policy will lead to an increasing loss of legitimacy. Government power, as this suggests, is a two-edged sword. It can accomplish important public purposes by helping solve perennial collective action problems, but it can also be used in ways that antagonize significant numbers of people, such that citizens begin to believe that the government has become predacious rather than useful.

GOVERNMENT STRUCTURE: WHAT ARE THE ALTERNATIVES?

We now turn to an issue that has been lying just below the surface in the previous discussion. How can government be structured so that it can effectively solve collective action problems but be prevented from using its powers in ways that are arbitrary and predatory? In essence, how can government be constituted so that it has sufficient capacity to solve problems but be constrained sufficiently to maintain public belief in its legitimacy? This is an age-old question. Here, we survey several answers by examining the Leviathan state, federalism, and self-governance, and then we contrast polycentrism with these models of governance. For each of these government structures, we weigh two main concerns. The first is **governmental capacity,** which is the ability of the government to solve collective action problems, both large and small. The second concern is responsiveness, which is the extent to which government policies are influenced by preferences of different publics.

The Leviathan State

The Leviathan state gets its name from Thomas Hobbes, whose thinking we encounter frequently in this book. Leviathan state describes a national government with central control over all public functions within its borders. The national government is supreme within a country and enjoys substantial powers to execute public policies. Variants of this model of government have been employed in many countries, including France at multiple points in its history, Nazi Germany, Argentina, Korea, the Soviet Union, and the People's Republic of China. As this list indicates, the model has been used in monarchies, totalitarian states, communist regimes, military dictatorships, and even occasionally democracies. Thus, there is no necessary connection between a Leviathan state and how government leaders are selected or tied to a nation's people.

The idea behind the Leviathan state is that it will have the greatest possible capacity to repel threats to the security of the country, whether those threats are from external enemies or from internal discontents. By centralizing power, the state is able to intervene in social and economic matters with a minimum of effective opposition. If land needs to be acquired to build roads, if soldiers need to be mustered to fight a war, if small businesses need to be consolidated into a large national corporation, if capital needs to be raised to underwrite large-scale infrastructure projects, if taxes need to be levied to redistribute wealth from one economic class to another, if rivers need to be dammed to create lakes and hydroelectric facilities, if new modes of agriculture need to be implemented—the Leviathan state can act decisively to inhibit free riding and holding out. In short, the Leviathan state has enormous power to make things happen.

The single greatest problem with the Leviathan state is its lack of responsiveness to the array of preferences that exist within societies. This may seem obvious in the case of Leviathan states that are nondemocratic. But consider the problem even in the case of a Leviathan state where government leaders are selected democratically. What is the practical necessity for leaders to consider or be influenced by the preferences of minorities? The minority groups may be racial, ethnic, religious, economic, social, or based upon some other type of common interest. Minority groups—particularly minority groups that are well defined, with preferences that are stable and distinct from those of the majority members of society—can be ignored with impunity. They cannot prevent the state from acting. Why should the government leaders care about the concerns of such minority groups? In a Leviathan state, minorities can do little, if anything, to make their views count. They can resort to violence, but this will invite the full weight of the state down upon them. They can try to emigrate, but that is likely to be costly and perhaps impossible if other countries refuse to allow them to cross their borders. In essence, minorities can do little to avoid policies that they find onerous or unfair, even in democratic Leviathans.

The problem, however, is even worse. In Leviathan systems, even the preferences of majorities can be disregarded. When information about the actions of government leaders is difficult to obtain, it may be a practical impossibility for people to learn how policies are being implemented. Notice that acquiring such information is a collective action problem. What incentive is there for any individual person to expend the effort and resources to obtain information about government actions? In a Leviathan state, the costs of acquiring information that may cast the government in an unfavorable light may be extremely high, since the government may actively attempt to suppress such information and punish those people who try to obtain it. Control of information allows government leaders to engage in corruption with almost complete impunity. Moreover, such control of information can make it virtually impossible for political opponents to mount effective campaigns against incumbent political leaders.

For this same reason, the public will be incapable of obtaining much information about government leaders who trade favors with organized interest groups. Political officials will have strong incentives to offer protective economic policies to these organized groups in return for private side payments that line their own pockets. This exchange of political favors for policies that protect politically organized economic interests, the phenomenon known as rent seeking, will be discussed at length in a later chapter. Suffice it to say for now that rent seeking is likely to be especially prevalent where there is a high degree of centralization of government power and authority, as in the Leviathan state.

A further negative consequence of a centralized government is the likelihood that the bureaucracies assigned to carry out government policies will be much larger and consume more resources than necessary. The reason is that information about the minimum number of staff and minimum level of resources for implementing a particular policy is difficult to ascertain. The public is not in a position to know. Political leaders do not know, and have little incentive to try to find out. Only the personnel in the bureaucracies that are supposed to be implementing the policies are in a position to estimate the mix of resources needed. But their incentive is always to overstate the resources required. With more staff and more resources, the bureaucracy grows, salaries swell, advancement becomes more rapid, prestige for department heads grows, free time increases, and opportunities to branch out into additional policy activities expand. In short, government grows. This phenomenon is due to what is called the principal-agent problem, which we introduced in Chapter 3 and which we will discuss further in a later chapter. Like the rent-seeking problem, the principal-agent problem is particularly pervasive where government authority is centralized, such as in the Leviathan state.

A final limit of the Leviathan state is its one-size-fits-all approach to policy implementation. Even if all the other problems with the Leviathan state could be solved—that is, even if the potential for its unresponsiveness to public preferences, the possibilities for rent seeking, and the likelihood of bloated bureaucracies could all be successfully addressed—it would still be unsuited for solving many policy problems. In a now-classic book, Vincent Ostrom argued that one of the chief limitations of central governments is that they seek to impose uniform policy solutions within their jurisdictions.[1] Uniform policy solutions are inevitably too stringent in some areas and too weak in others. Part of the reason that Ostrom suggests for this problem is that the costs of gaining information to make and implement policies is high, and a Leviathan government has little incentive to bear the costs of gaining this information. Another part of the reason for this problem is that the knowledge of alternative solutions to fit national policies to local conditions is likely to be limited or even absent. Leviathan governments are too often unable to identify what sorts of policies might work better in a particular local context, because there are no local governments that are trying different sorts of policy solutions and thereby producing information about what works and what does not.

Federalism

An alternative to the Leviathan state is a system of government known as **federalism**. This type of government is based upon a separation of policy responsibilities between a national level of government and one or more lower tiers of governments, such as states (as in the United States) or provinces (as in Canada). The key feature of federal systems is that there are policy responsibilities for which each of the levels of government are separately responsible.

Federal systems permit enormous variability in how policy responsibilities are divided, but what all federal systems have in common is that each level of government possesses at least some sovereignty. That is to say, lower levels of government are not mere instruments created by the national government to assist in the implementation of policies, nor is the national government merely the product of the states or provinces acting together.

Consider, for example, the recent case of welfare reform, and how having a federal system for allocating authority offers the possibility to rearrange policy responsibilities. Box 5.1 offers an overview of the factors that led to the 1996 welfare reform. Notice that one of the main criticisms of the old system was a complaint about the ponderousness of the Leviathan policy arrangement. The presence of a federal structure with both a central government and fifty state governments offered reformers of the welfare system the option of restructuring the program by giving states responsibility for trying to design improved ways of moving low-income families out of reliance on government assistance by encouraging greater work effort.

Federal systems share some attributes with the Leviathan state. One attribute in common is a central government that can address collective action problems that afflict the nation as a whole. Threats to national security can be met by the raising of a military from all provinces. Environmental pollution spilling from one state across the borders of others can be met by national emission controls that limit the volume of pollutants spewed from factories and homes regardless of the state of origin. Standards for weights and measures and the value of money can be agreed upon and enforced by the national government, thereby reducing the uncertainties associated with carrying out trade over an extensive geographic area. Taxes can be levied from across the whole country for the purpose of redressing extreme inequalities in the distribution of resources, both across regions and across income strata. The infrastructure required to move people and goods across large distances can be established and paid for by the national government. In all these ways, and many more, the existence of a national government conveys substantial utility. It permits the resolution of collective action problems that spill across large geographic areas and involve publics that are distributed in multiple states or provinces.

Federalism, with its division of sovereignty, has important differences from the Leviathan state—differences that make it much more responsive to public preferences. The existence of provincial or state governments means that there are sources of political power independent of the national government. This holds distinct advantages. It creates a strong possibility that there will be politicians at the subnational level from political parties other than the majority party at the national level. Politicians at both the national and subnational levels know that the states are springboards to elective office at the national level and vice versa. Thus, politicians and their political and ideological backers in the states have an incentive to bear some of the costs of collective action associated with gathering and disseminating information about the actions of

Box 5.1   Welfare Reform, Federalism, and Poverty

IN 1996, a Republican-led Congress and a Democratic president agreed to pass the **Personal Responsibility and Work Opportunity Reconciliation Act.** The plan completely overhauled the welfare system in the United States. It did so primarily through the means suggested in the title of the legislation: making recipients responsible for taking work opportunities. This reform concentrated on two particular areas: influencing recipient behavior and transferring responsibility for implementation of welfare from the national government to the states.

Economist Rebecca Blank, director of the Joint Center for Poverty Research at Northwestern University and member of the Clinton administration's Council of Economic Advisers, presents an excellent discussion of the factors that have driven changes in this policy area.[1] She reports that three areas of the previous welfare regime contributed to its demise.

First, the program followed a one-size-fits-all approach that offered little flexibility to address the individual needs of recipients. The development of the system into the seemingly one-size-fits-all program stemmed, in large measure, from corruption of the system during earlier periods, when local caseworkers had discretion in deciding who qualified for the programs. Specifically, black southerners who should have been considered eligible for such assistance were frequently deemed ineligible. To avoid this problem, the government created stricter guidelines for acceptance, which often took away the ability to mold the program to the specific needs of recipients. This lack of discretion to meet the dissimilar needs of specific recipients led to suggestions that state governments could better tailor programs to the needs of beneficiaries.

Second, many Americans and politicians misunderstood or misrepresented the profile of welfare recipients; it became too easy to stigmatize recipients. The profile generally held that those helped by welfare programs were young (often teenage) minority mothers of illegitimate children living in inner cities. In fact, this profile mostly did not jibe with reality. A substantial minority of recipients but the majority of the longest-term recipients are single mothers with little or no work history and are disproportionately likely to be African American. But most recipients do not live in inner cities, and most are not teenage mothers. Most are not minorities, and most spend relatively short periods of time on welfare during their lifetimes.

Third, and most important to students of policy analysis, the incentives created pernicious unintended consequences. That is, instead of assisting poor people struggling to make ends meet at work or struggling to get work, the prior program actually served as a disincentive to work. Many critics of the welfare program asserted that it created a culture of addiction to welfare and an impediment to getting off welfare. However, this view again did not match the reality. One-quarter to one-third of those who qualified for some of these programs never applied for them. Further, of those single parents who received such programs, only 7 percent received the programs for ten years or more. Fully two-thirds of recipients participated in the program for less than two years, and three-quarters did so for less than three years. This seems to reflect less an addiction to the programs than an outcome of cyclical employment patterns among the poor who have the fewest skills and are most susceptible to economic swings. Nevertheless, the American ethos of self-support still led many to have a distaste for those receiving assistance rather than working.

There are rational explanations as to why one might have chosen not to work under the old system. Blank calculates that given the pay level for low-skilled Americans, even if a husband worked full-time and his wife worked half-time (to take care of the children the other half), only 72.5 percent of families would earn enough to reach the poverty line. This is before taxes and does not include rent, insurance, or bills. The situation is worse for single mothers. Low-skilled women earn little due to the pool of jobs available, and women typically receive less pay than men in any job sector. This means that while working full-time at a wage level above the average for low-skilled women, only 22 percent of women would earn enough to meet the poverty line.

Again, this does not include taxes, medical insurance, child care, rent, or bills. The single parent had little incentive to work when considering how payments were adjusted to earnings. The Earned Income Tax Credit (a cut in income taxes or even a subsidy in lieu of taxes for poorer Americans) depended on how much the individual earned. The same inverse relationship occurred for food stamps. For single parents (particularly mothers), Aid to Families with Dependent Children, the main "welfare" program, was also reduced when more income was earned. Thus, not only would benefits be scaled back for recipients who were working, but the recipients would also have to pay taxes and pick up child-care costs that they did not have while not working. In sum, much of the nonwork under the old system was due to the perverse disincentives to work.

The welfare reforms passed by Congress and signed by President Clinton in 1996 directly promoted behavioral changes for recipients. At the core of the reforms was the demand that recipients get jobs. The passage of this welfare reform package prompted cheers from many and complaints from others who feared that the government would push a significant portion of low-income Americans into the streets. The original intent of the previous program had been to assist single mothers with children, specifically widows with children. As the norm that women should not work diminished and the perception grew that moneys were going to support births outside marriage, support for welfare diminished. Too often, the former program failed to provide workers at the margins of poverty enough help to keep working and gave nonworkers few reasons to engage in work. Because most recipients moved in and out of the system anyway, it is clear that these incentives still did not overwhelm people's desire to work—they only made it difficult to stay working. That is why Blank suggests that the behavioral incentives of the new program may work better.

Just as important, however, the new welfare system devolves responsibilities for fashioning the welfare program to states and local communities. The one-size-fits-all approach has been replaced with an approach that gives discretion to subnational governments to adapt welfare assistance to local needs and contingencies. The question, of course, is whether the states and local governments will be able to find policy solutions that help move individuals into economic self-sufficiency without re-creating the pathologies that led to the removal of this discretion in the first place.

1. Most of the intellectual foundation for this box stems from Rebecca M. Blank, *It Takes a Nation: A New Agenda for Fighting Poverty* (Princeton, N.J.: Princeton University Press, 1997). Arguments and examples should be attributed to Blank. The authors accept responsibility for any mistaken translation of her arguments.

politicians in the majority party at the national level. Citizens, therefore, are able to make informed and thus better choices of political leaders in federal systems. Citizens benefit from being able to make implicit or explicit comparisons of the behavior of political leaders and the consequences of their policy actions at different levels of government. Consequently, leaders must be more responsive to their needs. Democracy, then, will be a more effective check on the actions of government leaders and will result in policies that are more closely aligned with the preferences of majorities at both the subnational and national levels.

An important consequence is that politicians at each level may be more cautious about engaging in corruption. In federal systems, side payments from organized business interests to politicians in exchange for protective policies, while still present, should be reduced in both size and scope. Again, this is because information about such side payments will be more widely available and less costly for citizens to acquire. Indeed, depending on which level of government has primary responsibility for the regulation of economic activity, a system of federalism may reduce rent seeking to a very low level.

Political scientist Barry Weingast has hypothesized that if states have responsibility for economic regulation and the national government enforces a policy of open trade across state lines, rent seeking by organized businesses, and the associated higher prices that such businesses charge, will simply result in consumers purchasing products from businesses located in states where rent-seeking policies have not been awarded.[2] Weingast's argument is that when rent seeking occurs at the state level, businesses that face competition at the national or international levels that have won protections from state governments tend to lose market share and experience a decrease in profitability. State governments may therefore be reluctant to grant such protections, inasmuch as tax revenues from these companies and their employees will begin to disappear, crimping what the state government can afford to do across a host of policy areas.

The qualification in Weingast's argument is worth noting: the key to the value of federalism in reducing rent-seeking efforts by business is the scope of the market within which a particular business competes. Businesses that do not face competition from businesses located in other states or countries can indeed benefit from trying to seek protections from state governments. You need not look hard to find examples of the latter. As an experiment, do a search on the Internet for the rules in your state that govern licensing of cosmetologists, barbers, dog groomers, taxi drivers, or funeral directors. In each of these occupations, the effective market is typically local. What you will find in many states is that the trade associations representing these occupations have won protective regulations from state legislatures limiting the entry of new competitors into these occupational markets.

The flip side of the Weingast argument is that organized interests may target the national government to obtain rent-seeking policies. Politicians at that level may be quite willing to produce policies that benefit organized interests in exchange for electoral resources. Unlike politicians in state governments (at least some of the time), politicians at the national level encounter few obstacles to engaging in such exchanges. The same is true with regard to the principal-agent problem. There are likely to be few countervailing forces at the national level effectively stopping bureaucracies from becoming bloated. State governments are somewhat constrained in how oversized and inefficient they can become, because they will begin to drive off businesses and productive capital if taxes become too high relative to the services that are provided. The national government is much less constrained. Businesses and productive capital have fewer options about relocating, since the costs of moving across national borders may be substantial. In short, rent seeking and the government growth associated with the principal-agent problem are likely to be as prevalent at the national level as they are in the Leviathan state—for all of the same reasons.

As discussed in Chapter 3 in the section on permanent minorities, the problem of minorities is not necessarily solved in federal systems. A moment's reflection on the long, mean history of discrimination against African Americans and other racial, ethnic, and religious minorities in the United States should suggest that the preferences of minorities can be systematically ignored, even in a federal system. The same might be said with regard to the historical treatment of the native peoples of Canada. Federalism offers no guarantee that majorities will not disregard the interests of minorities.

To be sure, it may be possible for groups that are in the minority in several states to relocate to a single state where they constitute a majority. The example of Mormons and their exodus from the Midwest to Utah attests to this possibility. Alternatively, minority groups that face discrimination in some states may be able to relocate to a state where the discrimination is not so severe. The example of the relocation of gay men and lesbians to San Francisco and Hawaii from less tolerant places is evidence of this type of mobility. But the fact remains that some minority groups may be unable to have their preferences fully valued anywhere, because majorities in every state have preferences that are antithetical to those of the minority groups.

Self-governance

Self-governance is ubiquitous in the United States, as well as in other parts of the world. Self-governance includes neighborhood organizations that conduct crime watch programs, monitor deed restrictions, and represent the neighborhood when developers try to win zoning exceptions or variances for a nearby project. Other examples include volunteer fire departments, many emergency medical and rescue units, many rural water districts, most irrigation districts, many flood control and levy districts, and even cemetery districts. One of the most common forms of self-governance is the enormous array of nonprofit organizations that have been created by groups of people to carry out a dizzying number of activities. These organizations range from social groups for veterans; to social activities, housing, and meals for college students (for example, college fraternities and sororities); to cotton gin and grain silo cooperatives for farmers; to emergency shelters for abused women and children; to child-care facilities; and on and on. In short, these organizations are responses to preferences of groups of individuals for particular types of policy goods and services.

Self-governance is so common that it is easy to overlook when discussing the size and scope of government. Yet it is responsible for many of the policy activities that people take for granted. How does self-governance differ from Leviathan and federalist forms of government discussed here? It differs in two main respects.

First, one of the things that all formal governments have is an organizational structure with full-time professionals carrying out specified duties. Self-governance generally operates without full-time professional staff. There may be part-time paid staff or a paid jack-of-all-trades who does everything from overseeing programs to handling financial matters to sweeping the floors. These people are most often not government employees but private citizens. In general, however, there is no paid staff. Consequently there is little formal organization in the conventional sense. The same people may hold the same positions year after year. Elections may be rare. Instead, self-governance mainly depends on volunteers who serve in offices for a period of time and are responsible for making sure that the activities of the organization are carried out.

The second way that self-governance organizations differ from formal governments is that they tend to be restricted to a single policy function or a circumscribed set of functions, and their ability to exercise coercion is limited. Indeed, the main tool that such organizations may have for obtaining cooperation may be moral sanctions. That is, they may appeal to the good intentions of individuals. This tool is often quite effective. Indeed, in face-to-face communities, self-governance often demonstrates remarkable capacity. This is because people tend to value their reputations. Repeated free riding or holding out tends to tarnish reputations. People tend to take offense when others too often take advantage of them.

What happens, however, when moral sanctioning proves ineffective? There is no single (or simple) answer to this question. In some places, extralegal threats of violence may be used. Some self-governing organizations have recourse to the formal system of government via the courts, which gives the organizations the ability to wield a big hammer to enforce agreements and contracts. Recourse to the legal system gives self-governing organizations the ability to credibly threaten free riders and holdouts with the possibility of coercion, including fines and even arrest. These organizations can sue people who renege on agreements or violate contracts. Such recourse, however, tends to be expensive. Also, many self-governing organizations lack this recourse, since the organizations are not in the conventional sense agencies of government. The more common recourse is thus to rely on the social capital that exists in local communities. As we saw in Chapter 4, social capital results from the desire of people to be friendly and maintain generally positive reputations.

Self-governance, because it depends on voluntary contributions of time and labor, tends to be fragile. Because self-governing organizations typically rely heavily on voluntary compliance to be able to get things done, they tend to suffer from the exhaustion of good intentions. People grow weary of contributing their time, resources, and energies, especially when confronted with an array of other needs and opportunities.

Moreover, beyond a relatively small scale, self-governance tends to collapse. When problems are too large to be solved through face-to-face interactions, social capital often proves an inadequate mechanism for inducing collective action. The absence of formal governance structures can begin to look capricious and arbitrary. As problems grow in scale and complexity, administrative systems, made up of trained employees who are compensated to do particular tasks and who are overseen by professional managers, become necessary to ensure a consistent flow of policy goods and services. Some tasks are simply too complex or too essential to leave to volunteers. Hence self-governance, while valuable and useful, is limited as a structure for addressing important classes of policy problems.

Polycentrism

Polycentrism is a structure of governance that contains elements of each of the three forms of government discussed above. The term polycentrism derives from poly, which means "multiple" or "many," and centric, which refers to centers or locations of authority. Polycentrism is a structure of governance made up of multiple, overlapping jurisdictions of varying geographic scope.

Polycentrism describes the overlapping governments, small and not so small, that characterize much of the modern structure of governance in the United States. Consider, as an example, any typical U.S. metropolitan area. Such places often have dozens or even more city governments lying adjacent to one another. Overlapping them, in whole or in part, may be a number of school districts, hospital districts, water and sewer districts, low-income housing special districts, museum districts, mass transit authorities, counties, and of course, state and federal government agencies. Within these nested, polycentric structures, scores of self-governing organizations may come into and out of existence to address myriad public purposes. Self-governing organizations, such as churches and other nonprofit organizations, provide low-cost day care for children, organize summer youth programs, and offer enrichment programs for the elderly. Likewise, neighborhood organizations provide recreational services, such as small parks, play equipment for kids, and community pools; provide policing services through crime watch programs; and periodically clean up common neighborhood areas. In other words, polycentrism is a governance structure composed of nested and partially overlapping public organizations, from narrowly local organizations up through the national level (and potentially even the international level), each with jurisdiction for a circumscribed set of public functions.

The key strength of polycentrism is that it permits the structure of governance to be "sized" to the scale of particular public problems. Some problems, such as water pollution, extend beyond state borders but do not involve the whole country. Other problems, such as air pollution, can extend even beyond national boundaries. Still others, such as traffic congestion, can involve multiple cities and even counties within a large metropolitan area, but rarely involve entire states. Recall from Chapter 2 that a public is defined in terms of groups of people who are potentially affected by the consequences of an activity or problem. Optimally, we would like to size governance structures to the scope of each of these public problems.

Notice how the Leviathan state and federalism are likely to be poorly sized to fit well the scale of most public problems, except when a public, through a quirk of fate or coincidence, happens to match the boundaries of the nation as a whole or an individual state. Self-governing organizations, because of their flexibility, in principle might be sized appropriately to encompass any given public; but for reasons we've already seen, they tend to collapse when problems move beyond local boundaries. By contrast, polycentric systems, because of their nested and overlapping structures, can be sized to respond to the preferences of publics that may vary enormously in scope. That is to say, in a polycentric system it is possible to structure governance mechanisms that correspond to each of the publics that confront particular policy problems.

One of the main criticisms of polycentric systems is that holding public officials accountable may be difficult or impossible, given the numbers and layers of governing organizations that make up these systems. This is not a trivial issue. While some of the leaders of these organizations may be elected, others may not be. In cases where the leaders are elected, citizens have the option to "throw out the bums" if they are dissatisfied with the behavior or policy actions of the elected officials. And to be sure, there are other outlets for citizens to voice their preferences. Newspapers, weekly journals, civic clubs, neighborhood organizations, and churches all can be a forum for citizens upset with government actions to express their discontent.

Notice, however, that polycentrism offers an additional mechanism for holding public organizations accountable for inadequate policy performance. While not costless, citizens often can vote with their feet. **Voting with the feet** means relocating to a jurisdiction in the geographic area that more closely matches a citizen's set of preferences. The power of this mechanism was first identified and explained by economist Charles Tiebout.[3] What Tiebout and others who followed him have shown is that where there are numerous government jurisdictions and where the costs of moving are relatively low, a dynamic is set in motion whereby governments seek to tailor their policies to attract and keep citizens. The argument is as follows: as with markets for private goods (for example, food, clothing, furniture, and cars), there can be a marketlike dynamic where producers of public policies (that is, governments) seek to attract consumers of public policies (that is, citizens) by fashioning a mix of service offerings and tax burdens that will appeal to citizens with similar preferences.

This responsiveness of polycentric systems allows groups that would otherwise be in the minority to influence public policies, but only up to a point. Through their mobility decisions, such groups can cluster into jurisdictions more to their liking. Some of these jurisdictions may be predominantly made up of a particular ethnic or racial group. Others may be organized around golf courses and be filled with golf enthusiasts. Still others may be organized around tennis facilities, residential airports, or horse and saddle clubs. Where jurisdictions are small, there may be dozens of relatively homogeneous groups of residents.

There is another, and potentially more serious, limitation of polycentric systems. They face difficult collective action problems. Governance structures have to be adapted to or created for each new policy problem in order to achieve an appropriate geographic scale. Members of affected publics (that is, the various people who are potentially affected by the consequences of an activity or problem) must be able to find one another and forge some sort of governance organization to cope with the problems that turned them into publics in the first place. This may mean the creation of regional authorities that overlay existing governments. Or it may mean creating a new authority within a community to cope with a problem that affects a subset of the population living in a city or metropolitan area.

Establishing new governance mechanisms is costly and time consuming, and it requires some degree of cooperation and coordination with existing government organizations. Cooperation and coordination may be difficult, if not impossible, to obtain, depending on the circumstances of a given public issue. Mass transit, for example, is a policy area where such problems often occur. Mass transit systems, if they are to be of much utility, need to connect suburbs to central cities, as well as to one another. But such systems tend to be controversial, both because of fears about an influx of "undesirable elements" into upscale neighborhoods and because of legitimate concerns about who should pay for the system and how much. The difficulties of organizing a coordinated effort among adjacent jurisdictions can doom a mass transit system. Houston, for example, tried for years to build a light-rail transit system, but the city was never able to overcome the objections of people in adjacent jurisdictions. Eventually the plans for a rail system were scrapped, and the existing bus system was simply expanded.

Furthermore, consider the difficulties faced in trying to implement policies that involve redistribution of resources across social classes or across geographic areas. The policy of busing to redress racial segregation has proved notoriously difficult to implement in metropolitan areas with many jurisdictions, because families (especially white families) have chosen instead to exit from any jurisdictions that were part of the busing plans. Likewise, it is difficult to maintain redistributive income transfers, which involve shifting money from higher income people to those with lower incomes, in metropolitan areas; people in jurisdictions where there are few poor households may object to paying for programs benefiting residents of other jurisdictions. Moreover, if such policies become very generous, and thus expensive, those taxpayers bearing a disproportionate share of the burden may begin to exit the metropolitan area altogether.

In sum, polycentric systems of governance have both positive and negative features. Because polycentrism is the system of governance that typifies much of what exists in the United States, we will have much more to say about it in the final section of this book, beginning with Chapter 8.

CONCLUSION

Government is a necessary instrument for solving many collective action problems. Governments are organizations that can legitimately mobilize and use coercion. But governments can be dangerous instruments. They can become predacious toward their own citizens, as well as a threat to their neighbors. The question is, How can we benefit from the capacity of governments to solve problems while preventing them from becoming unresponsive to the needs and preferences of publics?

Several ways of organizing government have been discussed in this chapter: the Leviathan state, federalism, self-governance, and polycentrism. At one end of the spectrum, the Leviathan state is most likely to be able to implement policies but least likely to be responsive. It is also the most likely to suffer from corruption and be undemocratic. At the other end of the spectrum, polycentrism is highly responsive but often finds it difficult to implement large-scale policies.

Key Terms

eminent domain *p. 80*
governmental capacity *p. 84*
federalism *p. 86*
Personal Responsibility and Work
    Opportunity Reconciliation Act *p. 88*

self-governance *p. 91*
polycentrism *p. 93*
voting with the feet *p. 94*

Suggested Readings

Hirschman, Albert O. 1970. *Exit, Voice, and Loyalty.* Cambridge, Mass.: Harvard University Press.

Keynes, John Maynard. 1836. *The General Theory of Employment, Interest, and Money.* London: Macmillan.

Lindblom, Charles. 1977. *Politics and Markets.* New York: Basic Books.

Miller, Gary. 1981. *Cities by Contract.* Cambridge, Mass.: MIT Press.

Ostrom, Vincent. 1989. *The Intellectual Crisis in Public Administration.* 2nd ed. Tuscaloosa: University of Alabama Press.

Ostrom, Vincent, Charles Tiebout, and Robert Warren. 1961. "The Organization of Government in Metropolitan Areas: A Theoretical Inquiry." *American Political Science Review* 55: 831–842.

Peterson, Paul. 1981. *City Limits.* Chicago: University of Chicago Press.

Pigou, A. C. 1920. *The Economics of Welfare.* London: Macmillan.

Tiebout, Charles M. 1956. "A Pure Theory of Local Expenditure." *Journal of Political Economy* 64: 416–424.

Notes

1. Vincent Ostrom, *The Political Theory of a Compound Republic: Designing the American Experiment*, 2nd ed. (Lincoln, Nebraska: University of Nebraska Press, 1987).

2. Barry Weingast, "The Economic Role of Political Institutions: Federalism, Markets, and Economic Development," *Journal of Law, Economics, and Organization* 11 (April 1995): 1–31.

3. Charles M. Tiebout, "A Pure Theory of Local Expenditure," *Journal of Political Economy* 64 (1956): 416–424.

6

The Market as a Collective Action Mechanism

INTRODUCTION

Collective action does not always imply a dilemma. Certain mechanisms are capable of solving societal problems without the need for centralized control. We usually refer to such mechanisms as markets, and we will do so throughout this book. Many public policy analysts mistakenly believe that public policy begins where markets fail. While this is in large part true, we are becoming more aware that thriving markets do not spontaneously emerge. Markets require that property be secure. This chapter explores the institutional foundations of markets.

MARKET INSTITUTIONS

Capitalism is an economic system based on private ownership of property in which production, distribution, and exchange of goods and services are conducted through competitive markets. It is an institutional system in which markets thrive. In an earlier time in which ideologies dictated political activity, it was thought that capitalism required little or no government. **Socialism,** an alternative ideology or idea, is based on the premise that capitalism will fail to provide adequate production and allocation of goods and services in an economy. Instead, under socialism, the government is responsible for production and allocation decisions. Government policy under socialism is meant to make better economic decisions in a centralized rather than a decentralized manner. Relatively recently, most nation-states have adopted the view that markets are necessary for the production and allocation of goods and services. When democratic government and a market-based economy are conjoined, the resulting system is known as **liberal democracy.** A liberal democracy recognizes that properly designed markets allow individual preferences to play the major role in production and allocation, just as democracy gives expression to individual preferences in the political arena. To create institutions where markets thrive, governments must have limited powers.

The reason why markets work is simple. Markets require people to act on their own volition and according to their own preferences. When people produce something, it is because they expect a reward, a profit. The incentive is built in for individuals to produce things that other people want. When someone buys something, it is because that person gets more satisfaction from that product than he or she would from another use of his or her money. Individuals doing what they want for themselves make a market work. It is very simple. There are limitations to markets (see Chapter 7), but the basic idea is persuasive and powerful. Voluntary action must lead to society's being better off after market transactions than before.

A **market** is a social structure that allows people to produce, buy, and sell goods and services without limitation by others. Markets require people to be

The greatest symbol of the free market and capitalism is the Pit at the New York Stock Exchange. *Porter Gifford/Liason International.*

secure in their property. If not, stealing will be a better economic occupation than producing and selling goods and services.

A very important foundation of liberal democracies is the design of market institutions. Institutions are formal rules and informal norms that influence the way individuals behave. Formal rules that help produce thriving markets include prohibitions against stealing, one method of providing secure property rights. Individuals realize that if they are caught stealing, the consequences might be fines, imprisonment, or both. Laws, then, try to induce people to behave differently. However, formal rules are rarely enough to make markets work as effectively as possible, and norms also play a critical role.

Norms induce people to act in certain ways by giving them social incentives to be honest, among other things. Religious norms, such as "Thou shall not steal" or "Though shall not covet," are one kind. So is the attempt by a vendor to keep a good reputation. It may or may not be illegal to sell an inferior product for an inflated price, but in a close-knit community it would not be smart, because business would suffer. All markets require norms, and some markets have operated well without formal rules. However, public policy focuses on rules, because we understand less about how to manipulate norms to produce better outcomes in society. Norms evolve over time and become a part of what we call society. It is foolish not to acknowledge the existence of norms, primarily because the decision about which formal rules are needed is going to be contingent on what norms are in place in a given community.

This emphasis on the importance of norms may seem overblown, but the policy analyst must take norms seriously. Policy analysts who ignore norms will be biased toward fixing problems that do not exist. For example, a typical mistake made by policy analysts is to identify a situation where a collective action problem potentially exists and ignore the fact that individuals may very well have solved the problem themselves. The discussion in earlier chapters of self-governing institutions for the solution of collective action problems shows that individuals in certain situations can solve these problems without relying on a coercive authority. What can happen when a central authority uses formal rules to fix collective action problems that have been solved by individuals? Individuals will lose their incentive to solve such problems as they wait around for government to do so.

Using a market example, individuals in a common market may have generated ways, such as through talking to one another, to identify which vendors provide good products and which ones sell lousy products. If individuals think government regulation of products is successful and thus no lousy products should exist, they may quit talking to one another. If they buy a lousy product, instead of telling others, they may instead get angry at the government for not solving the problem. This is why liberal governments should take care in developing and imposing formal rules for structuring markets and other policies. As Box 6.1 indicates, this is why the Federal Trade Commission (FTC) exists to police the marketplace and doesn't leave citizens on their own to seek reme-

Box 6.1 Consumer Fraud and the Federal Trade Commission

WHEN CONSUMERS are defrauded, one of the most common means for seeking redress is use of the courts. Home buyers often end up suing construction contractors for poor or unfinished work on their homes. Groups of consumers can also work together in class action lawsuits. These lawsuits require someone to bring a group together or even start a court proceeding without all members even being aware of the lawsuit. Finally, state agencies may investigate and sue fraudulent companies. In 1992, for example, the California Consumer Affairs Department investigated Sears, Roebuck and Company's automotive repair shops for systematically charging customers for unneeded repairs. Sears settled the dispute by offering over $46 million to Californians who had had automotive repairs to their cars.[1] In each of these ways of rectifying damages, the incentive is to win money from those who defrauded customers.

There also may be serious disincentives to seeking restitution, however. The federal consumer protection agency, the Federal Trade Commission (FTC), exists to protect the public against fraudulent advertising and business practices. Unfortunately, the FTC's procedures for handling suspected fraud actually act as a disincentive to those with legitimate fraud claims.[2] Even worse, the mode of operation at the FTC may actually promote false accusations against companies by parties that have not been defrauded. The FTC allows only limited restitution to defrauded consumers, so there is little incentive to spend time and energy to punish a fraudulent company. Another perverse incentive stems from the commission's paying for the whole cost of the prosecution. As such, competitors can bring unwarranted complaints against others just to frustrate them and cause them to waste energy fighting bogus complaints. Thus, governments must be aware of how they create policies and institutions to handle market exchange; otherwise, they may inadvertently worsen, rather than solve, problems.

1. *Los Angeles Times* (Sept. 3, 1992); *San Francisco Chronicle* (Sept. 3, 1992).
2. Richard Posner, *Economic Analysis of Law,* 4th ed. (Boston: Little, Brown, 1992), pp. 370–372.

dies against consumer fraud. However, as the box points out, the FTC does not employ the most effective types of regulation to ensure consumer protection.

In this chapter, we consider three successive ideas. First, Thomas Hobbes's Leviathan will be extended as a way to understand the role of government in markets. Second, we will consider Adam Smith's argument about the benefits of markets and the role of government. Smith's prescriptions for government are not as draconian as those of Hobbes, but there is a major role for government in his *Wealth of Nations* and other writings that often is unrecognized by scholars and policy analysts. Finally, we will describe in finer detail the role of institutions in the development and success of capitalism.

HOBBES AND PROPERTY RIGHTS

We have already mentioned much about Thomas Hobbes in this book. The reason is that Hobbes was the first philosopher to recognize the fundamental dilemma of governance: a nation-state strong enough to enforce laws to make citizens abide by the law is also strong enough to break the law. Plato, Aristotle, and those who followed them clearly understood the weakness of government, but Hobbes posed this problem in its starkest form.

How do citizens keep the state from being a **predatory state,** that is, a state that makes policy to enhance its own resources? This public policy problem was ignored throughout much of the twentieth century, and we focus much attention on it in this book. Of course, Hobbes's answer is at the very best a quaint attempt to solve a difficult problem: the sovereign, or government, would need to be answerable to God. All this is nice and good, but such governments tend to be self-perpetuating autocracies. Hobbes's was a premodern, not a contemporary, vision.

Property rights are the lawful claims to possess, enjoy, and dispose of an item or good. In terms of property rights, Hobbes's dilemma becomes all too real. Restated, it reads as follows: a nation-state strong enough to protect property is also strong enough to confiscate it. Thus, the Leviathan approach to market institutions is more complicated than is typically thought. The typical view is that centralized authority can impose formal rules to provide property rights. It is not clear how a society imposes rules on those who govern so that they do not act in a predatory fashion.

Contemporary analytic democratic theory includes several theories of government that reflect this problem. The most illustrative of these is called the fiscal illusion theory. This theory predicts that governments that have tax structures that obscure the amount of money that is collected in taxes will collect more revenues than governments that make this summary absolutely clear. Thus, predatory governments will want to create a **fiscal illusion** in which individuals will not be clear about how much money is extracted from them. This model helps us understand why the U.S. government uses payroll deduction to keep individuals from knowing just how much the income tax is costing from week to week. But a better example consists of excise taxes, tariffs, and sales taxes. While these taxes all have more or less visibility, it is difficult for individual taxpayers to know how much they pay in a given year.

This begs the question, Why would governments want to have more rather than less revenues? The answer is basically the same as that of the following question: Why would an individual want to have more rather than less income? Like anyone or any organization, the government, at the very best, is going to want resources to solve problems. At the very worst, the government, just like any opportunistic individual, is going to want more resources simply because it craves more in order to provide greater benefits to supporters at the expense of nonsupporters. Societies can design democratic institutions so that governments face incentives to do otherwise, just as incentives can be designed to make individuals change their behavior. For better or worse, the basic, fundamental nature of governments is to be predatory in some way, even if such predation is meant, on the surface, to be good for people.

A basic implication of property rights derived from Hobbes is that investors in democratic nation-states must be concerned with government's changing the rules of the game. Let us give you an example. Suppose an upstart state, in terms of economic development, announces a policy guaranteeing that investors in plant and equipment will be able to keep a certain, large proportion of profits from investments. If you are an investor, should you believe the government? Not necessarily. Rules can change. Thus, the probability of predatory behavior will thwart a government's efforts to encourage economic investment in the economy by the private sector. Because a state that is strong enough to enforce property rights is strong enough to confiscate property, the government cannot be trusted without assurances that it will be trustworthy.

It is noteworthy that nation-states do develop strong economies. That is, investors occasionally receive and believe the signal from government that they will be able to keep a decent return on investments. When reviewing the historical record, there are diverse ways that governments have developed reputations as credible defenders of property rights. The ways that this credibility has been established are too numerous to be detailed in this book. However, as any analyst of the world economy can all too easily show, the ratio of failures to successes is all too high.

Why, then, do nation-states that have successfully developed economies continue to enjoy success relative to less developed countries? One very interesting answer is provided by Charles Lindblom.[1] Government enjoys political success by producing economic prosperity. Once an economy produces economic success, it must refrain from doing anything that would hurt economic growth. Lindblom actually decries this phenomenon as a limitation on democracy, but one positive benefit that this mechanism has is to limit the predatory nature of governments. Once a government oversees a developed democracy, it has an incentive to make sure that it does not confiscate so much wealth that the economy sours. Replacing Hobbes's God as enforcer are investors who hold the implicit threat of disinvestment if the government begins confiscating too much wealth. Thus, Hobbes's problem is more apparent in less developed than developed countries.

Jesus proclaimed, "Render unto Caesar what is Caesar's," asserting the legitimacy of government to coerce individuals to provide government resources under Christian principles. This creates a problem, because those who build a capitalist economy, investors, must be sure that Caesar will not take all that is produced. This continues to be a problem in democracies that have not yet produced thriving markets, because there is no guarantee that Caesar will not take more than his share.

All this means that one of the most important institutions of capitalism is limited government, the model being liberal democratic government. Many more institutions beyond this are important for economic success, but the most fundamental and difficult rules to design are meant to limit the government's ability to confiscate wealth in excess. There are no simple ways to design these rules for those states that have fledgling economies. Indeed, historical accident rather than rational design appears to explain the successes. Economic success breeds limitations on the state. This fact allows us to focus on solving other policy problems that occur in developed economies. The basic fundamental dilemma, as outlined by Hobbes, is more or less solved by the threat of disinvestment. Many other institutional design issues are important, the paramount one being how to design market institutions that make markets thrive, not just survive.

SMITH AND PROPERTY RIGHTS

Hobbes was not concerned with capitalism as we know it. Rather, he was concerned with simple societal order. Adam Smith, the philosopher and economic thinker who in 1776 authored *The Wealth of Nations*, one of the most influential books ever written, recognized that the production and allocation of goods and services is the issue that allows us to understand why states have economic success. The genius of Smith was that he found a way to explain to others why the success of individual businesses meant the success of a nation's economy. To understand his accomplishment, one needs to understand the context in which he wrote.

Like today, in Smith's time economists were ubiquitous, listened to, and often very wrong. Two schools of thought show this clearly. Physiocrats were economists who used a biological science analogy to explain how economies work. Money and resources are like blood. The way to understand an economy is to understand how the blood, or resources, flows across individuals. Needless to say, this analogy turned out to be a dead end.

More powerful, and even surviving to contemporary times, is the mercantilist school. These folks believed that the global economy is something like a zero-sum game, where gains for one country are losses for another. Thus, economic success depends on making gains at the expense of other economies. **Mercantilism** requires that a nation-state be all-powerful so that it can heavily regulate how its economy operates. If it does not do so, there is no guarantee that other states' economies will not overtake it in economic performance. Neo-mercantilism is alive and well in the protectionist movement, where a typical nation-state tries to minimize the effect of another economy on the performance of its own economy.

The logic of Smith's argument strongly indicated that mercantilism's flaw is in not properly understanding the "wealth of nations." Prior to Smith, the wealth of a nation was thought to be its supply of gold and other natural resources. Smith's genius was in showing that the wealth of a nation is in its ability to produce goods and services valued by its people. The best way to do this, according to Smith, is to allow the butcher, baker, and candlestick maker to operate as they choose. If they are selling their products in an open market, they have the incentive to produce goods that people like. With everyone operating this way, the best way to increase the wealth of nations is by letting people consume and produce goods under capitalism. Ricardo's contribution was to generalize this idea to the world economy, arguing that free trade among nations followed the same logic as Smith's free trade among individuals.

Smith has been understood ever since as the proponent of the economic concept of *laissez faire,* or "leave things alone." This idea was already in currency before Smith, and it is often viewed as a primary foundation of liberal government. The argument is that if a government leaves the economy alone, things will work better than if the economy is heavily regulated. Most laypersons have viewed Smith as someone who saw little role for government. This is not the case. Indeed, Smith was the head of the Scottish **Custom House,** and he wrote a book with the same name. Custom Houses were responsible for collecting taxes from all ships passing through British ports. In this book, he included prescriptions for how government should design international trade policy to better benefit the nation-state; he did not prescribe unfettered free trade (see Box 6.2).

Furthermore, *The Wealth of Nations* was hardly a book that had no role for government. We have documented that government has a significant role in the protection of property rights that is necessary for economies to flourish. Smith's real intention was to point out that the domestic economy could be better regulated, in a large-scale fashion, by allowing individuals wide autonomy in decisions about what to produce and consume. It was the first presentation of the idea that the decentralized market solves production and allocation problems better than more centralized mechanisms. However, there was a role for government to provide property rights and some goods and services.

The best way to understand *The Wealth of Nations* is by comparing the ideas in it to mercantilist schools of thought. Smith saw his book as an important corrective for economists who could see only the forest but not the trees. Only by conceiving how the butcher, baker, and candlestick maker decide how much and what to produce can one begin to see how economies operate. Smith identifies the gains from voluntary trade that allow economies to thrive. It is the voluntary exchange of resources that ensures that individuals are better off after trade than before. Thus, the wealth of nations is produced by individuals acting in their own interests.

This idea was indeed revolutionary, because the mercantilist notion is that two individuals, or more appropriately two states, face a trading situation in which there is clearly a winner and a loser. Two traders in Smith's world both gain, or they would not trade. This revolutionary concept is largely accepted in liberal democracies, but mercantilism is still popular when trade among nations is considered. It is still true, however, that even in a liberal democracy

Box 6.2   *Adam Smith as Customs Officer*

ADAM SMITH is frequently given credit for being the intellectual father of the economic concept of *laissez-faire,* and thus a commitment to free trade. In the 1700s, during Smith's life, all the European powers pursued the policies of mercantilism, which defined a country's economic power as the stock of gold and coin held in a government's treasury. Smith's greatest book, *The Wealth of Nations,* published in 1776, is a cogent, ringing condemnation of mercantilism and an endorsement of the advantages for society of relatively unfettered market exchanges and liberal trade policies.

Ironically, in actual work as a commissioner for Scottish Customs, Smith was diligent in carrying out Britain's mercantilist trade policies by collecting duties and taxes on behalf of the British crown.[1] Customs provided a major source of government revenue for Britain due to its dominance of the high seas and trade. Without modern communications, Britain relied on customs commissioners to search all ships for cargo to be taxed, collect duties from ship captains, and ensure that all traders met every government regulation or be punished severely. The commissioners for Scottish Customs had six ships, guns, and full crews at their disposal to ensure that the government's policies were followed and that all duties were paid.

Commissioners were also important advisers to Parliament on trade matters. Despite the opportunity that Smith had to promote to Parliament the tenets in *The Wealth of Nations,* he never did so, except through the publication of the book itself. According to documents covering his tenure as commissioner, Smith was a "good bureaucrat." Evidence suggests that he ordered crews to search exhaustively for ships trying to avoid duties and severely punished a ship's captain who did not have all of his cargo listed on his manifest. Smith often ordered ships' cargoes to be warehoused, a ploy practiced by some commissioners to add hefty storage fees to the duties that shippers had to pay. In essence, Smith inflated prices to the benefit of the government and not the consumer. Thus, one of the great ironies of history is that Smith, the revolutionary proponent of liberalized trade policies, spent his adult career advancing the mercantilist economic system that he had condemned as a false system for the creation of national wealth.

1. The following is drawn from Gary Anderson, William Shughart, and Robert Tollison, "Adam Smith in the Custom House," *Journal of Political Economy,* 93, no. 4(1985): 740–759.

like the United States this concept is sometimes forgotten or ignored. Box 6.3 indicates that even the free-trade Reagan administration resorted to mercantilist policies in trying to restrict the importation of Japanese automobiles to the United States.

THE BREADTH AND COMPLEXITY OF PROPERTY RIGHTS

So far, we have focused on a very basic notion of property rights, one that emphasizes the role played by institutions in guaranteeing that individuals will re-

Box 6.3 Voluntary Trade Restrictions on Japanese Automobiles

AMERICAN AUTOMOBILE manufacturers suffered greatly during the late 1970s and early 1980s. An economic recession kept many consumers from buying new cars. Worse, with the second major oil crisis in ten years, those consumers who did buy cars preferred smaller, more energy efficient cars. Detroit's "Big Three—General Motors, Ford, and Chrysler—had for decades specialized in large "gas-guzzler" cars, and their initial offerings of small cars such as the Vega, the Pinto, and the Omni were of poor quality and in some cases dangerous. The Japanese, however, had been building smaller cars for decades—cars that had increasingly earned a reputation as reliable and well built. Americans, in expanding numbers, began to buy Hondas, Toyotas, and Datsuns (later renamed Nissans). As a result, the largest U.S. manufacturing industry was losing money, laying off workers, and closing plants.

President Ronald Reagan, a Republican known for having a strong market orientation and a lack of sympathy toward unions, had a solid pro-free-trade profile. Early in President Reagan's first term, a rift broke out among his cabinet and prominent political leaders over a proposal by Republican Senator John Danforth of Missouri to impose trade sanctions against the Japanese due to the automobile trade imbalance.[1] Not anxious to be blamed for job losses but a firm believer in the evils of protectionism, President Reagan was left with a difficult decision, to which he developed an interesting resolution. To avoid imposing sanctions, the administration convinced the Japanese government to place "voluntary restraints" on how many cars Japanese auto makers could export. Facing the threat of congressional sanctions, the Japanese government agreed with President Reagan's plan to reduce its exports.

Thus, there was no explicit U.S. governmental policy that could be said to be protectionist or mercantilist, but the desired effect of lowering the number of Japanese vehicles exported to the United States was achieved. Nevertheless, this tacit policy led to non-free-market outcomes. The limited number of Japanese cars meant that demand for those available grew and, consequently, so did the price. The International Trade Commission (ITC) found that this raised the price an extra $1,300 per Japanese car and allowed U.S. car manufacturers to raise their prices by $600 per car.[2] Further, the ITC **voluntary trade restrictions** had saved 44,000 U.S. jobs. Those in favor of pressuring the Japanese into voluntary export restrictions argued that Japan did not open its market to American cars, so closing off access to U.S. markets was the best approach.

It is interesting to note that the Japanese government continued to restrict automobile exports to the United States even after 1985, when the Reagan administration stopped requesting it to do so. The threat of congressional sanctions was enough of an incentive that the Japanese automakers wanted to avoid them at the cost of profits. Further, the Japanese automakers found ways to sell their cars to Americans while still keeping within their voluntary limits. They began building assembly plants in the United States. Honda began to assemble the Accord, the best-selling car in the United States, in Marysville, Ohio. Toyota, Nissan, and Mitsubishi soon followed suit.

1. Clyde Farnsworth, "Car Import Curb Splits Cabinet," *New York Times* (March 5, 1998), p. D1; Clyde Farnsworth, "U.S.–Japan Trade Ties on Agenda," *New York Times* (March 23, 1981), p. D1.
2. Stuart Auerbach and David Hoffman, "Car Quotas to Be Left Up to Japan," *Washington Post* (Feb. 20, 1985), p. A1.

ceive gains from trade. Throughout history, economic development has been thwarted by the existence of thieves and pirates. The development of institutions that make thievery less attractive is very important. These institutions include things as diverse as common law, authoritarianism, international law, and war. But institutions of property rights are much more complex than simple rules against theft. These institutions are fundamental to market systems and the private exchanges on which markets are based. To understand this, let us first introduce the concept of common law.

Common Law

Common law is often referred to as *judge-made law*, in contrast to legislative, or statutory, law. In the English legal tradition, common law had an important place in regulating society. The English Parliament attained its power of law-making long after the legal system developed a very expansive code of what was right and wrong for individuals and businesses to do. This code was largely built on the idea that decisions rendered by judges should provide individuals guidance about how to do business, as well as how to behave, in a large number of potential interactions with others.

The basic principle of common law is clear: judges should render decisions that make it clear to citizens what actions are appropriate. This law should not be murky, or else judges would have the extraordinary task of sitting in judgment of a very large number of cases. Common law should make things clear. For example, if judges made decisions on grounds other than what was established by common law, dockets would become overloaded. In a perfect common law system, there would never be a lawsuit, because all actors would know the ultimate outcome of adjudication.

In such a case, **transaction costs** of individuals and the judicial system would overwhelm gains from trade. Transaction costs are all of the costs incurred when engaging in an exchange that is not part of the production of a product. These costs include the costs of legal counsel, costs of negotiation, and costs of hiring brokers. Transactions are not costless, as traditional economic theory assumes. Rather, these are real costs that influence the way goods and services are traded, as well as how disputes are resolved.

Unlike our system of **statutory law**, common law waits until after something has happened to take an action. Statutory laws are laws made by legislatures or, as in the case of regulatory rules, authorized by legislatures. For example, pollution regulation details how much an automobile can pollute, whereas common law requires a transgression before action is taken. Under common law, an individual who is hurt by some action of another has recourse in the courts. This means that a person harmed by pollution would have to file suit in a court to get some sort of redress. The individual doing the damaging action may have to pay damages in such a case. This system changes the incentives of people so that they do not harm others.

Common law has the advantage of being flexible. The body of cases decided by courts, known as case law, has developed important doctrines of common law that specify this flexibility. Statutory law, in contrast, is rigid. It is the place of the police and other authorities to make more flexible interpretations of statutory law. These authorities, however, do not necessarily have the incentive to ensure this important flexibility.

Right to Trespass

Why is flexibility important? Consider the following interpretations about trespass. If people own land, they have the right to keep others off the land. This appears to be a basic property right. Most local governments have ordinances or statutes against trespass. It is possible for a sheriff to arrest someone on the grounds that the person is on someone's property without permission. Common law would allow someone to sue if another violated trespass doctrine.

But what if a boat is on open waters when an unexpected storm approaches? Realizing catastrophe is possible, the boat docks at a nearby pier not owned by the captain. Suppose the owner objects. It is clear under common law that this, according to doctrine, is a "right to trespass." Under statutory law, such contingencies would need to be anticipated and the legal remedies written into legal code. Common law evolves to take account of contingencies.

Indeed, as Box 6.4 indicates, the common law has a doctrine of **right to trespass**. This principle is based on weighing the needs of the trespasser relative to the needs of the property owner. If the use of the property is of greatest value to the trespasser, as in the case of the boat in the unexpected storm, then there is a right to trespass. If not, there is a trespass that will produce a judgment in favor of the owner, and damages will be paid. Note that no prior statute tells the parties about the exact appropriate behavior. Rather, parties make decisions based on the tradition of common law.

The right to trespass is a simple idea, but it also illustrates a conception of legal principles that is important to all common law. To whom should the law assign rights? It should assign rights to those who make the greatest use of property. Clearly, the trespasser (in this case) makes greater use of the pier than does the owner, who suffers little from the pier's use. However, if someone simply wanted to have a party on the pier, it would not be so clear that the trespasser would be gaining more than the owner would lose.

Another example makes this clear. Suppose that some individuals decide to have a *bon voyage* party on an unsuspecting farmer's property. Let us say these partiers were going to drink, be merry, and then launch hot air balloons from the farm as a way to live it up. The farmer could rightfully argue that these partiers were wrongfully trespassing, because they could easily do damage to property for no other reason than to have a good time. They could do this elsewhere. Common law would clearly stand behind the farmer.

Box 6.4   *Right to Trespass*

ONE OF the most important precedents for the right to trespass is based on the needs of sailors in distress.[1] Early in the 1900s on Lake Champlain in Vermont, a boater and his family attempted to moor their boat to someone's dock to avoid an intense storm. The family was refused the right to dock, however, and their boat was destroyed by the weather. The decision in this case, *Ploof v. Putnam,* was that the dock owner was responsible for the damage to the boat because, according to common law principles, the boater's value in using the dock exceeded the cost to the dock owner's property rights. This does not mean a boater has no costs to his or her decision to trespass. According to *Vincent v. Lake Erie Transport Co.,* if the boat were to have damaged the dock during the storm, the boater would have been responsible for any repairs needed on the dock. This same logic has been extended to so-called Good Samaritan laws in many states.

Indeed, citizens may actually have a duty to the government and/or private citizens who trespass.[2] A common example occurs when firefighters destroy property to prevent the spread of a fire. Essentially, the immediate threat to the community creates a right for the government act and an obligation on the property owner to permit emergency personnel to take whatever actions they deem necessary. In fact, the government need not compensate the owner of the destroyed property. Perhaps the most interesting right to trespass cases occur among private citizens. At first, it may seem strange that property owners have obligations to those who may enter their property without permission. But a homeowner could be held legally liable, or even criminally liable, if a trespassing child were to suffocate inside an abandoned refrigerator whose doors had not been removed or were to drown in a swimming pool that was not properly secured against unauthorized entry.

1. Richard Posner, *Economic Analysis of Law,* 4th ed. (Boston: Little, Brown, 1992), pp. 174–175.
2. *Ibid.*

But suppose that a flotilla of balloons were in the airspace over the farmer's property and that one unlucky balloonist (let's call him Ken) runs out of propane (the gas that heats air to make the balloon fly) because of a defect in the propane tank. Ken must land on the farmer's property. In this case it is clear that Ken has made a greater use of the property than the farmer, or else Ken could not survive. This is the classic right to trespass. If the farmer sued Ken for trespass, Ken could simply defend himself because he had a right to trespass. Ken owes the farmer for any damages that he may have caused, but he is not guilty of unlawfully trespassing. Of course, such cases are not always so simple. What if Ken, knowing he had a right to trespass, simply decided to ignore his fuel situation, since he could always land on the farmer's property on a right to trespass? The farmer could then claim that Ken did not take "due care" in avoiding this trespass. The farmer could then win support for his trespass suit against the balloonist. This represents the complexity of common law solutions.

Many legal scholars have declared common law dead, because statutory law now attempts to deal with most regulations and transgressions. But the common law is not dead, for at least two reasons. First, statutes are not very detailed. They do tie the hands of judges, but when unclear, statutory law is often interpreted within a common law framework. Second, much statutory law is based on common law. While this is not the case in a majority of circumstances, it is true that our legal tradition is heavily influenced by common law. Indeed, Theodore Lowi, in a famous critique of American democracy, points out that Congress never is precise in specifying policy through statutes.[2] Rather, during the past century legislatures have been more likely to delegate to bureaucracies than to courts. It is ultimately up to courts to interpret statutes and bureaucratic actions, and the common law lives in many of these interpretations.

Most legal scholars understand that common law is too antiquated to be a serious method of regulating modern society. Richard Posner, formerly a law professor at the University of Chicago and now a federal judge, argues that even if such is the case, we as citizens should uphold the common law tradition by requiring legislatures to mimic the common law.[3] This idea has produced little groundswell of support. Rather than acting as common law judges, legislatures typically make decisions based on distributional criteria. These criteria concern who gains and who loses. It is not that legislatures ignore solutions to problems. Rather, distributional criteria are very important in legislative decisions, much more than in common law.

Contracts

We have focused thus far on common law, primarily so that we can emphasize the breadth and complexity of political institutions for defining property rights. Common law traditions pervade a number of areas of law that define property rights. One of the most important is **contract law,** which governs agreements between people. Like trespass, contract law is not nearly as cut-and-dried as many laypersons might think.

Suppose Acme Chemical is contracted to deliver a certain amount of hydrogen hydroxide to AAA Water Company. And suppose a hurricane wipes out Acme, or at least causes damages sufficient so that Acme cannot supply this chemical to AAA without undue stress and expenses. Under contract law, a court would find Acme to be in efficient breach of contract. This means that society is better off if courts allow such breach than if contracts were always enforced, no matter what the contingencies. If contract law held up otherwise, large-scale damages would be paid for contingencies of any type. This law not only would punish parties hurt by acts of God but also would lead to a diminishing amount of contracting and a tremendous increase in the transaction costs surrounding any contract.

According to some economists, such contracting and contract law is beneficial to society.[4] There are certain potential events that are not predictable within the confines of a contract. Furthermore, the very nature of trying to write out all contingencies would be very costly. Thus, contract law fills the void where contracts end.

Another example is the doctrine of a one-sided contract. How many times have you had to sign some document, usually quickly, signing life, limb, and property away if you do not hold up your end of a bargain, usually with some large corporation? How many people read all the fine print? It turns out that if such contracts are interpreted as being one-sided, all in favor of the corporation and not the consumer, these contracts can be found to be null and void. We do not want you to think that this interpretation is easy. (Always read the fine print!) But there are certain reasons why such contracts, in some cases, should not be enforced, simply because they give no incentives to the contracting party to take care in delivering the goods and services in an appropriate way. One example of such contracts are waivers of rights to bungee jumpers. If courts upheld the rights of vendors to not be liable in any way if a bungee cord breaks, there would be little incentive on the part of the vendors to provide safe bungee cords. Contracts are almost always found to be null and void if they are too one-sided.

Intellectual Property Rights

Probably the most challenging and complex dimension of property rights has to do with intellectual property. This is also probably the most illustrative of the place of law in assigning rights and creating incentives for individuals to produce goods and services that will make society better off than if the rights were not established. What is intellectual property? Suppose you design a better mousetrap. Why did you do it? Probably to make money. But what if once your design is publicized, someone begins marketing a product based on your design? Is this property that has been appropriated by another person, or is it simply the free market in action? Intellectual property rights assign a claim on some idea for a certain period so that individuals will have an incentive to innovate.

These property rights are bestowed on inventors (**patents**) and authors (**copyrights**) so that individuals will have an incentive to innovate. Patents and copyrights are not immortal. Why not? Because there is no reason to provide monopolistic privileges to inventors and writers once they have been given incentive to produce. Homer, the Greek storyteller who lived and wrote more than two thousand years ago, now has millions of relatives. If he wrote *The Odyssey* with the idea that all his heirs would inherit the rights to his book, the proceeds today would be split among such a large number of people as to make the rewards insignificant. It is more advantageous to society if such rights are limited in duration.

One exception in the intellectual property rights area is trademark law. Trademark law provides a property right to an identifying name or symbol for some product, such as Coca-Cola, the most identified trademark in existence. Trademarks do not expire as long as the product is alive. Why allow such trademarks to be so long-lived? They provide a service to consumers, allowing them to know what product they are buying and who they are buying the product from. There is no reason to let trademarks expire as long as the product is being marketed.

Securities

Securities are also governed by a very expansive law of property rights. If you own stocks, it is illegal for you to misrepresent what they are if you want to sell them. It is also illegal for individuals to use "inside information" to buy and sell stocks. For a stock market to operate effectively, numerous rules must be enforced. These rules can be thought of as restricting property rights. In short, if you are a trader in stocks, there are severe limitations on appropriate actions. The Security and Exchange Commission, an agency of the U.S. government, enforces these rules.

Taxes

Taxes also involve property rights. Taxes transfer property from individuals to the government. For example, everyone is painfully aware that if you earn a given amount of money, the federal government and probably your home state government tax a certain proportion of your income away. Why do they do this? The normative principle is that certain functions are provided by governments to make society better off, and taxes are necessary to ensure that these functions are funded. Local governments also tax property. If an individual is incapable of paying property taxes, government can seize the property. This is all done, as we have indicated with every example, with the express purpose of making society better off.

The U.S. Constitution was originally interpreted by the Supreme Court as prohibiting the taxation of income. The Sixteenth Amendment to the Constitution, which was not ratified until 1913, was required before the question about the constitutionality of the federal government's taxing income was settled. The income tax is now the primary method the federal government uses to fund its programs. States also use income taxes, as well as sales taxes. Local governments depend heavily on property taxes but also use other methods such as fees to fund programs and services. These taxes transfer property from individuals to the government.

Before the income tax became the predominate method for funding the federal government, tariffs were used. Tariffs are taxes on goods that are imported into the United States. Many think that tariffs are good taxes, because they fund the government by taxing foreign businesses. This is incorrect, however. Tariffs are paid by consumers who want to buy these products and workers and businesses who export goods to other countries. In the early twentieth century, the heavy use of tariffs to fund the federal government was very controversial and pitted domestic manufacturers of goods against other interests in society. In part because of international treaties limiting the use of tariffs, they now provide a fairly insignificant flow of funds to the federal treasury.

Land Use Regulation

Another kind of taking of property results in planning and zoning laws. Ever since the Supreme Court decided the *Euclid* case in 1926,[5] governments have had the right to restrict and regulate the use of land. The reason for this regulation has been the gains for society of regulating the appropriate use of land, for example, to keep a garbage dump away from a housing development. This is one area of law where statute has replaced common law. Note that planning and zoning laws provide a substantial limitation on property rights.

Contrast planning and zoning laws, which regulate land use without compensation to landowners, with eminent domain, where a government may seize property only if appropriate compensation is forthcoming. The Supreme Court in the *Euclid* case found that planning and zoning regulations did not constitute "takings." This was significant, because takings require compensation under the Sixth Amendment to the U.S. Constitution. Takings are situations where a government shows that a given parcel of land (say, for a highway) is needed for the public good. In such cases, individuals must be compensated at full market value. Eminent domain is a transgression of property rights to favor the public good.

The difference between land use regulation and takings is not as obvious as it first appears. In recent years local governments have attempted to require developers of land to make certain improvements to property, and sometimes even to surrounding public areas, before land uses are allowed. As Box 6.5 shows, the Supreme Court, in *Dolan v. City of Tigard* (1994), found that governments are limited in their ability to make these demands. The Court ruled that the takings clause of the Constitution prohibits governments from requiring developers to provide improvements that are not associated with the social costs caused by development. This was an important limitation of land use regulation, because courts have generally interpreted *Euclid* very liberally.

Box 6.5   *Dolan v. City of Tigard*

THE RIGHT of private persons to use their own property sometimes comes directly into conflict with claims that the public interest should take priority. Nowhere is this collision more common than in local planning and zoning cases. *Dolan v. City of Tigard* has rewritten, at least in the margins, the rules by which these conflicts are to be decided.[1] The background of this case is as follows. Florence Dolan wanted to expand her hardware and plumbing store located in Tigard, Oregon. Even though the expansion was to take place on her property, the city placed conditions on her expansion plans.

First, the city claimed that the extra space of the increased building size would lead to increased water runoff. The city's plan for storm drainage included improving drainage and using floodplains to absorb extra runoff. Therefore, the city required that the Dolans cede to the city a small area of their property that had been designated as a floodplain. Second, a larger store would affect traffic patterns. The city also required that the Dolans cede another 15-foot stretch of their property for pedestrian and bicycle traffic to ease additional traffic problems. The requirements affected 10 percent of the Dolans' property. The Dolans filed suit against the city in a case that eventually wound its way to the Supreme Court.

The Court decided in a narrow 5-to-4 decision that the exactions, or requirements for permits for developing private property, were an uncompensated taking. Thus, the city would need to compensate the Dolans for the restrictions put on their building permits. The majority argued that the city did not sufficiently show that the actual building would negatively affect the general public. The outcome requires cities to show that any conditions placed on land use be proportional to the actual development itself rather than merely fitting into the cities' general zoning plans.

The case is controversial because the city, by all accounts, had legitimate concerns about how traffic and flooding would be affected by development. The key controversy was whether one viewed the city's zoning plans as an appropriate response to the extra water runoff and traffic that would result from the Dolans' expansion plans or as a violation of the Dolans' Fifth Amendment rights in holding their expansion plans hostage for purposes unrelated to the expansion itself. The case significantly influences recently established environmental protections, such as safeguarding wetlands. *Dolan v. City of Tigard* forces governments to explicitly show how very narrowly defined projects will directly affect the environment in order to place exactions on land use. This changes what had been typically considered planning and zoning decisions into compensable "takings."

1. *Florence Dolan, Petitioner v. City of Tigard*, 93 Sup. Ct. 518 (1994). For background, see "Dolan v. City of Tigard: Takings Clause No Longer a Poor Relation," *Washington Legal Foundation Legal Backgrounder* 9, no. 24 (July 29, 1994); Paul Kamener, "A Quest for an Invigorated Takings Clause," *Recorder* (Aug. 26, 1994), p. 7; Michael Berger, "Property Owners Have Rights, Too," *Los Angeles Times* (July 3, 1994), p. 5; Arlene Zarembka, "A Green Light to Ignore the Environment," *St. Louis Dispatch* (July 14, 1994), p. 7B.

War

The final property rights institution we consider, war, may appear somewhat unusual. War is thought of in many ways, mostly negative. However, in some cases **war as an institution** is used as a means of solving international problems in a similar, but more dramatic, way to solving domestic problems through coercion. War, among other things, is often about property rights.

The Gulf War of 1991 is an excellent example of how war is used as an institution for regulating property rights. Iraq invaded Kuwait in an attempt to solve a collective action problem. The Organization of Petroleum Exporting Countries (OPEC) attempted to fix the price of oil by limiting production and exports. As we know, collective action problems are situations where individuals (or in this case, countries) have an incentive to cheat. Kuwait was a major cheater. It continually, as a matter of policy, exceeded its quota of output and exports. There were also other issues involved, such as disputes about the ownership of oil fields and even the legitimacy of Kuwait as a sovereign country. But Iraq's invasion of Kuwait can be thought of in the same way as a government using coercion to force someone to provide for the collective good.

Of course, Western governments saw things differently. To the West, war served as an opportunity to limit the power of a major oil-producing country, although the stated purpose of the attack was to free Kuwait. War is obviously a complex institution, but it can serve the same purposes as the other property rights institutions described in this chapter.

CONCLUSION

Thriving markets do not usually just emerge spontaneously. Markets are governed by a diverse set of institutions that define property rights. The more developed and refined an economy, the more complex are its property rights institutions. In this chapter, we have seen merely the tip of the iceberg. Market institutions are so varied and diverse that it would be impossible to lay out all institutions in a single column, let alone a single chapter. We have focused primarily on formal rules. Norms for the governance of markets are far more diverse. It is rare that individuals making repeated market interactions have not developed a set of norms to govern their actions.

This chapter is meant to give students of public policy an appreciation for the diversity and importance of institutions for governing property and, therefore, markets. Too often public policy analysts contrast government solutions and market solutions. Not only is market activity facilitated (and sometimes hindered) by government activity, but governance of many types is required for markets to thrive.

Key Terms

capitalism *p. 98*
socialism *p. 98*
liberal democracy *p. 99*
market *p. 99*
norm *p. 100*
predatory state *p. 102*
property rights *p. 102*
fiscal illusion *p. 102*
mercantilism *p. 104*
Custom House *p. 105*

ITC voluntary trade restrictions *p. 107*
common law *p. 108*
transaction cost *p. 108*
statutory law *p. 108*
right to trespass *p. 109*
contract law *p. 111*
patent *p. 112*
copyright *p. 112*
Euclid case *p. 114*
war as an institution *p. 116*

Suggested Readings

Debreu, Gerand. 1986. *Theory of Value: An Axiomatic Analysis of Economic Equilibrium*. New Haven, Conn.: Yale University Press.

Feldman, Allan. 1980. *Welfare Economic and Social Choice Theory*. Boston: Klewer Academic.

Friedman, Milton. 1962. *Capitalism and Freedom*. Chicago: University of Chicago Press.

Hayak, Friedrich. 1937. "Economics and Knowledge." *Economica* 4: 33–54.

Libecap, Gary. 1989. *Contracting for Property Rights*. Cambridge, England: Cambridge University Press.

Posner, Richard. 1992. *Economic Analysis of Law*. 4th ed. Boston: Little, Brown.

Williamson, Oliver. 1985. *The Economic Institutions of Capitalism*. New York: Free Press.

Notes

1. Charles Lindblom, *Politics and Markets* (New York: Basic Books, 1977).

2. Theodore J. Lowi, *The End of Liberalism: The Second Republic of the United States*, 2nd ed. (New York: W.W. Norton, 1979).

3. Richard Posner, *Economic Analysis of Law*, 4th ed. (Boston: Little, Brown, 1992), esp. chap. 19.

4. See, for example, Oliver Williamson, *The Economic Institutions of Capitalism* (New York: Free Press, 1985).

5. *Village of Euclid v. Ambler Realty Company*, 47 Sup. Ct. 114 (1926).

7

Limitations of the Market

INTRODUCTION

Markets have features that make them especially attractive. They allow individuals to obtain a mix of goods and services that match their preferences very closely. Markets coordinate individual actions without the need for some external authority to determine the allocation and production of goods and services. This is why markets are often viewed as instruments of individual liberty.

Unfortunately, there are many circumstances where conditions do not exist for markets to function effectively. These are situations where goods or services have certain characteristics that make markets fail. Voluntary actions in some cases will not lead to a betterment of society. Market failures are clearly defined as collective action problems.

This chapter is primarily about when markets fail. Market failure is the primary justification for public policy interventions. We provide a typology of goods and services and explain why markets work well for some, work decently for others, and are unsatisfactory for still others. We also describe problems that occur when markets are not very competitive. Consumer choices are usually presumed to be informed. In some cases these choices are less informed than in others, and we discuss how consumer misinformation can make markets fail.

Some market failures are more controversial and subject to debate. Topics of debate include the importance of initial resource endowments and whether some just distribution should be a part of public policy interventions. Another problem is that some policy analysts do not believe people actually know what is best for them. If people do not know what is in their best interests, markets do not work very well. We take up each of these situations below.

A TYPOLOGY OF MARKET FAILURES: THE NATURE OF THE GOOD

Goods are all the different products and services that may be consumed, exchanged, sold, or made available in a society, both those produced and allocated through markets and those produced by government and nonprofit organizations. Goods vary in their underlying attributes. Some of those attributes can make it difficult, if not impossible, for markets to function appropriately in the production or allocation of the good. Two attributes of goods are useful for making this distinction: rivalrousness and excludability. A third potential problem, congestibility, which is not in the inherent nature of goods, is also an important component for predicting whether a market failure exists.[1]

A **rivalrous good** is a good that if consumed by one person cannot be consumed by another, because one person's use means another will not be able to use the good. A hamburger is rivalrous. If you eat it, another person cannot. Clean air is not rivalrous. If it is available for me to breathe, it is also available for you to breathe.

Excludable goods can be owned by a single person, so ownership rights can be defined. My car is an excludable good. To get into it or start it, you must have the proper keys. This is not absolute, of course. You may moonlight as a car thief and thus have the skills to steal my car despite my efforts to exclude your use of it. For some goods, it is very difficult to exclude potential consumers. Roads are such goods. While it is possible to set up toll booths on some roads, it is often so expensive to keep people from using the road that it isn't worth the effort. Sidewalks are even more nonexcludable. Once a sidewalk is built, it is nearly impossible to keep people from using it. Notice that **pure public goods**, like national defense, clean air, and the others described above, are goods that are neither rivalrous nor exclusive. These will be subject to extreme collective action problems, in that they will be only minimally provided for—if provided for at all—by voluntary contributions.

Goods become **congestible goods** when the numbers of individuals using them create a market failure. Suppose you are out for a hike in the forest and you come upon a berry field. If few people pick berries in the field, this good does not present a policy problem. A berry that one person eats cannot be eaten by another, so the berries are rivalrous; however, there is little reason for someone to exclude others—to try to exercise ownership rights—when there are enough berries to go around. But change the example just a little. Suppose you are hiking with a few hundred of your closest friends. Now the berry field will quickly become congested. If there is congestion, without clear ownership rights (rights that would often be too costly to impose), people pick too many berries, and the result is that no berries are left for others. The result is a tragedy of the commons, where too many consumers harvest free fare and deplete the common area. These goods that are nonexcludable, rivalrous, and congestible are called **common pool resources**.

A **toll good** is a good that is excludable but not rivalrous. Individuals may have an incentive to produce such goods and charge for their use. Because the goods are not rivalrous, however, too many people will be excluded from the use of toll goods than is best for society, since one person's use does not inhibit another's. Toll goods will therefore be underproduced by markets. Indeed, because one person's consumption of the good does not subtract from another's use of the good, the optimal price should be zero. Obviously, no one would produce a toll good under that arrangement, and thus toll goods are underproduced. As toll goods become more congested, the optimal price is greater than zero to reflect the effect that congestion has on people's use of the goods. However, even with congestion, toll goods will be underproduced.

Goods that are excludable and rivalrous are referred to as **pure private goods.** Described in more detail in another chapter, pure private goods will be produced and traded at a level that is good for society—if there are well-defined property rights in force. Individuals voluntarily produce and trade such goods in a way that makes society better off. The invisible hand of the market works to make collective outcomes desirable even though individuals are merely looking out for their own interests. Thus, collective action problems occur when goods are not rivalrous, excludable, or congestible.

When congestion is a problem with a rivalrous and excludable good, we usually refer to it as a private good with **externalities.** Externalities are either negative or positive benefits accruing to others not involved in the direct production or consumption of goods.

Many negative externalities are referred to as nuisances or pollution. The noise coming from your neighbor's stereo that disturbs your sleep in the middle of the night is a negative externality. However, a person listening to her favorite music in a sparsely populated rural area produces no such externality. The fumes emanating from the cars and buses in front of your apartment or house are also such negative externalities. So is the acid rain that poisons the lakes and forests in the northeastern areas of the United States. Negative externalities are overproduced because individuals who produce or consume such goods have no incentive to base decisions on the costs of such actions to society.

Positive externalities are social benefits that accrue from the production and consumption of rivalrous and excludable goods. Neighbors who keep a clean and beautiful landscape provide positive benefits to a neighborhood as a whole, and if everyone did so, aesthetic and property values in a neighborhood would be high. However, individuals have the incentive to keep their yards only as nice as is right for them, and such positive benefits to a neighborhood will generally be underproduced.

Note that the production of positive externalities looks like the production of pure public goods. It is in everyone's interest that they be produced, but individuals will not have an incentive to produce them, above and beyond what they individually value, because others will free ride and enjoy the benefits without paying the costs. National defense is a classic example of a pure public good. The idea is that a country defends all citizens. But notice that individuals will have an incentive, if asked to pay for defense, to say they really do not value defense very much and thus not pay. Voluntary action will result in no provision of national defense. One of the most common rationales for having coercive governments has been for the provision of national defense. Indeed, historically it appears that having a military was one of the motivations for the development of modern nation-states.

To recap, it is useful to think of goods as having two properties: excludability and rivalry. Congestion is a situation that can also lead to market failures. We have identified the following scenarios that are of most interest and relevance for policy analysis: (1) pure private goods, (2) pure private goods with externalities, (3) toll goods, (4) toll goods with congestion, (5) common pool resources with congestion, and (6) pure public goods. It would be useful for such typologies to provide clear and distinct categories, but unfortunately, such definitions have eluded the policy analyst's grasp. Thus, it is possible to reformulate one good as another for the purposes of policy analysis.

For example, it is possible to reformulate a private good with positive externalities as a pure public goods problem. Clean air is a public good. However, if we do not have clean air, it is often because of some use of property, such as steel production, that causes air pollution. Air pollution may also be caused by automobile drivers. Trying to get businesses and individuals to stop polluting is like trying to get people to provide for the common good. We could formulate a problem like this as one where private goods have consumption and production externalities. But we could also formulate this problem as one where clean air is a public good and will be underproduced when individuals do not reduce their emissions into the air. Public policy analysts typically prefer to formulate this problem as one of private goods with externalities, but you can see the point. It is possible to think of this issue from two vantage points.

For policy analysis, deciding the category to which a good belongs is the first step in offering policy solutions that connect to collective action problems. This decision is often referred to as determining the **nature of the good,** although congestion has little to do with the nature of the good. Table 7.1 summarizes the information we have learned about the nature of the good. When we refer to the nature of the good, we are making the first important decision in defining the nature of the policy problem that exists. Knowing the nature of the good is hardly sufficient for knowing the correct policy solution, but it will provide guidance for understanding the nature of the collective action problem that policy is meant to solve. Thus, this determination is an important, if incomplete, first step in understanding whether social problems exist. Understanding the nature of the good is necessary for identifying potential solutions to these problems.

The Physical Nature of Goods

Many policy analysts stop at the physical nature of goods when discussing the nature of goods. Doing so is often fine, but other characteristics of goods may also become important when doing policy analysis. These other features can

TABLE 7.1 The Nature of the Good: Excludability and Rivalry, with Congestion Effects

Type of Good (outcome of market)	Examples
Excludable and Rivalrous Private goods (produced and consumed at the best level)	Shoes
Excludable and Rivalrous with Congestion Private goods with negative externalities (externalities are overproduced)	Automobiles
Excludable and Nonrivalrous Toll goods (toll goods are underproduced)	Rural roads
Excludable and Nonrivalrous Toll goods with congestion (toll goods with congestion are underproduced)	Urban roads
Nonexcludable and Rivalrous Common pool resources (common pool resources are overconsumed)	Cod
Nonexcludable and Nonrivalrous Pure public goods (pure public goods are not produced)	National defense

be discussed under the umbrella concept of the physical nature of the good. Consider common pool resources, toll goods, and public goods in which the physical nature can be important for understanding how to solve market failures.

Fisheries are common pool resources. Once a fishery is congested, overconsumption can be expected. Let us consider two different kinds of fisheries, salmon and lobster fisheries. What is the difference between these two? No, lobsters do not swim upstream to spawn. Indeed, lobsters are pretty immobile. In contrast, salmon swim great distances over the course of a year, depending on the species. In essence, salmon are migratory. Nonetheless, salmon may also be overfished, because fishers can readily identify key areas in their migratory routes.

When trying to figure out how to reduce overfishing, do the differences in the physical characteristics of lobsters and salmon matter? The institutions that are appropriate for managing these fisheries will depend greatly on these physical characteristics. For lobster fishers, self-organization may be possible. Lobster fishers will be more likely to know one another, and thus they may be able to monitor and sanction one another. A policy analyst trying to find out

Lobster fishers prepare to set their pots. Every fishery in the United States has been depleted to some extent by overfishing. *Thomas Croke/Liason International.*

how to reduce the excess harvesting of lobsters might want to first look at self-organized institutions to see what is wrong. It may be that state efforts to make fishing groups more autonomous in dealing with the problem of over-fishing would be appropriate.

As for salmon, such self-organized solutions appear much more difficult. The **Cod Wars** between Britain and Iceland (see Box 7.1), as well as more recent disputes between the United States and Canada, suggest that overfishing issues are on an international rather than local scale. It appears that any solution to these types of overfishing problems would best be handled through diplomatic and other means of solving problems between and among governments.

Monopolies and Oligopolies: When Markets Are Not Competitive

Scale is another physical attribute of goods. Some goods can be produced only with a large initial outlay of production costs. These costs, referred to as fixed costs by economists, are the resources that must be invested before a good can be produced and provided to the public. The usual example offered by policy

Box 7.1   The Cod Wars on the North Sea

CONFLICTS RESULTING from the depletion of common pool resources can be severe. In a series of conflicts from the late 1960s through the 1970s, Iceland and Britain battled what have been called the Cod Wars.[1] Hostilities were high, and the two nations frequently stood at the brink of a legitimate shooting war while frantically pursuing peaceful negotiations. This leads one to the central question: Why would two relatively peaceful nation-states push each other to open hostility—to the point of ramming fishing boats into each other, cutting fishing-net lines, and using gunboats to shoot both blanks and real ammunition at each other? Each of the following factors worked to create the high-stakes situation: ecology, economics, culture, domestic politics, and international political bargaining.

International political economy scholar Jeffrey Hart has described exactly how the confluence of the above-listed factors led to the open conflict between these countries. First, a general fear existed that the stock of cod, haddock, scaithe, and halibut off the Icelandic coast would be depleted over time because of overfishing. This is the ecological explanation. If fishers took more fish than the sustainable level would provide, the decrease in the stocks of these fish would ruin fishing in the waters for extended periods, reduce the economic payoff for fishers (since the volume would be reduced), and greatly disturb the oceanic ecosystem. This fear provided an important bargaining chip for the Icelandic fishers, since they could argue for a universal reduction in what foreign fishing fleets could take from waters off Iceland's coast.

The second important factor leading to the Cod Wars stemmed from economics. Iceland relied on fishing for 80 percent of its economy. The British were fearful that up to 100,000 jobs could be lost if they were denied access to the area, but this represented only a small percentage of jobs. The scale of fishing boat volume also differed between the two nations—the enormous British trawlers could take a huge catch back to Britain, while smaller Icelandic boats left port every day and did not have the same volume capabilities as the British ships.

There was also a major cultural factor leading to the conflict. The small coastal Icelandic towns had relied on fishing for the basis of their economy for centuries. Fishing

analysts is utilities—for instance, electricity. Before electricity can be sold, lines must be run and a power plant built.

The electric utility is called a **natural monopoly** by policy analysts. Natural monopolies are those firms that produce products requiring high fixed costs relative to variable costs—in this example, the costs of producing electricity and ensuring that it reaches consumers. The usual belief is that products requiring high fixed costs will not be produced, because potential producers will be afraid that competition will result in returns insufficient to cover the initial fixed costs. Because all potential firms believe this, no firm will enter the market. This logic results in policies that either grant firms a monopoly or actually call for government to produce the product or service itself. If a firm is granted a monopoly, then governments usually regulate the pricing of the product.

for cod had been woven into Iceland's entire social fabric. Watching enormous British ships take their staple away offended many Icelanders. The British, too, had a cultural tie to the fish. Cod fished from those waters provided the substance of a very British meal—fish and chips.

While these factors provided the backdrop for the Cod Wars, how political leaders handled the actual conflict through international and domestic politics directly influenced the unfolding of events. Indeed, both sides agreed to provide safeguards against overfishing and ensured that Iceland's percentage of the catch would increase. Nevertheless, domestic politics in Iceland fueled the conflict by closing off particular international diplomatic channels. The electoral fortunes of the incumbent government require a successful economy. As such, economic pressure can make international economic agreements difficult to negotiate. When leftist parties who were sympathetic to fishers took office in Iceland, they demanded policy changes that eventually led to a deterioration of relations with Britain. Public opinion sympathies remained so solidly behind the small-scale Icelandic coastal fishers that the bold statements made by different parties drove the negotiation demands so high that even some technical fishing experts in Iceland disagreed with the position of negotiators.

The extremity of Iceland's position meant that Britain had to respond strongly, even though it had been willing to offer significant concessions to Iceland. One of the main reasons the sides eventually came together, despite the domestic political sources driving them apart, was their mutual membership in the North Atlantic Treaty Organization (NATO). An Icelandic NATO air base had been important because of its geographically strategic position. Each side realized the importance of NATO's success, and in the end, Britain was willing to cede to many of Iceland's demands. What drove the final agreements toward Iceland, however, was the intense domestic political pressure in Iceland relative to Britain, where domestic politics were geographically far away from the battlefield of the Cod Wars.

1. Jeffrey Hart, *The Anglo-Icelandic Cod War of 1972–1973* (Berkeley: Institute of International Studies, research series no. 29, 1976).

Monopoly pricing is higher than typical competitive market pricing. This is true because monopolists can reduce quantity so that they can optimize profits. Monopolists cannot charge anything they want, but rather, they reduce quantity in a way that ensures that people buy the product at a quantity that produces the greatest amount of profit.

The existence of natural monopolies depends on technology. For a very long time, telephone service was considered a natural monopoly. Telephone wires, like electrical wires, needed to be run in order for service to be established. This need caused high fixed costs. The Justice Department of the federal government realized that technology had changed, and in the early 1980s it determined that local and long-distance telephone production is not the same. Local telephone service continues to have high fixed costs, but microwave and other technologies make long-distance service different. The government broke up AT&T and allowed other providers to provide long-distance service. MCI Corporation was the first to realize the advantages of these changes, providing long-distance services at reduced rates to customers long faced with regulated, and high, prices for long-distance service. This exemplifies the idea that natural monopolies can become potential competitive markets at another point in time.

Other firms are referred to as monopolies even when their fixed costs are not high enough to make them natural monopolies. U.S. Steel, General Motors, and Microsoft are examples of firms that appear to fit the description of monopolies but where the pace of technological change raises legitimate questions about whether they pose the dangers to society usually associated with monopolies. They have large market shares, at least in certain historical times. These firms may or may not have competitors at any particular point in time. More important, however, they have potential competition. As long as governments do not accord these types of firms monopolistic power, markets, although possibly slowly, may make them act as if they are in a competitive market.

However, oligopolies, which are industries in which the number of producers is small, may act as cartels and behave in a noncompetitive manner. In reality, the large automakers, U.S. Steel, and perhaps Microsoft are oligopolies. That is, they have a very large market share, but not a 100 percent market share, and there exist a small number of competitors with a large market share. Policy analysts must realize that oligopolies may or may not create a market failure. Indeed, economic theory offers dual predictions: sometimes oligopolies are able to collude and price as monopolies do, and other times collusion may fail, rendering oligopolies no different than competitive firms.

For oligopolies to behave like monopolies, they must cooperate with one another and limit quantities. We have seen that the international OPEC oil cartel tries to do just that. OPEC sometimes succeeds in collusion, and other times it fails. The reason cartels often fail is that these producers must overcome collective action problems. There is always an incentive for a member of a cartel not to cooperate and to sell the product for a lower price than the cartel has established. Of course, we also know from Chapter 4 that long-run interaction can lead to cooperation, meaning that it is quite possible that collusion can work. Whether oligopolies are colluding or not is often a policy controversy that involves the U.S. Justice Department's implementation of antitrust policy.

The key for policy analysts in making sure that monopolistic and oligopolistic behavior does not cause markets to fail is to ensure that a firm's behavior will not allow collusive behavior. The Sherman Antitrust Act, passed by the federal government in the late 1800s, is designed to do just that. The act is simple. Section I makes illegal the behavior of firms that allows them to combine to act anticompetitively in any market. Thus, Section I tries to prevent oligopolistic power. Section II bans any noncompetitive actions from a single firm that has strong, or "monopolistic," market power. Section II deals with potential problems resulting from "unnatural monopolies" acting in an anticompetitive manner.

The latter includes prohibitions on predatory pricing. Very large firms may try to run smaller businesses out of the market by pricing their products below actual cost. In the short run such firms lose, but in the long run competitors are driven from markets, and the firm in question can act more like an unregulated monopolist. As discussed in Box 7.2, the actions of Microsoft have drawn the attention of the Justice Department because of alleged violations of Section II.

In summary, anticompetitive behavior by firms, whether natural or not, may keep free markets from operating effectively. Policies such as price regulation, government provision, and antitrust are meant to ensure that firms do not take advantage of the fact that they have too much market power. However, governments always must be careful, because anticompetitive behavior does have a down side for the companies themselves. Firms that act like oligopolists and monopolists may be making long-term mistakes. New contestants may enter the market; these newcomers may be more attuned to consumer preferences, and large firms may suffer in the long run. Most analysts of the domestic automobile industry interpret the success of foreign competition in this light. Ford and General Motors once thought they had an iron-clad grip on the U.S. automobile market, and they have been paying for this presumption for the last twenty years.

INCOMPLETE INFORMATION AND TRANSACTIONS COSTS

Another impediment to the effective operation of markets is incomplete information. Typical models of markets assume individuals have complete information. Of course, this is not the case. However, some markets operate effectively, and others less so, because consumers do not have complete information. It is this distinction in markets that makes the concept of incomplete information important.

Consumers are frequently uncertain about the quality of the merchandise they seek to buy. What do consumers do about this uncertainty? Obviously, they try to determine the quality of the products they buy. This is relatively easy to do with goods that require a simple search when identifying and buying them. **Search goods** are goods for which, with an inspection before purchasing, the consumer can determine quality. For example, clothes are a search good. A consumer can look them over, check the stitching, evaluate the materials (polyester versus cotton), and so forth. Markets for clothing work relatively well because consumers can become well enough informed upon inspection of goods to make informed choices.

Another type of goods, **experience goods**, is not so easy for consumers to judge. Experience goods require some amount of use before consumers

Box 7.2   Microsoft Antitrust Case

Most Americans recognize the name Microsoft; it is perhaps the most dynamic company in the world today. The company so dominates aspects of the Information Age economy that the U.S. government brought antitrust suits against the company, claiming it has attempted to monopolize the Internet browser market. Both the government and Microsoft have raised interesting points concerning antitrust issues. The largest lesson stemming from this confrontation concerns the Information Age application of the monopoly laws that were written for the Industrial Age.

In the antitrust case filed in 1997 by the federal government and twenty states, Attorney General Janet Reno claimed that Microsoft had a "chokehold" on the Internet browser market.[1] Two issues stood at the core of this argument: first, that Microsoft had illegally bound its World Wide Web browser Internet Explorer with its Windows operating system, and this led to **predatory pricing,** which consists of setting prices below costs in order to injure competitors; and second, that the company applied illegal tactics to hurt competitors.

Microsoft countered the government's arguments directly. First, the company claimed that the government's argument of predatory pricing was ridiculous, since the Internet browser was offered free, as was Netscape's browser. How could the prices be predatory against the consumer when no price was charged by either company? Second, Microsoft claimed that during the period in which it was accused of hurting Netscape, Netscape controlled 70 percent of the Internet browser market with a product that Microsoft admitted was superior to its own. Third, Microsoft asserted that the government's use of discussions and employee e-mail did not prove that it had attempted to injure Netscape. Rather, Microsoft, like any other business, wanted to beat its competitors. Thus, discussion concerning cutting off Netscape's "oxygen" was not unlike the competitive discussions of other businesses.

The primary thrust of Microsoft's defense relied on describing the government's case as being out of touch with the computer industry. Microsoft, Netscape, Sun Microsystems, and other computer software companies all have grown meteorically. Microsoft felt that competitors could dislodge its own position quickly, even without government interference. Microsoft also argued the unfeasibility of decoupling its Internet browser software from its operating system software. Claiming that the synthe-

can judge their worth. Markets do not work as well for such goods, because consumers will be uncertain about the quality of these goods. One classic case is the market for used cars.[2] This market is influenced by the fact that consumers are uncertain about quality and have legitimate fears that any car that is offered on this market may be a lemon. It is well known that driving a car off the new car lot will result in thousands of dollars of losses from the value of that car. Why does this happen? Buyers are wary of people who sell cars after a short period of ownership. Why would people sell a car when they would lose so much money? Why would people buy a car when they were wary that the owner was trying to dump a lemon? This all drives the prices of used cars sis between the Internet and software was the future of computing, Microsoft argued that integrating these software products would be essential to its success. Further, the company argued that the consumer benefited from Microsoft's decision to tie the software together and offer it at a lower price.[2]

The Microsoft antitrust case has far-reaching implications. As we move into the new information-based economy of the twenty-first century, the Sherman Antitrust Act, which when passed in the late 1800s was concerned with railroad and oil monopolies, may no longer fit contemporary situations. Government oversight of market monopolies in an era of rapid technological change may require different criteria of corporate wrongdoing than those concerning simple market share at a particular point in time. Even the government seems to acknowledge something new. The government's lead lawyer claimed that the notion of price competition, which is central to the notion of predatory pricing, has been replaced by the notion of competition in innovation.[3] It may be difficult to use laws that were written to cover tangible products and exchange in cases that involve intangible qualities such as innovation in the high-speed production and exchange of information.

Shortly before publication of this book, Federal Judge Thomas Penfield Jackson ruled strongly in favor of the federal government. He found that Microsoft was guilty of predatory pricing, the latter a more controversial interpretation of the Sherman Anti-Trust Act. Jackson ruled that breaking up the company would be appropriate punishment. Under Jackson's ruling, Microsoft would become two companies, one that sells the Windows operating system, another that sells application software.

Microsoft is appealing the ruling, and the federal government wants to expedite the appeal directly to the Supreme Court so that appeals will not take years to adjudicate. Microsoft wants the appeals process to take a conventional route in which the Federal Court of Appeals is the next step. If Microsoft gets its way, a final decision may be reached only after the information age (and its markets) looks much different than it does today.

1. Jube Shiver and Leslie Helm, "U.S., 20 States File Antitrust Lawsuits Against Microsoft," *Los Angeles Times* (May 19, 1998), p. A1.
2. T. J. Rodgers, "What's Good For Microsoft . . . ," *New York Times* (Oct. 20, 1998), p. A31.
3. "Iron Horse Laws vs. Space Age Ideas," *St. Louis Dispatch* (Oct. 23, 1997), p. 14C.

down. The logical conclusion is that the only individual willing to sell is someone who owns a lemon. The only buyer is someone willing to buy a lemon because the price is so low. This means markets for used cars do not work very well. An owner who buys a minivan, only to undergo a divorce and a reduction in the number of children to drive around, will not be able to sell, without great loss, the minivan in favor of the sports car that he or she thinks will help attract a new mate. The only used cars on the market will be lemons, so only those wanting to chance it with lemons will be buyers.

In a market with lemons, prices are deflated because individuals will not know the true quality of the good. Typically, regulations against lemons, along with, say, required warrantees for cars that are not too old, will make these markets work better. The point is that these types of markets do not work well without some institutions for solving the problems generated because consumers have inherent uncertainty. Markets for experience goods work better if there is some way to assure consumers that these goods are not inferior.

A final type of goods, called **postexperience goods**, provides a greater challenge to markets. The quality of postexperience goods is very difficult to judge. These goods and services require one to actually experience the consumption and then wait before judging the quality. Medicine is one such good. A consumer may like a doctor because of a great bedside manner, returning over and over to this "very good doctor." But years later, the consumer may find out the doctor failed to diagnose a simple form of cancer. How to make the market for medical care operate effectively is a perennial problem.

Another example is education. For many people, the main reason for being in college is to receive a diploma. The diploma has value because it signals prospective employers that its holder has completed a rigorous course of study, maybe with excellence. But when in college, you may value only getting the diploma, not the education. Unfortunately, you are failing to recognize the value of the education that you are receiving. If everyone else is also valuing the diploma and not the intrinsic value of being an educated person, the quality of education you and others receive will be unimportant, and this will send a message to the educational administrators. They will be forced to pander to your tastes and those of others. In time, they may quit caring about the quality of your education. They may simply try to make it as easy as possible for you to receive a diploma. Administrators will put pressure on department chairs and faculty members to pass as many students as possible. Indeed, administrators may begin to define the mission of the university in terms of maintaining enrollments and the proportion of students who receive diplomas. Education will be sacrificed. Retention, not learning, may become the university's motto. In the long run, the degree and diploma you receive may have diminished value. Thus, in the long run, higher education will become less important vis-à-vis other training mechanisms in society. But in the short run, educational administrators and students continue to pursue the seemingly best short-run solution, because they have little choice to do otherwise.

Government regulation is often the policy prescription for situations where individuals have high uncertainty. In addition, secondary markets for information are often created in such situations. Usually, government regulation is not enough. Licenses for doctors are hardly a panacea for poor medical practice. Neither is accreditation for educational institutions. A free press and word of mouth are usually necessary for the workings of markets where consumer uncertainty is high. Alternatives to free markets are also possible. Most countries do not provide health care using a market mechanism for this reason. For years the United States has been investigating alternatives to the market for health care, because the market clearly does not work well for this type of postexperience good.

The Problem of Insurance

When individuals face a great deal of uncertainty, they can, in certain situations, purchase insurance to protect themselves from large-scale or even catastrophic losses. Thus, we have car, homeowners, and other types of insurance. On the one hand, insurance allows individuals to function in uncertain markets where they otherwise could not do so. On the other hand, insurance creates distortions that hinder markets in performing well.

To understand the strengths and weaknesses of insurance, let us consider someone who seeks to buy car insurance. Having an insurance market does enable people to afford automobiles, but insurance also causes a form of market failure. One problem is called **moral hazard.** Simply put, individuals who have insurance will be more careless. If people have insurance and are less careful, they will pay only a fraction of the costs when accidents occur. The other problem is called **adverse selection.** Adverse selection is the problem that occurs because those who are more careless will seek insurance at a higher rate than those who take care. Insurance causing these problems therefore can distort markets.

Moral hazard rears its ugly head in the following way. If you know you are well insured, you may be more likely to be careless, from leaving your car doors unlocked to driving aggressively. If something goes wrong, you pay only a small price. Now imagine what would happen if everybody were a bit more reckless than they would be if they didn't have car insurance. There would be more wrecks, more damage, more injuries, and more death. And insurance premiums would ultimately be higher than they would be if moral hazard did not exist. Because insurance premiums were higher than they otherwise would be, safe people would find insurance to be a bad bargain. Thus, people who took risks would buy insurance, and those who did not would take their chances. Insurance is much costlier than would be the case if moral hazard and adverse selection did not exist.

Effective medical care is also hindered by problems with insurance. Healthy people may shun insurance, while unhealthy people buy it. If only the ill or those likely to be ill bought health insurance, what would happen? Incredibly large expenditures for insurance are the norm for the ill, including those with past histories of cancer, and the elderly. Policy efforts to reform health care are largely trying to solve problems that occur when private markets govern health care and adverse selection distorts the markets.

Transactions Costs

Uncertainty produces transactions costs. One way that consumers learn about products is through trying to find out information about cars, doctors, and universities. But this information can be costly. Transactions costs can also make markets perform poorly. Indeed, high transactions costs for postexperience goods are the reasons the markets for these goods do not perform well.

Ronald Coase, a Nobel Prize–winning economist, showed that if no transactions costs existed, the market failures we have described in this chapter would not really lead to a failure of voluntary markets.[3] People would be willing to bargain and overcome the problems that policy analysts fret over if no transactions costs existed. But, as Coase pointed out, in the real world, transactions costs are never absent. Thus, policy analysts must be concerned with a world where transactions costs are important.

Good public policy should aim to reduce transactions costs. Doing so means that consumers have a better ability to choose products to buy. But it also means that policy solves problems so that businesses and consumers are left satisfied with market outcomes. Why is this so? If policy prefers one segment or section of society to another, this leads to additional transactions that may occur among two or more groups. In short, bad policy leads to high transactions costs.

For example, suppose government policy endows a small factory with the right to release an enormous amount of polluted effluents in a neighborhood. Let us suppose that the value to do this was small to the factory (an alternative technology could clean the waste very cheaply), but the costs to the neighborhood were large. This would give the neighborhood an incentive to pay the factory to clean up its emissions. Now suppose that lawyers from both groups sat down to negotiate a deal to have the neighborhood pay the factory to clean up its emissions. The transactions costs from such a deal could exceed the amount of money that the factors might obtain from the neighborhood. If the government had given the rights to the neighborhood to determine the effluent level it found acceptable, then the factory would have automatically changed its behavior without negotiations. Public policy, when dealing with transactions costs, indicates that rights should be assigned, if feasible, to those making the most valued use of property.

More generally, policy analysts need to pay attention to transactions costs. Whether these be the costs of information, insurance, or bargaining, the higher the transactions costs, the more likely that market failure is a major problem. Following from this, one major goal of policy analysis is to reduce, or even minimize, transactions costs. If this is done, it is because there exist few gains from trade, meaning that policy has done almost as well as the market in reducing market failures.

UNACCEPTABILITY OF INDIVIDUAL PREFERENCES

A different kind of market problem is created when people have preferences that society finds unacceptable. The problem here is not market failure in the traditional sense. It is the emergence of markets for goods or services that society would prefer not to have produced. Notice that there is an important presumption at work here: the presumption is that markets will tend to spring up to satisfy the demand for goods or services if there are enough people with particular preferences, regardless of the acceptability or unacceptability of those preferences. Only a moment's reflection is necessary to realize how frequently markets have come into existence to serve preferences that most members of society would deem unacceptable. Illicit drugs, prostitution, child pornography, stolen goods, ivory, endangered exotic animals, archaeological artifacts from ancient ruins—markets have sprung up to bring together buyers and sellers of each of these products, and many others that you or we might find reprehensible.

The government typically does not maintain a property rights structure to help reduce transactions costs in these markets. Such markets nonetheless exist. Without a government to maintain a property rights structure, extralegal means, such as violence and threats of violence, are used to enforce property rights. Obtaining reliable information about the quality of goods traded in illicit markets is a particularly common problem. Occasionally, however, government policies lag behind popular sentiments, so enforceable property rights may exist in some markets where the preferences driving the market have come to be deemed unacceptable by large majorities of people. Such was the case for imported ivory for a long time, just as it was true for slavery in the southern states until the end of the Civil War. Today it is the case for such items as tobacco products, assault weapons, and fur coats.

What can be done to stop people from consuming products that majorities of people find unacceptable? This is a tough problem. Markets emerge around preferences, regardless of the acceptability of the preferences that give rise to the goods or services exchanged in such markets. Nevertheless, societies can try to inhibit the production and/or consumption of such products. Individual monitoring and moral sanctioning are often effective in reducing the level of consumption of illicit goods. The consumption of pornography is doubtless less than it would be in the absence of moral sanctions. Education is sometimes effective. Explaining the environmental costs associated with the trade in ivory has probably reduced the level of consumption of ivory, at least to some extent.

It is also possible to try to raise the cost of purchasing such goods through the imposition of steep taxes, thereby decreasing demand for the goods. Taxes on cigarettes and alcohol have this effect. Or the government may criminalize the ownership and exchange of products that are viewed by society as unacceptable. This is the method used to inhibit markets in illicit drugs, child pornography, and lots of other things. Like taxes, the criminalizing of a behavior raises the costs of engaging in it. Being arrested, prosecuted, fined, and sent to prison are costs. The probability of having to bear such costs keeps many people from participating or trading in criminalized activities.

How can we distinguish between acceptable and unacceptable preferences? There are at least three ways of trying to make this type of distinction. One way is to realize that some preferences lead to behaviors that may be pleasurable in the short run but are harmful to the consumer in the long run. This is an instance of a postexperience good, as discussed above. The consumption of illicit drugs, and even tobacco products, often falls into this category. The consumption of these products may bring some consumers immediate pleasure. The consumers may like the sensation that is obtained from taking a drug or smoking a cigarette. But over the long run, these products damage organs, impair the ability to function normally, and shorten life expectancies. They are bad for people. Unfortunately, most consumers of these products begin consuming them at a young age, when people tend to feel immortal and believe that bad things will happen only to other people. Only after an extensive period of consumption do the negative effects begin to show up. In the case of postexperience goods that are harmful to individuals who do not fully appreciate the danger until it is too late, it is therefore not inappropriate for society, acting collectively, to take measures inhibiting the production and consumption of the goods.

A second way to distinguish between acceptable and unacceptable preferences is by reference to negative externalities. The consumption of some goods, while not harmful to the consumer or producer of the good, may be harmful to people who are not part of the original transaction. This is the sort of argument often given about the consumption of so-called recreational drugs. These drugs may or may not be harmful to the drug user, but the drugs often create a need for the user to obtain a good deal of cash to maintain his or her drug habit. When this need for cash begins to take the form of burglary, robbery, and assault, the drug habit has spilled over to the rest of society, with negative consequences. Notice that this same sort of argument is made with regard to the trade in ivory. Ivory is not harmful to either the owner of the ivory or the hunters who produce the supply of ivory. But ivory comes from elephants, which are an endangered species in the wild. Each piece of new ivory harvested comes at the expense of an animal that is threatened with extinction. The argument is that all of us, even those of us who live on other continents, are better off if elephants continue to exist as a species. Hence, the ivory trade harms all of us if it leads to the extinction of elephants.

A third way to distinguish acceptable from unacceptable preferences was discussed in an earlier chapter. This was the "veil of ignorance" proposed by the social contract theorist John Rawls. What Rawls proposed was that we need to differentiate between preferences for policies or actions that are an advantage to us and do not harm others and policies that are an advantage to us but do harm others. The former he would treat as acceptable preferences, while the latter would be unacceptable. Rawls asks us to pretend that we are behind a veil so that we do not know anything at all about our personal attributes or possessions. Nor do we know the probabilities that should be assigned to the likelihood that we are male or female, old or young, black or white, rich or poor, right-handed or left-handed, talented or just average. Consequently, we must determine preferences for policies or actions based on their merits rather than our own selfish impulses. If a policy preference seems acceptable even without knowing the specifics of your own attributes, then the policy preference is presumed to be acceptable. In the following section, we show how the veil of ignorance can be used to help sort out difficult moral questions about preferences.

USEFUL VERSUS INAPPROPRIATE DISCRIMINATION

Everybody discriminates every day. We have to. We discriminate among restaurants in trying to select ones that will offer good food that has been prepared in a safe, clean way. We discriminate among cars as we drive down the road when trying to stay a safe distance from those that might be driven by inexperienced or inebriated drivers. We discriminate among neighborhoods during a late-evening walk or jog when we avoid streets that are not well lit or where there are cars cruising slowly by. We discriminate among people when we go in a store and try to identify salesclerks, rather than customers, to help us select suitable products. As these examples illustrate, it is impossible, and doubtless inadvisable, to try to avoid making discriminations. The issue is distinguishing between helpful discrimination and inappropriate discrimination.

Consider the issues that a sales manager faces in trying to hire salespeople. What kinds of factors should the manager legitimately take into consideration? The manager wants to ensure that the sales force that is put into the field will be able to connect with clients, provide clients with accurate product information, and make as many sales as possible. The example could involve any number of products, but let us assume it is medical examination equipment for physicians' offices. Knowledge of the product line and experience in sales are clearly acceptable traits to consider. What about the personal grooming of prospective salespeople? For example, should the manager take into account things like hair length, tattoos, or the presence of jewelry that pierces noses and cheeks? Perhaps personal grooming is an appropriate consideration, given the importance of salespeople looking professional in doctors' offices.

But what about the ethnic or racial characteristics of potential salespeople? Is it appropriate to discriminate against African Americans or Hispanic Americans simply because the majority of physicians are white? Is it appropriate to discriminate against smokers or people who are overweight? Is it appropriate to discriminate against people with physical disabilities? In short, if you were the sales manager, how would you handle these issues, especially if you knew that your own income and advancement were contingent upon maximizing sales from your sales force?

If these questions were simple, they wouldn't be the sorts of problems that have convulsed the political process in the United States, as well as many other countries, for such a long time. But the questions must be answered. Discrimination is inevitable and often helpful. The tough question is how to decide on what basis discrimination is appropriate and legitimate, and on what basis discrimination is inappropriate and leads to reprehensible behavior. Often the way these issues are settled is through available democratic processes. Some of these issues, however, are never fully settled. They continue to be the source of perennial political conflicts.

CONCLUSION

Markets are powerful instruments. They allow individuals to obtain satisfaction for many of their needs and preferences. Markets, however, are not perfect. Many situations lead to shortcomings and failures of market processes. We have reviewed many of these situations in this chapter. The nature of goods makes a huge difference in the ability of markets to operate properly. Some goods are not excludable; others are not rivalrous; still others have problems of congestion. These attributes can mean that markets do not perform well in producing appropriate levels of such goods. Likewise, the physical attributes of goods make a difference. It is difficult to establish property rights structures for goods that are migratory, such as salmon. Other goods have properties that lead to natural monopolies or allow a small number of firms to collude with one another to restrict supply and thereby increase prices.

Incomplete information and the difficulties of obtaining needed information to make informed decisions often hobble markets, especially markets for services like education and medicine. Other problems emerge when we try to protect ourselves from the vagaries of nature and one another by purchasing insurance; moral hazards and adverse selection commonly occur. Transactions costs can be high enough to make it difficult to benefit from market exchanges.

Furthermore, markets may emerge when we prefer that they did not. Markets often exist to supply goods or services that large majorities of people find distasteful or objectionable. But making careful distinctions between acceptable and unacceptable preferences is itself difficult. Nowhere is it more difficult than in the area of discrimination with regard to personal attributes. When is discrimination appropriate and useful? When is it inappropriate and reprehensible? These issues are at the heart of much of the politics in the United States—something we will explore later in this book.

Key Terms

rivalrous good *p. 119*
excludable good *p. 119*
pure public good *p. 119*
congestible good *p. 119*
common pool resource *p. 119*
toll good *p. 120*
pure private good *p. 120*
externality *p. 120*
nature of the good *p. 121*

Cod Wars *p. 123*
natural monopoly *p. 124*
search good *p. 127*
experience good *p. 127*
predatory pricing *p. 128*
postexperience good *p. 130*
moral hazard *p. 131*
adverse selection *p. 131*

Suggested Readings

Arrow, Kenneth. 1974. *The Limits of Organization*. New York: W. W. Norton.

Coase, Ronald. 1937. "The Nature of the Firm." *Economica* 4: 386–405.

Mueller, Dennis. 1989. *Public Choice II: A Revised Edition of Public Choice*. Cambridge, England: Cambridge University Press.

Musgrave, Robert, and Peggy Musgrave. 1980. *Public Finance in Theory and Practice*. 3rd ed. New York: McGraw-Hill.

Samuelson, Paul. 1954. "The Pure Theory of Public Expenditure." *Review of Economics and Statistics* 36: 386–389.

Schwarz, John. 1988. *America's Hidden Success*. Rev. ed. New York: W. W. Norton.

Weimer, David, and Aiden Vining. 1999. *Policy Analysis: Concepts and Practice*. 3rd ed. Upper Saddle River, N.J.: Prentice-Hall.

Williamson, Oliver, and Scott Masten. 1999. *The Economics of Transaction Costs*. New York: Edward Elgar.

Notes

1. The following discussion is adapted from David L. Weimer and Aidan R. Vining, *Policy Analysis: Concepts and Practice*, 3rd ed. (Upper Saddle River, N.J.: Prentice-Hall, 1999), pp. 74–94.

2. George Akerlof, "The Market for 'Lemons': Quality Uncertainty and the Market Mechanism," *Quarterly Journal of Economics* 84(1970): 488–500.

3. Ronald Coase, "The Problem of Social Cost," *Journal of Law and Economics* 3(1960): 1–44.

IV

Public Policy in the United States

8

Policy Analysis in the American Political Context

INTRODUCTION

For much of this century, the American people have looked to the national government for solutions to important public problems. From the first days of Franklin Roosevelt's New Deal, Washington, D.C., has come to be the epicenter of politics in the United States, with the president as the policymaker most responsible for articulating the needs, problems, hopes, and aspirations of the American people. The scores of agencies, hundreds of programs, millions of employees, and billions of dollars that collectively make up the federal government represent the triumph of the view that the federal government is the best, if not the only, venue for solving the ills of modern society.

In this chapter, we focus on the institutional context in which policymaking is conducted in the United States. In particular, we look at how the federal government has come to occupy the focal point of policymaking activity. We show evidence that the states and local communities have increased their capacity for making and implementing public policies since the dark days of the Great Depression. This is a healthy development. The reasons why are discussed in the later sections of the chapter. In particular, we discuss the tradeoffs between the "top-down" approach to policymaking that has dominated American politics since the Great Depression and a more organic, "bottom-up" approach to policymaking that appears to be emerging in recent years. The chapter concludes with a set of design principles for recommending top-down versus bottom-up strategies for policymaking.

THE ASCENDANCY OF THE NATIONAL GOVERNMENT

The Great Depression, which began in 1929 and lasted until the entry of the United States into World War II, changed virtually every aspect of American life. At its depth, over a quarter of the American work force was unemployed, millions of American families lost their life savings as banks collapsed, tens of thousands of farmers lost their land and equipment to foreclosures, wave after wave of workers took to the railways and highways in search of work for themselves and food for their families, and everywhere was strewn the detritus of an industrial society in despair.

While the election of President Franklin Roosevelt in 1932 did not bring an end to the Great Depression, it did mark a fundamental change in the role of the national government in American life. To cope with the national economic emergency, Roosevelt pushed through Congress an array of new federal programs, collectively known as the **New Deal,** that were designed to bring relief to farmers and industrial workers; stem the tide of starvation and homelessness in the cities; stabilize the banking, financial, and insurance systems; and give hope to the country that better times would come again soon. As explained in Box 8.1, these emergency relief agencies were so numerous that they soon came to be known as the **alphabet agencies.**

The traditional system of federalism—the division of authority between the national government and the states—underwent a fundamental transformation with the New Deal. The previous system of federalism, which has often been described as **layer cake federalism,** involved the assignment of distinctly different and nonoverlapping responsibilities to the national government on the one hand and to the states and local governments on the other. As depicted in Figure 8.1, each level of government, like the layers of a layer cake, had its own set of policy activities that rarely crossed the boundaries between levels of government.

Subnational governments had primary responsibility for public safety, education, social welfare, the construction of most roads and other public improvements, most regulation of business activity, regulation of workplace conditions and product safety, and most other day-to-day issues involving the American public. The national government was responsible for national security; regulation of international and interstate commerce; large-scale capital improvements, such as the development of railroads, canals, and waterways; and the promotion of a handful of individual economic sectors, such as agriculture.

By and large, the earlier system was characterized as a bottom-up form of policymaking. The center of gravity in American politics was in the large cities, counties, and state capitals. Many of the most important policy initiatives originated in subnational governments. The nation's capital was still basically a sleepy small town with little importance in the daily lives of most citizens.

Box 8.1   Franklin Roosevelt's Alphabet Agencies

THE TURNING point of the Great Depression was the election of President Franklin Roosevelt and the initiation of his agenda, which soon became known as the New Deal. Unlike his predecessor, Herbert Hoover, Roosevelt aggressively expanded the role of the federal government to combat the Depression. Roosevelt established new agencies with the goals of employing people, improving the nation's infrastructure, constructing government facilities, and reenergizing depressed sectors of the economy. These agencies included, among others, the Civilian Work Administration (CWA), Civilian Conservation Corps (CCC), Farm Security Administration (FSA), Federal Emergency Relief Administration (FERA), National Youth Administration (NYA), Public Works Administration (PWA), Tennessee Valley Authority (TVA), and perhaps the best-remembered agency, the Works Progress Administration (WPA). So many new agencies were established by Roosevelt that they soon became known as the alphabet agencies.[1]

The accomplishments and scope of projects undertaken by the alphabet agencies remain impressive. The TVA dug channels for flood control, established roads for commerce, and dammed rivers to provide electricity to an extensive area in the southeastern United States. The PWA started the first subway system in Chicago to complement its elevated trains, dug the Lincoln Tunnel connecting Manhattan to New Jersey, and built the Grand Coulee Dam on the Columbia River, which became the electrical source for much of the Northwest. Not surprisingly, the lake produced by the Grand Coulee Dam took the name Roosevelt Lake. All together, there were thousands of projects undertaken.

Perhaps the most impressive of all of these agencies, however, was the WPA. Some 8.5 million people found work with the WPA. There were 650,000 miles of road, 125,000 public buildings, 75,000 bridges, 8,000 parks, and 800 airports constructed by the WPA. Some familiar projects include the Tri-Borough Bridge that links Manhattan, the Bronx, and Queens; New York's La Guardia Airport; and the San Diego Zoo. The WPA also assisted the arts through the creation of the Federal Arts Project, the Federal Writers Project, and the Federal Theater Project. Many new post office buildings were constructed by WPA workers and adorned with murals painted by WPA artists. The WPA constructed numerous high schools at this time, and thanks to the WPA many university campuses added buildings, including the building in which the authors of this textbook now work.

1. For information on these alphabet agencies and specific projects, see *http://newdeal.feri.org/library/index.htm* and Walter I. Trattner, *From Poor Low to Welfare State: A History of Social Welfare in America*, 6th ed. (New York: Free Press, 1999).

With the New Deal, Washington, D.C. became centrally important in American politics and in the lives of Americans generally. To be sure, the ascendancy of the national government was not entirely without critics. Numerous lawsuits were brought against Roosevelt's new programs, and the Supreme Court invalidated many of his administration's early efforts to fight

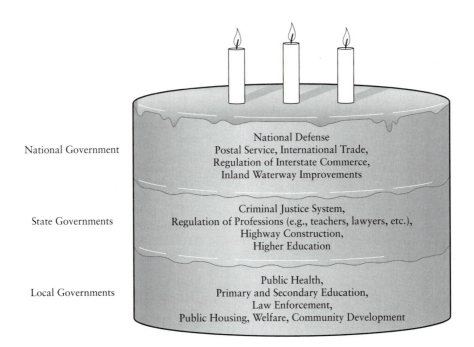

National Government — National Defense
Postal Service, International Trade,
Regulation of Interstate Commerce,
Inland Waterway Improvements

State Governments — Criminal Justice System,
Regulation of Professions (e.g., teachers, lawyers, etc.),
Highway Construction,
Higher Education

Local Governments — Public Health,
Primary and Secondary Education,
Law Enforcement,
Public Housing, Welfare, Community Development

FIGURE 8.1 Layer Cake Federalism

the Great Depression. But within a few years, the Supreme Court capitulated and began to find room in the Constitution for most of his initiatives. In the context of the economic emergency facing the country, neither the administration nor the Congress worried much about whether or not these initiatives fit well within the preexisting system of federalism.

The national government took over the primary responsibility for protecting the general welfare of individual citizens, in particular with the passage of the Social Security Act, which provided pensions for many elderly people, benefits for the blind, assistance to children in households headed by mothers only, compensation for workers laid off in mass firings, and insurance for persons injured on the job. Many of these policies were modeled on programs that had already been developed in the more innovative states, especially in the arena of social legislation. In an important sense, the national government's preemption of state and local policy activities was made feasible because the national government was able to learn from policy successes in states that had experimented with providing greater social protections to their citizens.[1]

At Roosevelt's behest, Congress created programs to put people to work building local courthouses, park facilities, university buildings, streets and sidewalks, drainage systems, dams across rivers, and hundreds of other local projects. National programs were created to employ local artisans to create paintings, sculptures, and murals to decorate local buildings. The national government began actively regulating a host of economic sectors, including agriculture, banking, insurance, finance, pharmaceuticals, telecommunications, energy production, transportation, shipping, mining, and more. In short, the national government, sometimes with the active cooperation of the states and local communities and sometimes not, assumed responsibility for scores of activities traditionally left to the subnational governments. The reason was clear and, for most people, compelling: to get the United States on its feet again.

The vastly expanded role of the national government was not reversed after the economic crisis of the Great Depression ended. While many New Deal programs were terminated as the country mobilized for World War II, the fundamental alteration in the roles of the national government vis-à-vis the states continued in the postwar period. Indeed, in most respects, this new top-down approach to policymaking became even more firmly entrenched after the war. One of the lessons that many people had taken from the performance of state and local governments during the Great Depression was that these governments lacked the competence, capacity, and in many cases interest in addressing social and economic problems. This assessment was in many cases unfair. To be sure, state and local governments were no match for the destructive power of the worst recession in American history, but many of them were capable of addressing the more normal problems facing their citizens.

Adding to the negative assessment of the state and local governments was another, much more pernicious reality. State and local governments—especially, though not exclusively, in the South—were often adamantly opposed to improved social welfare programs because they might be used to treat black Americans as equals with white Americans. Until the middle of the 1960s, southern states and local governments maintained a set of segregationist laws and ordinances that were used to discriminate against African Americans. These restrictions collectively were known as **Jim Crow laws.**

These laws regulated virtually every aspect of an African American's life, including where that person could live, go to school, and eat. They restricted where a black person could sit on buses and trains. They restricted the types of educational opportunities and jobs available. They prevented most African Americans from voting or serving on juries. These laws were enforced by regular police and judicial officials, as well as through extralegal mechanisms of organized militias such as the Ku Klux Klan and its weapons of intimidation and terror. Outside the South, government officials in many large cities tolerated, and even supported, discrimination against African Americans. Segregated housing for blacks and whites, together with inferior public services and bad schools in black neighborhoods, were not uncommon in northern cities. It should be no surprise, therefore, that the reluctance and outright opposition of many state and local governments to reverse segregationist policies contributed to a negative view of subnational governments and a pessimistic attitude about their ability to foster a fertile, positive environment for bottom-up policymaking.

One of the factors reinforcing the ascendancy of the national government in the postwar period was a quiet, but noteworthy, occurrence: the professionalization of the federal bureaucracy. Even before the Great Depression, most jobs in the federal government fell under civil service rules, which required that federal employees be hired and promoted on the basis of their competence for the job rather than on the basis of partisan allegiances or political connections. It's not clear what difference these civil service rules made prior to the New Deal, but after the New Deal, they had an important impact. In part, this was due to the huge increase in the number of federal employees. With the growth of the federal government, more government jobs fell under civil service requirements. At the same time, universities across the United States were quickly expanding in size and beginning to produce tens of thousands of new graduates (many of whom were funded through the G.I. Bill, which paid the college expenses of the veterans of World War II). Many of these graduates were earning degrees in specialized fields, such as financial accounting, mechanical and civil engineering, biology, economics, rural sociology, political science, and public administration, and finding jobs working for the federal bureaucracies.

These professionally trained employees greatly added to the capacity of the national government to identify problems, propose solutions, and implement programs that originated from within the executive branch agencies. In short, federal bureaucracies were staffed by people with better education and greater qualifications than was typically the case in state and local bureaucracies—reinforcing the view that state and local governments were laggards in the federal system and reinforcing, as well, the inclination to rely on top-down policymaking.

POLICY IMPLEMENTATION IN A TOP-DOWN FEDERAL SYSTEM

While the national government becomes the locus of policymaking activity in the postwar period, lower levels of government did not disappear. Their roles changed. Increasingly, they became instruments of the national government, used to implement national policies and provide political support for increases in federal spending. A new term was coined to describe this altered set of relationships between the national government and lower levels of government: **picket fence federalism.** In this system of federalism, the federal government utilized lower levels of government to deliver programmatic goods and services to the ultimate recipients of federal assistance. As shown in Figure 8.2, each of these vertical relationships (that is, pickets in a fence) centered on individual policy areas: one for agricultural research, another for commodity stabilization, one for mental health, another for vocational training, one for

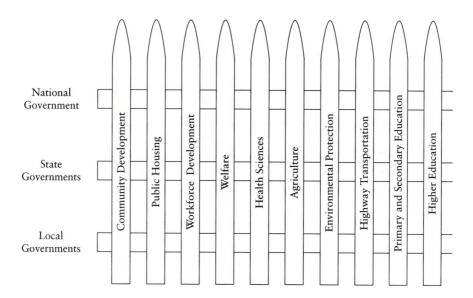

FIGURE 8.2 Picket-Fence Federalism Figure adapted from *Classics of Public Administration,* Fourth Edition, by Jay Shafruitz and Albert C. Hyde, copyright © 1997 by Harcourt, Inc., reproduced by permission of the publisher.

highway transportation, another for medical research, one for public housing, another for welfare, one for support of primary and secondary education, another to subsidize colleges and universities, and on and on.

One of the chief features of this form of federalism is that political allegiances form vertically across levels of government in a particular policy area. Together, policy professionals from all levels of government work to maintain public commitments to the particular policy area in which they work. These alliances among policy professionals work to the advantage of each "picket" (vertical alignment) within the picket fence system of federalism. Within each distinct functional policy area, policy specialists at the national level develop close alliances with policy specialists at lower levels. Professionals at the national level provide revenues, and thus job security, to professionals at the lower levels. Policy professionals at the national level look to their counterparts at lower levels of government and among think tanks and interest groups for support rather than to Congress or voters from the various states. Professionals in cities, counties, and state agencies provide political support for the initiation of new programs and enhanced funding at the national level. Professionals at lower levels of government, in turn, look for support to their counterparts in higher levels of government rather than to local voters or local elected officials. Loyalty among professionals working in each policy area is the glue that holds together the "pickets" that make up this type of federalism.

This system of federalism came under attack during the 1960s and 1970s, as new interest groups entered into the political system and began to argue that the close allegiances that existed within each separate policy area were too insular and exclusive. In many cases, these attacks led to an opening up of the policy subsystems that surrounded the functional policy "pickets." New voices and new viewpoints were introduced. Conflict among policy professionals and advocates became more common. Often there were fights over the details of policy initiatives and the relative roles of federal versus state and local governments.

Not until the late 1980s and early 1990s, however, were there serious calls for alterations in this system of federalism. In the 1980s, as the national government began to run up huge budget deficits and was forced to scale back new spending, federal lawmakers increasingly resorted to mandating actions by lower levels of government without providing the required funds to carry out the required actions. These laws, known as **unfunded mandates,** were met with hostility by state and local governments, and the situation began to cause a growing number of governors and mayors to demand a fundamental alteration in the relationship between the national government and lower levels of government. In response to these demands, Congress in 1995 passed a law prohibiting the passage of future bills that failed to provide the funds needed by lower levels of government to carry out Washington's mandates. This law, while almost completely unenforceable on future Congresses, nonetheless expressed the dissatisfaction of lower levels of government with top-down policy mandates of the national government.

Despite the vastly increased importance of state and local governments in the post–World War II period (about which we will have more to say below), it is interesting to note how much the picket fence system of federalism continues today. One indicator is the frequency with which the national government chooses to implement national policies by delegating the delivery of services to organizations and public agencies at the state and local levels. Table 8.1 shows the major programs of the national government that operate on an intergovernmental basis. These programs involve transfers of moneys to subnational governments, such as state agencies, counties, cities, towns, special districts, school districts, and Indian tribes, which are, in turn, responsible for delivering final policy goods and services to individual beneficiaries. At the same time, these programs impose constraints on state and local governments with regard to eligibility restrictions to be used in identifying beneficiaries, reporting requirements, maintenance-of-effort requirements, and a variety of other features. The largest of these programs are Medicaid (medical coverage for the poor), Food Stamps (nutritional assistance to the poor), Lower Income Housing Assistance (subsidies for housing rehabilitation for the poor), Highway Planning and Construction (construction and repair of the federal highway system), and almost two dozen other programs with outlays in excess of a billion dollars.

The food stamp program is one of many policies oriented toward alleviating poverty in the United States. *Mary M. Steinbacher/PhotoEdit.*

POLICY INSTRUMENTS IN A TOP-DOWN FEDERAL SYSTEM

The top-down policymaking approach that has characterized the United States since the early days of the New Deal period has led to the development of a variety of mechanisms by which the national government attempts to influence the behavior of subnational governments, business enterprises, and individual citizens. The most prominent of these mechanisms are positive inducements, such as fiscal instruments and tax incentives, and negative sanctions, such as regulatory rules. Other types of policies have also been used extensively by the federal government, including information provision and public goods. Each of these types of policies is introduced here and discussed at length in the next chapter.

Positive inducements, such as fiscal instruments, are used by the national government to obtain desired behaviors by offering a positive motive to do something—a carrot. **Fiscal instruments** involve the direct transfer of funds from the government to a recipient in return for compliance with strictures about how the recipient will utilize the funds. In the picket fence federalism discussed above, fiscal instruments are the primary means by which the national

TABLE 8.1 Major U.S. Government Programs That Operate on an Intergovernmental Basis

U.S. Agency	Program	FY97 Outlays
Department of Agriculture		
	Food Stamps	$19.51
	Special Supplemental Nutrition Program for Women	3.55
	State Administrative Matching Grants for Food Stamps	1.95
Department of Housing and Urban Development		
	Lower Income Housing Assistance Program—Section 8 Moderate Rehabilitation	19.98
	Community Development Block Grants/Entitlement Grants	2.90
	Public Housing Comprehensive Grant Program	2.34
	Public and Indian Housing	2.03
	HOME Investment Partnerships Program	1.19
	Community Development Block Grants/State's Program	1.15
Department of Labor		
	Job Training Partnership Act	2.79
	Unemployment Insurance	2.24
Department of Transportation		
	Highway Planning and Construction	21.25
	Federal Transit Capital and Operating Assistance Formula	2.44
	Federal Transit Capital Improvement Grants	1.69
	Airport Improvement Program	1.35
Department of Education		
	Title I Grants to Local Educational Agencies	5.71
	Special Education Grants to States	3.01
Department of Health and Human Services		
	Medical Assistance Program (Medicaid)	93.64
	Temporary Assistance for Needy Families	11.02
	Family Support Payments to States Assistance Payments	3.79
	Foster Care Title IV-E	3.29
	Social Services Block Grant	2.49
	Child Support Enforcement	2.10
	Child Care Mandatory and Matching Funds	1.96
	Block Grants for Prevention and Treatment of Substance Abuse	1.29
	Low-Income Home Energy Assistance	1.19
Federal Emergency Management Agency		
	Disaster Assistance	3.39

Note: FY97 outlays are in billions of dollars for U.S. federal domestic programs, with more than $1 billion in outlays to subnational governments (i.e., state governments, counties, cities, towns, special districts, school districts, and tribes).

Source: Bickers and Stein Database of U.S. Domestic Assistance Programs, available from the authors.

government gets subnational units of government to implement policies in ways that national policymakers desire. In some cases, the federal government transfers income directly to individual citizens. Such programs are few in number but very large in size. Table 8.2 indicates what these programs are. They include Social Security, Medicare, benefits for veterans and their dependents, pensions for workers in a handful of occupations deemed by the federal government as critical to the nation's economy, and agricultural stabilization and assistance programs. In all of these cases, the national government uses its revenues to reward particular types of behaviors, such as participation in the armed forces, or to assist persons facing unavoidable problems, such as old age, health problems, or crop losses.

A second major form of positive inducement used by the government to produce desired behaviors by businesses and individuals is **tax incentives.** Like fiscal instruments, tax incentives operate as carrots rather than sticks. These policies, however, do not involve direct outlays by the government. Instead, they represent tax revenues that the government forgoes. Known as **tax expenditures,** these policies operate on a voluntary basis. Recipients of tax incentives choose to engage in a behavior that the government is seeking to promote and in return are rewarded with the financial benefit provided by the tax expenditure. Table 8.3 shows the most important of the U.S. government's tax incentives. By far the biggest is the home mortgage interest deduction. This tax policy encourages home ownership by reducing the effective cost of a home mortgage. It has also been criticized for contributing to suburban sprawl in American metropolitan areas and for the deterioration of the inner city. Other big tax expenditures include the state and local income and personal property tax deduction, which allows citizens to avoid paying federal taxes on income that is taxed by subnational governments; the partial nontaxability of

TABLE 8.2 U.S. Government Programs in Which All Recipients Were Individual Persons, 1997

Program Area	FY97 Outlays
Social Security program payments	$384.18
Medicare	229.42
Veterans' and dependents' benefits	18.83
Pension payments for railroad, longshore and harbor, and coal mine workers	8.67
Agricultural stabilization and assistance programs	6.96
Other	0.06
Total	$641.11

Note: FY97 outlays are in billions of dollars.

Source: Bickers and Stein Database of U.S. Domestic Assistance Programs, available from the authors.

TABLE 8.3 Selected U.S. Government Tax Expenditure Policies, 1994

Tax Expenditure	Federal Revenue Loss
Home mortgage interest deduction	$51.2
State and local income and personal property tax deduction	23.7
Partial nontaxability of Social Security and railroad retirement benefits	22.2
Earned income tax credit (EITC)	19.6
Charitable contribution deduction	16.5
Real estate tax deduction	13.1
Extraordinary medical expenses deduction	3.8
Child and dependent care exclusion	2.7

Note: Amounts are in billions of 1994 dollars. Amount for the EITC includes refunds.

Source: Christopher Howard, *The Hidden Welfare State* (Princeton, N.J.: Princeton University Press, 1997), p. 28.

Social Security and railroad retirement benefits, which allows recipients of government-provided retirement income to avoid paying taxes on most of this income; the earned income tax credit, which provides a subsidy to low-income households; and the charitable contribution deduction, which is an indirect government subsidy to churches and charities that receive contributions from taxpayers with large enough tax obligations that their deductions exceed the threshold of the standard deduction.

Negative sanctions, such as regulatory instruments, are also used by government to induce desired behaviors. Regulatory instruments are akin to sticks. They impose constraints on behaviors by making it painful to engage in certain actions. For example, the national government restricts the permissible behaviors of cities, counties, special districts, local schools, public universities, and states if they accept funds from the federal government to carry out particular policies. Using regulatory instruments such as mandates specifying sidewalk shapes and physical access to public facilities, regulations requiring seat belt laws, procedures for inspecting surface mines, and requirements for monitoring air quality over urban areas, the federal government induces lower levels of government to comply with policy preferences set at the national level. These government-over-government regulations are the proverbial "other side of the coin" of picket fence federalism.

The national government also regulates the behaviors of private actors. Prior to the Great Depression, the national government began to regulate the banking system through control of the currency. Using antitrust powers passed in 1890 and amended from time to time thereafter, the government regulated corporate mergers and acquisitions that might create monopolies. From the turn of the century, it had begun to regulate the transportation industries, including railroads, waterways, trucking, and later aviation. Likewise, it had begun regulating the communication industries, including telephones, telegraph, and broadcasters.

The first big surge in federal regulation of private interests, however, occurred during the New Deal, as the national government sought to stabilize and shore up a host of business sectors. The national government moved heavily into the regulation of industries deemed crucial to the national economy. These included, most especially, financial sectors, such as the stock markets and securities exchanges, insurance, and banking. Likewise, the national government began closely regulating agricultural methods and production levels. It began to regulate electricity production and distribution, pipelines, coal mining, aluminum and steel production, and timber production. In most cases, the primary goal of the national government during this period was to regulate production levels and pricing patterns. In other cases, such as fighting forest fires, dredging harbors, damming rivers, and building massive hydroelectric projects, the goal was to expand or stimulate new economic activities.

In the 1960s the regulatory activities of the national government shifted again, this time in a direction that had been historically delegated to states and local communities. The national government began actively **policing** categories of behaviors. The U.S. Constitution grants to the states the task of policing, which from the beginning of the country has always been understood to include more than the county sheriff or city police force. Policing includes oversight of public health, safety, and welfare. Consequently, states and local communities have long regulated such things as doctors, dentists, lawyers, land surveyors, veterinarians, dairy producers, and funeral directors, and even activities such as hair styling and cutting, tattooing, well drilling, and street cleaning.

Beginning in the heady days of Lyndon Johnson's Great Society programs during the mid-1960s and continuing into the 1970s, the federal government began to police activities that cut across multiple economic sectors and that touched on virtually every aspect of life. Key to these policing activities was the regulation and provision of information about products. Consumer protection laws were passed to guard against misleading advertising and unsafe products; clothing fabrics were subjected to testing and regulation to reduce the danger from fires; refrigerators were required to be redesigned; children's toys were to be tested and potentially removed from the market; housing quality was regulated, including prohibitions on the use of lead paints, the safety of stairs, and fire protection standards to be employed; workplace safety regulations were passed that applied to virtually every corporation and firm in the country; automobiles were regulated to enhance the safety of occupants, to reduce emissions, and to increase fuel economy; and food products were subjected to new regulations. We will confront these types of policies again in the next chapter in discussing the use of information provision as a distinctive category of public policies.

Among the most important of the new regulations during the 1960s and 1970s were those pertaining to the provision of public goods. Public goods include things that if provided to one person are provided to all persons within a particular area. Examples include the regulation of water quality, air quality, pesticides, herbicides, and toxic wastes. Another example is antidiscrimination laws, which were passed to create a more level playing field in industry and government for women, minorities, veterans, and more recently people with physical disabilities. While most of these antidiscrimination regulations are now widely accepted, the most famous of them—affirmative action—has been controversial almost from its inception in the early 1970s, with supporters arguing that it has allowed women and minorities to overcome systematic barriers to advancement in schools and the workplace and critics arguing that it is a form of reverse discrimination, systematically giving advantages to minorities at the expense of nonminorities.

GROWTH OF POLYCENTRICITY

The growth of the national government, in conjunction with its frequent practice of utilizing subnational governments and local organizations to carry out its policies, has produced a curious unintended consequence. It has led to the development of a much more polycentric political system in the United States.

Signs of enhanced polycentricity abound. In the postwar period, government employment at the state and local levels has far outpaced the growth in civilian employment by the federal government.[2] Consider the following. In 1950, federal government civilian employees numbered just over 2.1 million; state governments employed just under 1.1 million persons; and local governments employed 3.2 million persons. By 1997, the number of federal government civilian employees had grown to 2.8 million, an increase of 33 percent. State employees in 1997 numbered almost 4 million, an increase of 277 percent from 1950. Local governments had increased their ranks to over 10 million persons, an increase of 217 percent.

These overall totals tell only a portion of the story about the enhanced policy capacity at the subnational level. Of the 2.8 million civilian employees of the federal government in 1997, over 58 percent worked either for the Postal Service or in national defense and international relations–related jobs. Of the remainder, almost one-quarter were engaged in financial administration or in jobs that kept the federal government itself running from one day to the next. Relatively few jobs in the federal government were directly connected to the day-to-day implementation of federal policies. By contrast, approximately 64 percent of state government employees were involved in actual policy implementation, as opposed to the administration and overhead tasks associated with keeping government operating. At the local level, the proportion of employees engaged in policy implementation was even higher. Approximately 92 percent of local government employees were engaged in the implementation of policies. At this level of government, only 8 percent of the public employees were primarily engaged in administrative and overhead tasks associated with keeping the government operating.

This asymmetry in policy engagement can be illustrated by looking at welfare policy. At the federal level in 1997, there were fewer than 9,000 full-time employees working in agencies that carry out welfare policy. At the state level, over 200,000 welfare agency employees worked in this policy area. At the local level, over 250,000 full-time employees were engaged in welfare policy formulation and delivery.

Or consider surface transportation (that is, streets, highways, and mass transit). In 1997, the federal government had fewer than four thousand full-time employees working in this area; states had over a quarter of a million employees operating in this area; and local governments had almost half a million employees engaged in surface transportation. Such numbers, of course, cannot tell the whole story about policy capacity. Certainly a substantial number of the street and highway department employees at the local level are engaged in manual labor, filling potholes and replacing the asphalt on city roads. Likewise, many local welfare agency employees are intake workers, whose primary task is filling in forms and recording client information.

Nevertheless, in each local and state agency there is likely to be a subset of officials who spend a portion of their time thinking about how to better implement the policies and programs in which they have come to have years of hands-on experience. Given the sheer number of local and state governments, the accumulated capacity of these officials should not be underestimated. As of the 1997 *Census of Governments,* in the United States there were, in addition to the 1 national government and 50 state governments, over 3,000 counties, approximately 19,000 municipal governments, almost 17,000 townships, 14,000 school districts, and almost 35,000 special districts. In all, there are over 80,000 governments in the United States. This is a lot of government— most of it at the local level.

There is more to this story, however. During the nearly half a century of picket fence federalism, it was not only state and local governments that acquired substantial experience and capacity in dozens of functional policy areas. Community organizations sprang up across the country to advance policy issues and implement social and educational programs. The organizations that make up this sector, collectively known as the **independent sector,** include foundations and charitable organizations. As of 1993 there were almost 38,000 foundations, nearly double the number from the late 1970s. Charitable organizations are even more numerous and have grown even faster. Charities that are registered as 501(c)(3) organizations with the Internal Revenue Service are tax exempt; they are permitted to receive donations that are tax deductible; but they are restricted from engaging in political activities that are designed to influence the election of particular candidates. These organizations exist to promote the general welfare by offering education, providing benefits to the poor and other needy populations, serving as museums, or serving as places of worship.

It is significant that the periods of formation of organizations in the independent sector coincide with major episodes of new public policy initiatives by the national government. Relatively few nonprofit organizations other than religious entities existed prior to the New Deal. There was a surge in the formation of nonprofit organizations following World War II; another major surge occurred in the 1960s and lasted into the 1970s; and a surge beginning in the mid-1980s followed the efforts of the national government to create block grants giving greater policy discretion and autonomy back to states and local governments. As of 1993, there were almost half a million 501(c)(3) organizations, excluding religious organizations and private foundations. This figure is nearly double the number that had existed in the mid-1970s.

The growth of the independent sector has been stimulated by the same forces that have led to an increase in the capacity of state and local governments. The independent sector has come to be utilized as a primary vehicle for delivering public goods and services. Health care nonprofit organizations had annual funding as of 1992 of $261 billion—a figure that exceeded the U.S. defense budget.[3] Education and research organizations had revenues in 1992 of $78 billion, up from $49 billion in 1977. Social and legal services organizations had revenues in 1992 of $46 billion, up from $18 billion in 1977. Much of this growth has been stimulated by an increase in government reliance on local nonprofit organizations to carry out public policies. Consider, for example, the policies provided by Planned Parenthood, as discussed in Box 8.2. This agency, though private, carries out a number of services that government funds but is reluctant to do itself.

In the mid-1970s, about a quarter of the revenues of independent sector organizations came from government. By the early 1990s, this percentage had grown to almost one-third. In some subsectors, the increase in government sources of revenues has been even greater. For example, in the area of health services, nonprofit organizations in 1977 received 32 percent of their revenues from government; by 1992, revenues from government sources constituted 41 percent of their funds.

All told, the propensity of the national government to rely on lower levels of government and other intermediaries to implement public policies has led to a remarkable growth in the size, scope, and capacity of subnational government agencies and local nonprofit organizations. From their front-line involvement in scores of policy areas over the past two generations, these agencies and organizations have acquired substantial experience in the intricacies and issues that lie at the heart of public policy provision. The layering of these organizations and agencies, their increased proximity and interactions, and their growing experience and expertise in multitudes of policy areas have all added to the richness and capacity of the American political system as a polycentric system of governance.

Box 8.2 *Planned Parenthood and the Provision of Public Services*

THE FEDERAL government does not always administer every program it funds. One effective means of providing policy services is through nonprofit organizations. Nevertheless, some of these policies become controversial, and nonprofit service providers can get caught in the middle of a political fight. One such nonprofit service provider, Planned Parenthood, exemplifies how such subcontractors implement government policy goals while simultaneously lobbying the government to influence the very policy in which they are involved.[1]

In 1970, President Richard Nixon helped create Title X, a family planning program to be overseen by the Department of Health and Human Services (HHS). Specifically, the Office of Family Planning within HHS oversees the program. The Title X family planning program contains multiple goals related to reproductive health. Title X establishes goals, guidelines, and the primary funding source for these programs to be carried out by states in the form of categorical grants. In 1999, for example, the federal government provided $218 million for Title X family planning program projects. Essentially, the program attempts to service the needs of low-income women. Indeed, 85 percent of the recipients of Title X programs represent low-income women.

States usually subcontract with organizations such as Planned Parenthood to provide the services. Seventy-eight percent of Planned Parenthood clinics receive some Title X grant money. These clinics are spread through different regions of the United States. Services include comprehensive reproductive health services, abortion counseling, tests for sexually transmitted infections, reproductive cancer checkups and counseling, and sex education programs. Family planning issues, especially abortion, are hot-button issues to much of the public. Groups such as Planned Parenthood take much of the political heat for these issues.

During the Reagan administration, the regulations concerning pregnancy counseling by Planned Parenthood and other recipients of Title X funds were altered. No agency that received federal funds from Title X could provide abortion counseling. Opponents referred to this policy as the "gag rule," because agency staff and doctors were disallowed from mentioning abortion as an alternative to a pregnant woman.

As a result, Planned Parenthood, a reproduction rights proponent, joined other organizations in an unsuccessful lawsuit against the government's policy. Indeed, this gag rule continued until President Bill Clinton, in one of his first acts as president, repealed the regulation. Soon after, a newly elected Republican-dominated Congress tried to cut all funding to Title X programs. The controversy continues. Planned Parenthood agencies continue to receive Title X funds for policy implementation while Congress episodically is convulsed by efforts to eliminate those funds.

1. Robert Pear, "Reagan Bars Mention of Abortion at Clinics Receiving U.S. Money," *New York Times* (Jan. 30, 1988), sec. 1, p. 1; Tamar Lewin, "Groups Challenging Abortion Rules," *New York Times* (Feb. 2, 1988), p. A12; U.S. Department of Health and Human Services, Office of Population Affairs, FY1999 Budget: *http://www.hhs.gov/proorg/opa/titlex/ofp.html.*

TOP-DOWN VERSUS BOTTOM-UP APPROACHES TO PROBLEM SOLVING

One of the useful lessons of the federal government's response to the Great Depression is that there are circumstances in which a national response to policy problems is appropriate. One of the unfortunate lessons that many people took from this experience was that lower levels of government are ill-equipped to deal with policy problems. Reality is not so simple. There are benefits to a top-down policy approach, such as the federal government's New Deal programs in response to the Great Depression. And there are benefits to a bottom-up policy approach, as we will see below. The benefits and costs of each approach become clearer when considering three issues that policy analysts often confront: capacity to cope with crises, equity concerns, and policy efficiency. Below we will consider how the top-down and bottom-up approaches may be combined.

Capacity to Cope with Crises

One of the most common rationales for utilizing a top-down approach to policy problems is called upon when there is a widespread and immediate crisis. For example, in the Great Depression, the nation as a whole faced an immediate crisis that demanded an immediate response. The national government possesses the ability to act decisively to mobilize resources on a massive scale in response to a crisis. State and local governments are less able to do this. This is, in part, because state and local governments, due simply to their large numbers, find it difficult to coordinate their efforts with numerous other states and local jurisdictions. In a crisis, it is often difficult for large groups to choose a course of action and to implement a plan of attack. The national government, as a more or less unitary actor, does not face the same degree of coordination problems as do states and local governments.

Another advantage possessed by the national government in periods of national crisis is its ability to finance its activities by incurring deficits and running up a large national debt. Most state and local governments lack the authority to incur debt to finance their operating expenditures. The national government, though ultimately constrained by the forces of private credit markets, is not constitutionally prohibited from mobilizing tax revenues from current, as well as future, taxpayers. This gives it a decided advantage in responding to crises.

One of the factors implicit in the above paragraph is that there are some problems that have broad geographic coverage. That is, some problems are geographically large in scale. These include national economic recessions, air pollution, threats to national security, and the like. In such cases, it may make sense to employ a top-down approach to solving public problems. For instance, if air pollution is spilling out over large sections of the country, with particulates spewed from smokestacks in some states impairing air quality in other states, then the federal government may need to intervene to set acceptable air quality standards and establish monitoring procedures for all of the affected states.

Likewise, in the case of national security, a threat to one part of the country is potentially a threat to the whole country. Thus, the national government is properly the jurisdiction to devise strategies and mobilize people and resources to ward off such threats. In essence, the principle here is that the scale of the solution should approximate the scope of the problem. Problems that are geographically widespread require a response that encompasses the jurisdictions that underlie the affected areas. Often, though certainly not always, this is likely to be the national government. Below we explore ways in which a top-down response to widespread problems can be combined with bottom-up experimentation to find effective solutions.

Equity Concerns

One of the issues with which policy analysts often are asked to grapple is equity. This principle has two dimensions: horizontal and vertical. The aspect of equity known as **horizontal equity** holds that people in like circumstances should be treated alike. In this view, it is unfair, or inequitable, to treat two people differently who are the same in all relevant ways. Hence, for example, job discrimination against a black person who holds the same educational qualifications as a white person violates the norm of horizontal equity. The second aspect of equity, known as **vertical equity,** holds that persons should contribute to the betterment of society based on their ability to pay. In other words, people who are needy should be helped by people with greater incomes and wealth.

Horizontal equity is often used to justify a top-down policy action to equalize the treatment of people in different parts of the country. The idea is that a government that overlies local communities of different capabilities is in the best position to help equalize resources so that people will be treated equally, regardless of the particular place where they happen to live. For instance, an impoverished family who happens to live in Arkansas or Mississippi is probably far worse off than the same family who happens to reside in Connecticut, New York, or California. This is because Arkansas and Mississippi have a long history of providing paltry benefits to the poor, in part due to the relative poverty of the states as a whole; in contrast, Connecticut, New York, and California have a history of generous benefits to the poor, in part due to the relative wealth and economic robustness of these states. With a top-down approach, resources can be moved from jurisdictions where people are, on average, better off to be redistributed to jurisdictions where people are, on average, worse off, to bring about parity among people.

Vertical equity is used to justify trying to redistribute wealth and income to reduce the inequalities across economic classes. There are vast differences in the United States, and in many other countries, between households near the top of the economic ladder and households on the lower rungs. Taxing people with above-average incomes and providing those resources to people with below-average incomes is one way to try to reduce these inequalities.

Top-down policy approaches are often advocated as the best avenue for reducing these inequalities. The argument is that a particular local jurisdiction that tries to tax businesses and taxpayers of above-average income to provide benefits to low-income residents runs the risk of a retreat by businesses and high-income taxpayers to locations outside the local jurisdiction, along with the risk of an influx of needy people from less generous jurisdictions to the jurisdiction that has more generous services. The conclusion often drawn from these potential outflows of revenues and inflows of assistance to recipients is that local governments will be unwilling to attempt redistribution, and that this type of policy should properly be the responsibility of the highest level of government in a country. A top-down policy process is thus recommended to ensure that redistributive policies can be adopted to bring about greater vertical equity.

One of the key issues relating to bottom-up policymaking is its impact on equity. As discussed above, top-down approaches to policymaking are often advocated on the grounds that higher levels of government, such as the U.S. government, are best positioned to promote equity, especially the type of vertical equity that are created by redistributive policies. While there is merit in this argument, it overlooks the opportunities to engage in redistributive policies in a bottom-up policy environment. It is true that local governments and, to a lesser extent, states are constrained in their ability to pursue redistributive policies due to the possibilities for taxpayers of above-average income to react to increased tax burdens by fleeing the jurisdiction and for needy people to flock to the jurisdiction to consume generous assistance programs. But this is a constraint; it is not an insurmountable wall.

Local policymakers have a variety of means for supporting redistributive services. To assist needy households without increasing tax burdens, policymakers can provide seed moneys to, and help with, the fundraising activities of nonprofit organizations that provide services to the poor. Services rendered by nonprofit organizations are frequently encouraged and subsidized, if only in part, by local governments. Notice, however, that nonprofit organizations have a variety of funding sources, from government grants and contracts, to fundraising campaigns that elicit voluntary contributions from individuals and businesses, to grants from philanthropic foundations, to fees that recipients are charged to help defray the costs of services. These services have only a minimal impact, if any, on local tax burdens. Likewise, local governments themselves often solicit grants and contracts from private foundations, from the state, and from the federal government to help underwrite the costs of social services that help the poor. Another option often exercised by local governments is to enter into service arrangements for redistributive services, as well as a host of other programs, with other local governments or the state government to spread the tax burden to citizens across an area approximately the same size as the area in which most beneficiaries typically reside. In these ways and others, local communities utilize the bottom-up approach to public policymaking, even in policy areas that raise important equity issues.

Policy Efficiency

Another key concern of policy analysts is **efficiency.** Efficiency exists when resources are put to their best use. When beneficiaries of public programs are the same as the taxpayers paying for the programs or are closely tied to those taxpayers, it is possible for citizens of the jurisdiction to assess how important a policy issue is to them relative to the other issues that they want or need to address. When such decisions are far removed and when the tax revenues have been collected from people in disparate parts of the country, such tradeoffs are difficult to assess. In situations where the connection between those paying taxes for a program and the actual beneficiaries of the program is remote, it becomes tempting for policymakers to create programs that would not be supported if the beneficiaries of the program were required to pay for the program themselves.

In contrast, the closer the connection between recipients of a program and the level of government at which a program is formulated, the more likely that the program passed by policymakers will be supported by the taxpayers that must pay for it. In the case of policies that are made locally, the beneficiaries of a policy are co-located with the taxpayers who are required to fund it. Sometimes beneficiaries and taxpayers are the same people; other times they are in close proximity, such as schoolchildren are to parents and other local adults. Such proximity induces people to ask how important policies are—and then to agree to pay for them. Proximity encourages efficiency. This is a key reason why the bottom-up approach to public policymaking typically leads to more efficient uses of public moneys.

This advantage is directly related to the responsiveness of bottom-up policy solutions to local contingencies and priorities. The welfare problem in Alaska is far different than the one in New Jersey. Water policy in South Florida is different than it is in eastern Oregon. Air pollution is different in Los Angeles than in Dallas. The issue of teacher recruitment and certification is different in Minot, North Dakota, than in Madison, Wisconsin. A one-size-fits-all policy is unlikely to work well in each of these places, and it may not work at all in some of them. Policymakers at the state and local levels are much more familiar with the particular needs and circumstances of their communities. Moreover, they are more likely to be attuned to the priorities of citizens in their jurisdictions. In some cases, road building and basic infrastructure will be the predominant concerns; in others, expansion of cultural and artistic facilities may predominate; in still others, education and training of the work force may be the preeminent concerns.

While the top-down approach allows for a quick, uniform response to large-scale problems, notice that this kind of response can be a disadvantage on efficiency grounds. One of the advantages of a bottom-up approach is that it ensures innovation and experimentation. Public problems are often hard to solve. There is no guarantee that the first policy proposal that can win approval at the national level is the best, or even a good, solution to a problem. Having a multitude of state and local communities trying to solve a problem means that some of them are likely to try something that actually works.

CONCLUSION

One of the strengths of the American political system is that it permits us to avoid the choice of having to rely solely on either the bottom-up or the top-down approach in all circumstances. What is the best approach for moving welfare recipients into economic self-sufficiency? What is the best approach for retraining blue-collar industrial workers for Information Age jobs? What is the best approach for keeping children off drugs and in school? What is the best approach for training and certifying teachers? What is the best approach for reducing landfill usage? What is the best approach for increasing literacy among newly arrived immigrants? Fortunately, the polycentrism of the American political system allows us to fashion policy solutions to these and other issues that draw on both the top-down and bottom-up approaches to policy design.

As discussed in Chapter 5, one of the great strengths of polycentrism is that it allows the structure of governance to be "sized" to the scale of particular public problems. Part of what this means is that in a polycentric structure of governance, problems can be broken into multiple pieces so that each one can be addressed separately. The top-down approach might be used for issues relating to the financing of a policy activity, while the bottom-up approach might be used for the provision and implementation of the activity. In this way, polycentrism offers a governance structure that permits a top-down solution to vertical equity concerns while encouraging the innovation and efficiency gains that accrue from a bottom-up approach.

In the following chapters, we discuss in greater detail how the polycentric governance structure helps resolve persistent quandaries in public policy. We discuss the policy tools available for policy action, methods of policy analysis, and the role of bureaucracies in implementing public policies—all in the context of the American political order founded on a polycentric structure of governance.

Key Terms

New Deal *p. 142*
alphabet agencies *p. 142*
layer cake federalism *p. 142*
Jim Crow laws *p. 145*
picket fence federalism *p. 146*
unfunded mandates *p. 148*
positive inducement *p. 149*
fiscal instrument *p. 149*

tax incentive *p. 151*
tax expenditure *p. 151*
negative sanction *p. 152*
policing *p. 153*
independent sector *p. 155*
horizontal equity *p. 159*
vertical equity *p. 159*
efficiency *p. 161*

Suggested Readings

Derthick, Martha. 1971. *The Influence of Federal Grants*. Cambridge, Mass.: Harvard University Press.

Derthick, Martha, ed. 1999. *Dilemmas of Scale in America's Federal Democracy*. Cambridge, England: Cambridge University Press.

Hughes, Jonathon. 1977. *The Governmental Habit: Economic Controls from Colonial Times to the Present*. New York: Basic Books.

Katz, Michael B. 1997. *In the Shadow of the Poorhouse: A Social History of Welfare in America*. 10th anniv. ed. New York: Basic Books.

Lowi, Theodore J. 1979. *The End of Liberalism: The Second Republic of the United States*. 2nd ed. New York: W. W. Norton.

Ostrom, Vincent. 1984. *The Political Theory of a Compound Republic: Designing the American Experiment*. 2nd rev. ed. Oakland, Calif.: ICS Press.

Patterson, James T. 1995. *America's Struggle Against Poverty, 1900–1994*. Cambridge, Mass.: Harvard University Press.

Skocpol, Theda. 1992. *Protecting Soldiers and Mothers: The Political Origins of Social Policy in the United States*. Cambridge, Mass.: Harvard University Press.

Skowronek, Stephen. 1982. *Building a New American State: The Expansion of National Administrative Capacities, 1877–1920*. Cambridge, England: Cambridge University Press.

Smith, Steven Rathgeb, and Michael Lipsky. 1995. *Nonprofits for Hire: The Welfare State in the Age of Contracting*. Cambridge, Mass.: Harvard University Press.

Stein, Robert M. 1990. *Urban Alternatives: Public and Private Markets in the Provision of Local Services*. Pittsburgh: University of Pittsburgh Press.

Trattner, Walter I. 1994. *From Poor Law to Welfare State: A History of Social Welfare in America*. 5th ed. New York: Free Press.

Notes

1. One of the best treatments of state and federal efforts to develop social policies in the period before the New Deal is that of Theda Skocpol, *Protecting Soldiers and*

Mothers: The Political Origins of Social Policy in the United States (Cambridge, Mass.: Harvard University Press, 1992).

2. The source for the following figures on the numbers of governments in the United States and the tasks performed by government employees is U.S. Department of Commerce, Bureau of the Census, *Census of Governments* (Washington, D.C.: U.S. Government Printing Office, 1997), and the Web site at *www.census.gov.*

3. For comparative purposes, all revenue figures in this paragraph are in constant (1987) dollars.

9

Politics and Policy Choice

INTRODUCTION

As we saw in the previous chapter, the American political system is comprised of thousands of governments of varying sizes and policy responsibilities. This complexity contributes to the richness of policy experimentation and innovation in the United States. It also can be confusing, as different governments, sometimes in close proximity and sometimes separated by great distances, approach policy problems in different ways. As we have tried to show in earlier chapters and will show in later chapters, this is one of the strengths of the American political system, not a weakness. It gives citizens options about the sorts of policy goods and services that they can consume. And it affords policy learning inasmuch as policymakers are able to utilize the experiences of others in designing and reforming policies for their own jurisdiction. Yet this complexity of governance in the United States means that there is a seemingly bewildering array of policies from which public officials may choose in trying to find solutions to problems.

Another implication of this complexity is that the politics of policymaking can vary enormously from one jurisdiction to another. In some places, there may be well-organized agricultural and business groups; in others, unions may exercise a great deal of voice in the determination of policies; in still other places, environmental activists and human rights advocates may play particularly important roles in the policy process; and in some places, all these groups and others may play important roles. Indeed, looking at the country as a whole, there may appear to be an almost infinite set of potential alliances, short-term tactical moves, self-interested calculations, claims and counterclaims of interest groups, and posturing by politicians busily seeking reelection. The richness and fertility of all this political activity contribute to the complexity of governance in the United States. One of the goals of this chapter is to show that beneath the surface in politics, there is some predictability in the behavior of the people who are involved in policymaking, as well as in the kinds of policies that are debated and adopted.

In this chapter, we describe some of the patterns in the political process and how these patterns affect policymaking. We present several ways of categorizing policies, each of which is intended to highlight important aspects of the relationship between policies and politics that might otherwise escape attention. One way of categorizing policies is through **typologies** (classification schemes) that help differentiate the types of policies that are available to address different kinds of problems. These typologies help us understand the links between the kinds of political forces that often exist in policymaking and the policies that ultimately are selected for implementation. Typologies are useful because they allow us to group complex phenomena into a smaller set of categories that share characteristics, and in so doing permit us to generalize about relationships. Typologies are useful only as long as they allow us to see patterns that might otherwise go unnoticed. Thus, having more than one way to group policies and politics for inspection often reveals more than would be possible with a single typology.

POLICY BENEFITS AND COSTS: THE LOWI TYPOLOGY

The political scientist Theodore Lowi, in a seminal article in 1964, saw a connection between types of political conflicts and the policies that were at stake in the conflicts.[1] While Lowi refined his basic typology over time, the essentials of his scheme are still as useful today as they were over a generation ago. What Lowi showed was how the characteristics of policies are often related to distinctively different types of political struggles. He argued that policy characteristics beget politics.

Lowi's thesis was that to understand the direction that political conflicts take, it is useful first to differentiate policy proposals on the basis of who is likely to benefit and who is likely to bear the costs of a policy. He devised a typology that distinguished policies based upon whether the benefits were narrowly concentrated or broadly distributed and whether the costs were narrowly targeted or widely disbursed. A variant of this typology is shown in Table 9.1.

Lowi described policies whose benefits are concentrated and whose costs are also concentrated as **regulatory policies.** Examples of such policy issues include the regulatory disputes over the stock brokerage services and insurance benefits that banking institutions can offer, charges that electric utilities must pay to maintain excess capacity in the event of power outages elsewhere in the

TABLE 9.1 Lowi Typology

		Costs	
		Narrowly Concentrated	**Broadly Distributed**
Benefits	**Narrowly Concentrated**	Regulatory policies	Distributive policies
	Broadly Distributed	Constitutive policies	Redistributive policies

electricity system, disputes over the access charges that telephone carriers can charge for computer services, and so forth. These are issues in which large businesses on both sides have huge amounts of money at stake. These kinds of policies, Lowi argues, produce political conflicts involving well-organized and mobilized interest groups on both sides of the issue. Each side is willing and able to stay politically involved, pouring mounds of money into the campaign coffers of politicians and hiring legions of well-connected lobbyists in hopes of winning favorable outcomes, both in the legislature and later in the administrative processes of regulatory agencies. Only occasionally does this type of conflict attract intense public attention or get caught up in presidential election campaigns. By and large, these are battles that animate large businesses and well-organized interest groups.

Consider, by contrast, the policy struggles that lie at the other end of the diagonal on this typology, where both benefits and costs are broadly distributed. In this cell are **redistributive policy** conflicts, which Lowi argues often rise to the highest plateaus of the political process, involving political parties, presidents and presidential candidates, and intense public opinion. These battles involve transfers of wealth, income, rights, or privileges from one large class of people to another large class of people. Examples of such battles include such things as Social Security reform, proposals for universal access to publicly funded health care, and even proposals to extend or curtail affirmative action. A classic example of this type of political conflict is found in Box 9.1, which recounts the efforts during the Reagan administration to create a new program for the elderly for which the elderly themselves would have to pay the costs.

Political fights that emerge around redistributive policies involve issues that virtually everyone can understand. More important, virtually everyone knows whether they stand to benefit or bear the burdens of these types of policy initiatives. Consequently, these issues become potent tools for the political parties to define themselves in opposition to one another, rally supporters, and get peo-

Box 9.1   *Medicare and the Elderly*[1]

President Ronald Reagan came to office in 1981 promising to cut government spending. This concept attracted general support, but opinions often changed when specific spending programs were targeted. One such example was Reagan's attempt to reduce Medicare costs. Medicare provides health benefits to people over age sixty-five; it was then, and continues to be, one of the largest and fastest-growing programs of the federal government. Medicare is a redistributive program funded through taxes paid by working-age Americans. Both Reagan's cost-cutting plan and the way his administration attempted to implement it unnerved many elderly Americans and galvanized them into a powerful political force.

Reagan's proposed Medicare cuts included numerous requirements. First, the plan called for people who were over sixty-five years old and working to remain privately insured until retirement. Second, recipients would have to wait until the first full month after they became eligible to receive coverage. Thus, a person who turned sixty-five in early November could not collect until December. Third, every charge would be rounded down to the closest dollar rather than rounded up after $.51. Fourth, the plan was to increase the premiums paid by Medicare recipients. Fifth, the administration proposed a reduction in the costs of long-term care, including a requirement for payments for nursing home care, institutionalization, or both.

While each of these provisions struck some seniors as controversial, the fifth provision became the most controversial. The controversy over Reagan's cost-cutting measures concerning Medicare came to a head at the 1981 Conference on Aging in Washington, D.C. Just as the administration's plans became public, the conference met to cover current affairs and policies affecting seniors. Many felt that Reagan tried to rubber stamp his plans by packing the policy recommendation committees at the conference with sympathetic Republican supporters. This added to the intense debate concerning the impact of

ple to the polls to vote. Presidents and presidential candidates use these issues to raise campaign funds and build coalitions of interest groups and voters. In short, these issues become defining or cleavage issues that voters use to align themselves with parties and candidates and on which national elections often turn.

A more seemingly innocuous category of policy proposals falls in the cell where benefits are concentrated and costs are diffuse. These are often called distributive policy proposals, and they are associated with a relative absence of the sort of conflict and strife that news media typically report. The reason is simple. With diffuse costs, there are few incentives for the people who bear the burdens of these policies to organize or mobilize in opposition. Most of the time, these policy proposals go almost completely unnoticed by those who pay the costs. On the other side, however, those people who stand to benefit from these policies have strong incentives to work hard to get the proposals passed, due to the concentrated nature of benefits. Such policy proposals include local such policy changes on the elderly. In the end, Reagan lost support at the conference. The conference's report did support increased home health care programs, but it did so by requesting increased spending rather than reduced spending in Medicare.

This marked an important turn for the political mobilization of senior citizens and public policy concerning their specific concerns. Indeed, the *New York Times* joked that the senior movement had realized a "coming of age." This political force would become so powerful that later in the 1980s, Congress was forced to rescind legislation it had previously passed that provided catastrophic care for senior citizens. This catastrophic care measure had been promoted by the American Association of Retired Persons, the largest senior citizen interest group. But it was to be funded by levying a fee on Medicare recipients rather than through taxes paid by working-age citizens, as was the rest of the Medicare program. Senior citizens responded negatively to the requirement that they pay for this measure. The protests turned into a torrent, and even verged on violence. The protests were so intense that the chair of the House Ways and Means Committee, Dan Rostenkowski (Democrat, Illinois), had his car surrounded by a jeering mob of upset elderly constituents.

In short, as a result of the elderly population's increasing size and growing attentiveness to issues, it has become a powerful force in American politics. The elderly population has become an organized constituency group, able to mobilize to protect benefits and to defend against costs that might be imposed on the elderly.

1. Warren Weaver, "Coming of Age," *New York Times* (Dec. 6, 1981), sec. 4, p. 1; Warren Weaver, "White House Aging Parley Adopts Agenda for Decade," *New York Times* (Dec. 4, 1981), p. A18; Robert Pear, "Reagan Aides Map Proposals to Cut Health Care Costs," *New York Times* (Nov. 8, 1981), sec. 1, p. 1; "Mr. Schweiker's Proposals," *Washington Post* (Nov. 10, 1981), p. A18; Cass Peterson and Keith Richburg, "Home-Care Rules Issued," *Washington Post* (March 13, 1985), p. A21; Spencer Rich, "Schweiker Targets Welfare, Medical Plans for '83 Cuts," *Washington Post* (Nov. 9, 1981), p. A1; "The Reckless War on Health Costs," *New York Times* (Nov. 23, 1981), p. A26.

highway projects, harbor and waterway improvements, park facilities, and new courthouses and post offices. These projects provide tangible benefits to the workers, managers, and stockholders of the engineering and construction companies employed to build them; they also provide tangible benefits to local citizens. The problem with distributive projects, as we discuss in other parts of this textbook, is that in a representative democracy such as we have in the United States, where costs are borne by people in every legislative district, there are few impediments to the passage of far more of these projects than would be the case if local beneficiaries were required to pay the costs of building and operating the projects. As a consequence, distributive projects result in a strong tendency toward inefficiencies in how tax moneys are used.

At the other end of the diagonal from distributive policies are proposals that Lowi describes as **constitutive policies** that have diffuse benefits but concentrated costs. The kinds of political conflicts associated with these kinds of proposals have never been as fully developed by Lowi as the politics in the other categories. What he refers to as constitutive proposals are policies that establish broad-based rules by which society as a whole is to operate but that may impose high costs on violators of the rules. Examples of constitutive policies run the gamut of criminal, civil, and constitutional laws, including everything from arson to road rage, bankruptcy to zoning exemptions, and congressional apportionment to presidential impeachment.

Another political scientist, James Q. Wilson, offers a useful way to understand the politics associated with proposals with diffuse benefits but concentrated costs—Lowi's category of constitutive policy proposals.[2] Wilson argues that these proposals result from **entrepreneurial politics.** He uses the term entrepreneurial because the advocacy of a proposal with diffuse benefits requires someone who is willing to invest much of his or her own time, energy, and resources in the issue, much like a visionary businessperson who sees the potential for a new product or industry. Those who stand to lose from passage of this type of proposal may aggressively defend the status quo, trying to stall, delay, and obfuscate in order to wear the policy entrepreneur down and cause the issue to go away. Wilson sees this type of policy proposal occurring frequently in the area of environmental regulation, where benefits such as cleaner air, purer water, and unlittered seashores accrue to the public in general. Costs of these policies often fall heavily on automobile makers, utility companies, manufacturers, bottlers, and packagers. Passage of these environmental rules have often been associated with the hard work and long commitment of small numbers of impassioned policy advocates.

GOVERNMENT COERCION

One of the features of Lowi's policy typology is the distinction between those people who receive the benefits of policies and those people who must bear the costs. This distinction points toward a useful way of understanding the range of choices available to policymakers when designing policies. There is often a difference between the group of people or organizations that are directly subject to the application of government authority under a policy and the group of people or organizations that are the **target public of a policy.**

Indeed, most government policies differentiate between the people or organizations subject to official sanctions and the public that is intended to benefit from the policies. This is part of what makes policies—as well as the politics that gives rise to those policies—so complex. The exercise of government authority, which we have described in earlier chapters as the coercive power of governments, is often used to get one group to engage in actions that will result in a change in behavior or that will alter the welfare of another group of people or organizations.

Consider how much room this creates for policymakers to address problems while avoiding the imposition of costs on well-organized groups. By putting the burdens of complying with policy requirements on small, unpopular, or weakly organized groups, government coercion can be applied with less difficulty than would be the case if the coercion were to be applied to large, popular, or highly mobilized groups. At the same time, the target public of a policy can be advantaged by the change in behavior of the group to whom the coercion was actually applied.

Both the set of people directly subject to the application of government authority and the target public of a policy can be narrowly or broadly cast. Consider the following example. In every U.S. state, there is a policy that requires children below a specified age (typically fourteen) to be enrolled in a program of education. These policies, known as compulsory school attendance laws, are intended to benefit children. The target public is children. Notice that state and local governments enforce the policies by levying penalties on parents or legal guardians who fail to ensure that their children are in school (or officially enrolled in a home schooling alternative). In this policy, parents are the group that is subject to government authority.

Consider another example. The U.S. Food and Drug Administration requires that all processed food products carry labels that list each product's ingredients; the amount of fat, starch, and protein; and the percentage of the minimum daily nutritional requirements provided by the food product. The target public of the policy is consumers who rely on purchases of food products to eat and stay healthy. Consumers do not have to pass a test demonstrating their knowledge of different kinds of additives and ingredients. They are not even required to read the information displayed on food product labels. Grocery retailers and food producers, however, are subject to government coercion under this policy. Manufacturers and retailers that neglect to label food products properly are subject to fines and other penalties. Consumers benefit from the labeling requirements only if they choose voluntarily to take advantage of the information that manufacturers and retailers of food products are required by law to provide.

Sometimes the target public of a policy can be difficult to organize. This is particularly true when the target public is not a well-defined or well-organized group. Examples of policies without well-defined target publics sometimes include policies dealing with infrastructure construction for such things as new roads, bridges, runways, and harbors. Clearly, these policies confer direct benefits on the businesses that win contracts to build the projects, on the companies that supply materials used in the construction process, and on the workers who receive wages for working on the projects. These companies and workers are the entities that are subject to the application of government authority. By contracting with the government to build infrastructure projects, these groups obligate themselves to fulfill the terms of contracts that they make with the government as part of the construction process. Failure to fulfill their contractual obligations puts them at risk of a variety of penalties ranging from a slap on the wrist to draconian fines and forfeitures. Yet building contractors and their workers are not the target public of infrastructure projects. In a literal sense, they are the instruments of the government. The target public is typically those households and businesses that benefit from the increased efficiencies resulting from improvements in the infrastructure in an area. By decreasing the costs of transporting goods, improved infrastructure decreases the overall costs of goods. Thus, businesses may be able to reduce the prices they charge for their products and increase production, thereby permitting them to hire more workers and pay more taxes into local government coffers. Hence these projects, when successful, confer benefits on a broad, but not well-defined, target public.

Notice that it is possible for the group to which government authority is applied to be extremely small in number, but for the policy to have an impact on a large segment of the economy and society. For example, state and federal policies that dictate safety standards and fuel economy requirements to automobile manufacturers apply to no more than a dozen or so companies, but they have an impact on virtually everyone in the United States.

Likewise, since the mid-1990s, the U.S. government has required that all toilets sold in the country use no more than 1.6 gallons of water per flush. The history of this policy is odd, at best. The primary motivation behind this policy was apparently the need to find ways of reducing water usage in California due to chronic water shortages in that state. To head off toilet standards that would apply only in California, makers of plumbing fixtures, in an alliance with environmental groups, succeeded in having the low-flush toilet requirement written into federal law. These companies thereby managed to obtain uniform standards for the design and manufacture of their products, as well as to dry up the market in used plumbing fixtures. This law is of direct application to the score or two of companies that make toilets, and by extension to the plumbing companies that install plumbing fixtures. But the target public for this policy is enormous; it involves every person who buys or moves into a house or apartment built since the mid-1990s or has the need for a public restroom at a commercial establishment built since the date when the law became effective.

In sum, this distinction between the people who are directly subject to the application of government authority under a policy and the group of people or organizations that are the target public of the policy creates a wide array of choices about how policies can be designed to accommodate political pressures and demands.

POLITICAL ADVOCACY AND POLICY CHOICE

Recall that one of the key arguments of Lowi in devising his original policy typology was that policies beget politics. He argued that the configuration of benefits and costs or advantages and impositions produces the kinds of political conflicts that typically arise around policy proposals. Later, Lowi amended this simple precept by arguing that politics has an independent effect on policy proposals. He argued that how policies are advocated—that is, the language in which policy demands are cast—can lead in two very different directions with respect to the types of policies that receive consideration in the policymaking process.[3]

This thesis is based on the observation that the politics of advocating policy change is sometimes cast in terms of **absolute moral imperatives** and other times in terms of consequences. Absolute moral imperatives are principles of right and wrong and spring from ethical, religious, or moral standards. When political advocacy is cast in moral absolutes, arguments about change become equated with claims about principles and moral polarities; compromise becomes unacceptable; political conflict becomes a cause, perhaps even a crusade; and only radical transformation of underlying causes is admissible. By contrast, when political advocacy is cast in terms of **consequentialist arguments,** there is a tendency to seek measures that attenuate undesirable side-effects of behaviors. Building consensus becomes a key goal; politically workable compromise becomes the desired product; and incremental movement becomes the norm.

This divergence in the political terms used by advocates of policy change has a direct effect on the kinds of policy measures that are likely to be debated and adopted. Political advocacy cast in moral imperatives tends to push policymakers to consider policy proposals with more government intervention into private affairs and greater coerciveness. Policies advocated in terms of moral imperatives tend to be cast in criminal or penal terms, with stiff punishments meted out for transgressions of rules. The reason is simple: if the goal of a policy is to address root causes, it must punish evilness, not just reduce the undesired consequences of otherwise legal activity. Politics cast in consequentialist terms, by contrast, tend to encourage policymakers to adopt government policies with less intrusiveness into private activities and as little coerciveness as necessary to reduce negative consequences. This is because the goal, when focusing on consequences, is to find politically acceptable measures that help reduce the negative effects of behaviors rather than to try to eliminate the behaviors altogether.

These two fundamentally different approaches to political advocacy lead to the selection of policies with very different degrees of coerciveness. Policies involving less coerciveness are selected when political advocacy emphasizes the alleviation of consequences. Policies lying at the higher end of government coerciveness are advocated when the politics of the issue emphasizes moral imperatives.

TYPOLOGY OF POLICIES BASED ON COERCIVENESS

Looking at the degree of government coercion that is needed to achieve desired public goals is an important way to understand differences in policies. Policymakers always have a range of choices with regard to how coercive the application of government power will be when they are designing public policies. As we saw in the previous section, this choice involves not merely how best to achieve a desired objective. It is often a function of how the politics of the issue have been cast. That is to say, the kind and amount of official coercion can be as much the product of a desire to advance absolute moral imperatives as the result of a cold calculation of the precise ratio of benefits to costs necessary to achieve a particular end. Hence the policy typology presented in Table 9.2 involves both inherent differences in the coercion involved in different types of policies and the political logic that gives rise to those policies.

At the least coercive end of the continuum in Table 9.2 are **hortatory appeals,** which are essentially pleas or supplications by public officials to the general public to engage voluntarily in some sort of desirable behavior, such as recycling, not talking on cell phones while driving, or using headlights when traveling during busy holidays. Individuals are free to comply or not, as they desire. There are no penalties for failure to conform behavior to the hortatory appeal, other than the occasional twang of guilt that may result from peer pressure or an overbearing grandparent. Hortatory appeals are almost always means to promote desirable consequences. Political advocacy cast in moral absolutes typically combines hortatory appeals with calls for coercive measures, because appeals to civic duty or conscience, by themselves, are often viewed as having little power to transform underlying causes.

Somewhat more coercive, but still only modestly so, is **provision of information.** This type of policy entails such things as labeling requirements on foods, beverages, and medicines; full disclosure laws in commercial transactions; standardized weights and standards for products; and the like. Some coercion is involved, because manufacturers and packagers are required to comply with rules about what kinds of information they must provide and in what manner. Failure to follow these rules often involves modest fines. By and large, however, information provision rules of some sort are welcomed by responsible businesses that are interested in staying in business over the long run, because they permit potential customers to evaluate their products and encourage repeat purchases. From the point of view of consumers, and of citizens more generally, provision of information is almost always beneficial. If individuals want to ignore information, they can do so. The only penalty for ignoring information is that a person may make a bad decision that could have

TABLE 9.2 Policies, by Level of Government Coercion

Level of Government Coercion	Type of Government Policy	Examples
Noncoercive ↑	Hortatory appeals	"Seat belt" campaigns, U.S. government war bond drives during World War II, voluntary garbage recycling campaigns
	Information provision	Labeling requirements on food, beverages, and over-the-counter medicines; full disclosure laws in real estate transactions; standardized weights and standards for most products
	Positive inducements	Tax preferences (e.g., mortgage interest deductions and retirement accounts), grants (e.g., medical research, scientific investigations, and the arts), payments for agricultural land set-asides
	Government insurance	U.S. flood insurance program, crop insurance, unemployment insurance, workers' compensation (for workplace injuries), deposit insurance at banks and savings and loans
	Public goods	Air quality containment zones over urban areas, watershed protection districts, noise controls in national parks, harvest restrictions for hunters and fishers, childhood immunization requirements
↓ **Highly Coercive**	Negative sanctions	Criminal laws prohibiting murder, assault, robbery, theft, etc.; regulatory rules prohibiting predatory pricing, deceptive advertising, or selling tainted food or medical products; military rules prohibiting insubordination, absence without leave, or fraternization

been avoided. For people who are interested in making decisions that maximize their preferences, policies that require provision of information permit freely made, informed decisions. Information provision is a policy that tends to be associated with political arguments about consequences rather than moral imperatives. Information allows people to make better decisions; it doesn't force people to act in prescribed ways.

Box 9.2   Pell Grants for College Students

Nearly every college and university in the country has a seal that includes rays of light in the background or an old-fashioned oil lamp in the foreground. These symbols represent the intellectual period called the Enlightenment, in which reason became the basis upon which humans would relate to their surroundings. Colleges and universities have borrowed that image because they share the same goals: to allow reason to govern human action, intellectual philosophy to govern human relations, and scientific discovery to govern how we deal with our environment. These goals help explain why the U.S. government has established grant programs to help underwrite the educational costs of college students.[1]

Two fundamental reasons explain why a government would make education a primary public policy goal. First, citizens who are informed about economics, law, politics, and science better understand how society works. Education helps integrate or socialize people to become good democratic citizens. Second, society relies on productive citizens. An educated citizenry produces economic and social development. Helping students pay for college helps realize these goals.

The first major grant program was the **G.I. Bill** passed in 1944. The government feared that the multitude of returning soldiers would be too much for the economy to handle; there were not enough jobs to go around to support all of the returning soldiers. The G.I. Bill aimed to provide soldiers with new skills that would be needed in a postwar economy while keeping them from flooding the work force.

The second major grant program, the National Defense Education Act passed in 1959, was a result of the new role of the United States as a superpower. The launch of Sputnik by the Soviet Union in 1957, the first satellite ever to be put into orbit, created a panic in the United States so great that the U.S. government sought to obtain rapid advancements in scientific knowledge.

Positive inducements are used to promote worthy activities, which they do by inducing voluntary participation. These policies offer a financial reward, such as a grant payment or tax relief, to encourage a person to voluntarily engage in a desired behavior. Examples include tax preferences for things such as mortgage interest deductions, college savings, and individual retirement accounts; discretionary grants for medical research, scientific investigations, and promotion of the arts and humanities; and payments for agricultural land set-asides and dairy herd buyouts. Often the underlying motivation for these kinds of policies is the **positive externalities** that accrue to the rest of society if these activities are promoted.

For example, research grants do not involve merely advancing the academic careers of scientists. These grants, it is hoped, will lead to advances that benefit all of us, through improved scientific knowledge, medical discoveries, new technologies, and the like. Or consider the subsidy to home buyers via the mortgage interest deduction. This subsidy typically is justified on the grounds not just that

The third major grant program came in 1965 with the Higher Education Act. The Great Society programs of President Lyndon Johnson were designed to eliminate poverty. One important means for doing so would be to provide low-income people access to higher education. The idea was that assisting poor and minority students would help stamp out poverty.

The fourth major grant program was the Pell grant program, introduced in 1972. For the first time, the goal of the grant did not center on specific societal problems. Rather, the primary goal of the Pell grant was to increase access to higher education. There was no subtext; access itself became the primary motivation. The Pell grant program provided access to college for many low-income students who had never been unable to attend college. Pell grants provided about 78 percent of the cost of attending college in the mid-70s. That high percentage has dropped off somewhat, but 4 million students currently receive Pell grants. The amount a student and family can provide toward education determines the amount of the award along a sliding scale. Because the Pell grant reaches so many segments of society, it has often been referred to as the "universal G.I. Bill." Because its primary goal stands as universal access, the Pell grant moves beyond the somewhat narrower focus of earlier grants in refocusing attention on education's civic goals. Indeed, there has been an increasing movement toward helping all students gain access to higher education, even if they are not necessarily economically strapped. Direct loans from the federal government decrease the interest rate of repayment; tax credits for education costs also improve access to college.

1. James Perley and Mary Burgan, "Reauthorizing of the Higher Education Act," *American Association of University Professors* (Dec. 17, 1996), available at *http://www.igc.apc.org/aaup/reauthor.htm*; Institute for Higher Education Policy, "State of Diffusion," working paper prepared for the New Millennium Project on Higher Education Costs, Pricing and Productivity, August 1999; Jane Wellman, "Contributing to the Civic Good," working paper prepared for the New Millennium Project on Higher Education Costs, Pricing and Productivity, August 1999.

it helps home purchasers but that it stimulates a host of ancillary businesses, including the construction, plumbing, heating and cooling, and electrical trades; the manufacturing and distribution of household appliances and home furnishings; the lawn care industry; banking and insurance; and a host of other trades. As discussed in Box 9.2, this rationale is also often used to justify **Pell grants** and student loans, federal programs about which you may have close familiarity.

Participation in positive inducement policies is voluntary. A scientist can turn down the offer of a grant; a home buyer can choose to forgo the home mortgage deduction. It is important to add, however, that once individuals choose to participate, they are usually obligated to comply with certain conditions. These might include the submission of research reports or the filing of financial returns. Such conditions, however, are usually not onerous. The amount of government coercion is typically quite limited. Even in the event of failure to comply, the penalties are often little more than repayment of the original financial incentive.

The voluntary attribute of these policies and the relative absence of coercion implies that these types of measures are usually advocated because they produce desirable consequences. There is little in the way of an underlying moral imperative to these policies. They are promoted because they are useful and they are very popular.

Government insurance, sometimes known as **socialization of risk,** is similar to positive inducements in many respects. Government insurance involves some coercion, if not a great deal, and like positive inducements, it contains very strong elements of voluntary participation. These policies include such things as the federal flood insurance program, crop insurance, unemployment insurance, workers' compensation for workplace injuries, and deposit insurance at banks and savings and loans. These policies protect people from the financial misfortunes that can accompany bad luck or acts of God. Thus, these policies encourage people or businesses to engage in activities in which they might otherwise not engage for fear of financial ruin. When the activities are things like the production of the nation's food supply or participation in the nation's financial system, such policies serve useful public purposes. There is often a measure of coercion involved, because in return for protecting people or businesses from the risk of financial ruin, the government requires that certain standards of appropriate performance be maintained. Sometimes the penalties for failure to abide by appropriate standards can be fairly severe, including even criminal penalties. Also, the government typically requires that the recipients of the insurance put at risk some of their own resources in the event of a loss.

Without these provisions, insured persons would have nothing to lose by intentionally engaging in activities that were excessively risky. In effect, government insurance would reward irresponsible behavior and immoderate risk taking. This condition, which we encountered in an earlier chapter, is called moral hazard; it results when people engage in the very activities against which the insurance policy is designed to protect. It also means that people trying to play by the rules and accepting only appropriate levels of risk end up being required to pay the costs of insuring those who are irresponsible.

Government policies can be advocated because they mitigate undesirable consequences or because they advance moral imperatives. The latter argument is sometimes made for these policies because they can be used to promote goals that are widely viewed as morally good. The treatment of miscreants can show whether the argument is presented on moral grounds: if those who are found to abuse government insurance are subjected to harsh criminal penalties rather than monetary fines or forfeitures, it is a sure sign that they are being adjudged for sinfulness rather than error or misjudgment.

Public goods entail more government coercion than the previous types of policies. Public goods, as we saw earlier in the book, are things that, if provided to one person, are necessarily provided to everyone else, at least within a particular geographic area. The idea that public goods contain a substantial amount of coercion may strike some people as strange at first. But consider this: when government authority is used to produce a public good, then everyone, regardless of particular preferences, will receive the good. Public goods, in this sense, are not voluntary. For example, think for a moment about what happens when the government pursues policies that specify the volume of different types of pollutants that can be released into the air. Such regulations are designed to achieve a particular level of air cleanliness, which is a public good. Everyone breathes the air, including those people who would have preferred to breathe air containing fewer pollutants than the amounts permitted by the government.

Public goods take many forms, including air quality containment zones over urban areas, watershed protection districts, noise controls in national parks, harvest restrictions for hunters and fishers, and childhood immunization requirements. In all these cases, there is a prior political determination that a particular level of public goods is needed or will be permitted. Coercion is used to ensure its provision, both by requiring the payment of taxes that will be used to provide the public good and by inducing a change in behavior to actually produce the public good. Creating a public good such as a clean air containment zone over a metropolitan area may require that all automobile owners be compelled to purchase costly emission technologies and have their automobiles regularly tested. To ensure that this happens, the government may impose penalties ranging from fines to imprisonment for failure to comply or outright cheating. Creating a public good may mean compelling all parents of young children to have their children vaccinated against certain diseases. The public good is that society, as a whole, can be freed of diseases. But this works only if every family is successfully compelled to take its children to clinics or doctors for immunizations.

While it is possible to advocate public goods simply on the basis of the positive consequences that they provide, they often become the focal point of moral crusades. Clean air, pure water, undisturbed national forests, disease-free children—these are the sorts of things about which people develop strong emotional feelings. As a consequence, it is not uncommon to see advocacy groups utilizing the language of absolute moral imperatives with regard to these policies. These proposals tend to animate parties and candidates to affect the outcomes of national elections. Hence it is not uncommon to see politicians and policymakers use proposals for these policies to align themselves with mass sentiments and to mobilize voters.

The final category of policies is comprised of negative sanctions. These policies involve a very high degree of government coercion. Examples of negative sanctions include criminal laws against murder, assault, robbery, and theft; regulatory rules against deceptive advertising or selling tainted food and medical products; and military rules against insubordination, absence without leave, fraternization, and the like. These policies seek to regulate conduct and to prohibit undesirable behaviors. Violations of negative sanctions invite severe penalties. Long prison sentences are common. Indeed, the extent of government coercion in some instances, such as murder, can involve capital punishment.

In 1989, the Chinese government put down the uprising at Tiananmen Square with military force. *AP/Wide World Photos.*

The politics surrounding negative sanctions is frequently cast in terms of moral imperatives. This is not to say, however, that policy advocates do not engage in arguments about negative sanctions in terms of reducing undesirable consequences. Especially among professional policy analysts, consequentialist arguments about negative sanctions are quite common. In fact, studies about incarceration and different types of criminal sanctions are typically cast in terms of how to most effectively reduce the recidivism rate (that is, the rate that former felons commit additional crimes) or other behavioral measures.

Nevertheless, the pattern among the general public and most politicians is for discussions of these policies to be cast in moral language. These policies are typically established not merely because society works better (that is, has better consequences) when people abide by these rules but because some behaviors are viewed as being simply wrong—as morally reprehensible. This is one reason why advocates of policy change who cast their arguments in moral absolutes so frequently call for the criminalization of behaviors. This is a way of drawing the proverbial line in the sand. It is a way of saying that a behavior is wrong in an absolute sense—that a behavior is akin to sinfulness, not just an unfortunate error that had a negative impact on others in society.

CONCLUSION

In this chapter, we have looked at several ways of understanding differences in public policies. Your goal is to better understand the complexities that underlie policies. One way to do this is to see how the costs and benefits of policies are distributed and ask what impact this has on the politics that surround policy proposals. In looking at the differences in public policies, it becomes apparent that policymakers have a great deal of maneuvering room in how they design particular policies. One of the key decisions that policymakers make—a decision greatly affected by political pressures and demands—is the selection of which group of people or organizations will be directly subject to the application of government authority and which group of people or organizations will be the target public of the policy.

There are a number of types of policies for carrying out public purposes that differ enormously in the application of coerciveness. Politics, however, is more than the antiseptic choice of policy mechanisms. It involves concerns about consequences, passions, and sometimes moral outrage. Advocacy in terms of consequences versus advocacy in terms of moral absolutes is a crucial determinant of the kinds of policy proposals that get debated and selected. This determination often focuses on the type and amount of government coercion involved in public policies.

Key Terms

typology *p. 166*
regulatory policy *p. 166*
redistributive policy *p. 167*
constitutive policy *p. 169*
entrepreneurial politics *p. 170*
target public of a policy *p. 170*
absolute moral imperative *p. 173*
consequentialist argument *p. 173*

hortatory appeal *p. 174*
provision of information *p. 174*
positive externality *p. 176*
G.I. Bill *p. 176*
Pell grant *p. 177*
government insurance *p. 178*
socialization of risk *p. 178*

Suggested Readings

Dahl, Robert A., and Charles E. Lindblom. 1953. *Politics, Economics, and Welfare.* New York: Harper and Row.

Lowi, Theodore. 1964. "American Business, Public Policy, Case Studies, and Political Theory." *World Politics* 15: 677–715.

Lowi, Theodore. 1988. Foreword to *Social Regulatory Policy*, Raymond Tatalovich and Byron W. Daynes, eds. Boulder, Colo.: Westview Press.

Peterson, Paul. 1981. *City Limits.* Chicago: University of Chicago Press.

Ripley, Randall B., and Grace A. Franklin. 1991. *Congress, the Bureaucracy, and Public Policy.* Pacific Grove, Calif: Brooks/Cole.

Weimer, David L., and Aidan R. Vining. *Policy Analysis: Concepts and Practice.* 3rd ed. Upper Saddle River, N.J.: Prentice-Hall, 1999.

Wilson, James Q. 1980. *The Politics of Regulation.* New York: Basic Books.

Notes

1. Theodore Lowi, "American Business, Public Policy, Case Studies, and Political Theory," *World Politics* 15 (1964): 677–715.

2. James Q. Wilson, *The Politics of Regulation* (New York: Basic Books, 1980), chap. 10.

3. Theodore Lowi, foreword to *Social Regulatory Policy,* Raymond Tatalovich and Byron W. Daynes, eds. (Boulder, Colo.: Westview Press, 1988), pp. x–xxi.

10

Bureaucracy

INTRODUCTION

A **bureaucracy** is an organization that is designed to carry out the decisions of some larger entity. While many people use the term bureaucracy to refer to a government agency, we will show that a bureaucracy is much more than that. A reasonable definition is that a bureaucracy is a group of individuals charged with the responsibility of carrying out the policies of some large entity that cannot be managed properly using a single manager. Examples include the Social Security Administration (a government agency), General Motors (a private corporation), and the American Red Cross (a nonprofit organization).

The key issues we deal with in this chapter stem from the problems that result from the delegation of organization goals to individuals within organizations. Simply put, a large organization must depend on a multitude of individuals to do its business, and this delegation of responsibility often results in a slippage of performance. That is, bureaucracies do not necessarily pursue the ends of the organizations that they were created to advance.

Our interest in this chapter is in understanding how the delegation of responsibilities to individuals affects the performance of government bureaucracies. As we will see, the delegation issues associated with government bureaucracies vary across types of policy problems as well as by the structure of the political system in which the bureaucracy is embedded.

BUREAUCRACY: A MENTAL EXERCISE

To begin to understand bureaucracy, try a mental exercise. Imagine two scenarios. First, imagine your typical day. How many different kinds of bureaucracies do you encounter, directly or indirectly? What about the food you eat at breakfast, lunch, or dinner? How did it get to your table? Did it arrive on roads built with tax dollars and according to regulations created and monitored by government bureaucracies? Where was the food purchased? Did you buy it at a grocery store that is part of a chain of groceries (a private bureaucracy)? Or was the food purchased at a restaurant (another private bureaucracy)? Who ensures the safety of the food products (that is, the temperature of the refrigerator units in which it is stored, the separation of cleaning chemicals from food products, the labeling of food items, and so forth)? How did you pay for your food? Did you barter with goods that you had created with your own hands, or did you use money? If you used money, how did you get it, and how is its value regulated? What about the buildings in which you live and the buildings where your classes are located? Who built them? Did bureaucracies of one kind or another provide all these processes? According to what regulations are these products promulgated and monitored by government agencies? What about the classes that you are taking and the classes you register and pay for? All these are provided through a bureaucracy.

Second, imagine trying to "get away from it all." That is, imagine what you would have to do to live your life, even for a week or two, without encountering or interacting with bureaucracies directly or indirectly. What would you have to do to escape the clutches of bureaucracy? One approach is to go into the wilderness. How will you get there? On roads? No, they are built and regulated by bureaucracies. How will you get food supplies? Will you buy them? No, again bureaucracies are involved. Maybe you will hunt, fish, and forage, which sounds like a good method of avoiding bureaucracies. But with what tools and implements? Store bought? Or perhaps you'll make your own tools. How will you make them? With tools purchased from Sears or the local hardware store? Oops, again bureaucracy has intervened.

Let's go back to the beginning of this scenario. How is it possible that wilderness even exists near you? Perhaps you live in the remotest parts of Canada or Alaska, but probably not. If you are on privately owned wilderness, you are subject to arrest, fines, and even imprisonment for trespassing on lands owned by someone else. The owners of the land can summon the strong arm of government bureaucracies to remove you. If you are to legally escape into the wilderness, where will you go? There are true wilderness areas. That is because it is government policy to preserve wild or nearly wild areas for your enjoyment. In other words, wilderness itself is protected, monitored, and enforced by—you guessed it—bureaucracies.

Thus, the notion that a person or group can somehow avoid bureaucracies in the United States or any other developed country is a myth. It is possible to minimize your exposure to bureaucracies, but even if you stake out in the wilds of Alaska, state-supported expeditions might be launched to find you as a possible lost expedition. Our point, which has been made in an overstated manner, is that bureaucracy is a major part of everyone who lives in the United States. We can minimize but not eliminate the impact of bureaucracy on our lives, because bureaucracies have become a necessary component of almost everything we do.

WHY IS BUREAUCRACY A HALLMARK OF MODERN SOCIETIES?

Why is bureaucracy a hallmark of modern societies? One of the best and most widely accepted answers was provided by German sociologist Max Weber, writing just prior to the twentieth century.[1] His argument, put simply, was that the growth of bureaucracy is a function of the rise of a capitalist market system in which exchange is conducted not through face-to-face bartering but through impersonal monetary exchanges over large distances. Extensive exchanges over time and geography create a need for people to be able to have certainty that the goods and services that they purchase will be produced and delivered in an expected, predictable fashion.

Weber identified important criteria for the development of bureaucracies. These include the use by individuals of repeatable specifications for products, transported on agreed schedules, and in amounts that all parties in the exchange, wherever located, could assess using common measuring systems. Furthermore, these products could be exchanged for a known, predictable amount of currency. Underlying this system of exchange is a division of labor. Some people make shoes, some make bread, some make furniture, some transport goods, some build roads, some maintain systems of weights and measures, some help bring borrowers and savers together, and so on. Out of this highly developed division of labor, bureaucracies are born and flourish. Many bureaucracies are private and others are public.

What Weber was telling us is that bureaucracies emerge as the economy, and even the political economy, becomes more complex and "successful." This means that as societies develop and as individuals become more specialized, organizations must step in to do the work that once was provided by individuals, if it was ever provided at all. Barter economies simply require individuals to come together and make a deal. When political-economic interactions become more complex, decisions about price, quantity, transportation, and product availability become so difficult that no one individual can manage all these interactions effectively. According to Weber, modern bureaucratic organizations can be defined in terms of four distinctive features: hierarchy, impersonality, continuity, and expertise.

Hierarchy in an organization means a clear chain of command. This property has received much attention by those who study bureaucracy. Every bureaucracy has at least some **command-and-control** structure. The idea that individuals at the top of the chain of command will determine what underlings do presents a problem, because the principal-agent relationship between managers and subordinates is an important source of bureaucratic nonperformance. This property is an important component of the failures experienced by bureaucracies of all types.

Impersonality in an organization means it has a formal set of rules and procedures to ensure that it performs its duties in a consistent manner, regardless of the particular persons who happen to fill the positions in the organization at any given time. Formal rules are a hallmark of bureaucracy, which means that impersonality is a feature of bureaucracy. Thus, no member of a bureaucracy should be given special status due to personal attributes that are not connected to the goals and operation of the bureaucracy itself. Individuals are important only insofar as they fill a designated office or position. They carry out predetermined tasks.

This characteristic suggests that strong leadership, independent of the particular office that a person holds, should not make a difference in bureaucracies. As a practical matter, however, strong leadership can exist within bureaucracies. This is because the meaning of formal rules and the discretion of particular offices are always open to interpretation and reinterpretation. Power lies in the realities of an organizational situation. Strong leaders can shape an organization's decisions, because the complexity of an organization gives ambitious leaders multiple avenues for trying to induce subordinates within the organization to adopt their preferred courses of action. For the same reasons, however, bureaucracies provide opportunities for bureaucrats to stave off unwanted actions by leaders. Rules and procedures can be invoked to slow down the changes sought by a strong leader and maintain important elements of the status quo.

Continuity is the idea that the organization exists independently of the limited life spans of any particular employee of the organization; continuity is possible because the organization produces and retains written records of its actions. Bureaucracy exists to regularize interactions. Its memory is not simply the knowledge of its employees but also its records, which are retained for future reference. The idea is to bring predictability to exchanges over space and time. Thus, bureaucracy exists from generation to generation.

Expertise is a function of the specialization of tasks within the organization, which simply means that the organization itself has a well-defined **division of labor,** from managers to custodians and every position in between. Division of labor is the separation of tasks so that each activity or function within an organization is performed by different sets of people. Expertise in bureaucracies is part of what makes them so potent. They are able to bring together engineers, accountants, computer specialists, and dozens of other specialists, along with administrators and support personnel, within an organizational form that permits bringing to bear the different specializations on a given task. For example, consider the immense bureaucracies of Ford, General Motors, and the other automobile makers. These bureaucracies design, engineer, test, produce, and distribute dozens of different makes of highly sophisticated automobiles each year in quantities that often number in the hundreds of thousands of units. Despite all the flaws in how these companies operate, it is still a remarkable achievement.

Weber has sometimes been accused of assuming that bureaucracies inevitably drive out any room for individual attainment or personal accomplishments. This is due in part to his belief that bureaucracies promote rule by experts. He believed, but with regret that bordered on despair, that people increasingly were becoming cogs in the technocratic machine of modern rationalistic bureaucratic societies. He probably was too pessimistic about the room in modern societies for people to pursue individual callings or for people to seek individual fulfillment. But notice the key observation that Weber made: modern societies, because of the highly developed division of labor that underpins their economies, rely on bureaucracies in virtually every facet of human activity.

THE TASKS OF BUREAUCRACY

The growth of bureaucracy has produced many benefits for modern societies, but also many costs. Complex societies must organize in some manner, and the primary benefit of bureaucracies is that they enable large numbers of individuals to combine their efforts to produce complex products on a large scale. A single individual simply cannot conduct the business of a large corporation or government agency. Because bureaucracies are the producers of goods and services in a sophisticated and complex political economy, it becomes imperative to ask whether, or to what extent, bureaucracies do the job expected of them.

Some people might argue that bureaucracies are the best instruments we have for solving complex problems. Maybe this is true. The conventional wisdom, however, is that bureaucracies do not perform well, even though they exist functionally to solve complex problems. Moreover, much of the study of twentieth-century public administration is an attempt to design bureaucracies to eliminate what appear to be intrinsic flaws that hinder effective operation. In the following sections, we discuss three classes of problems or costs associated with bureaucracies: the delegation problem, rent seeking, and policy subsystems. These problems of bureaucracies can be understood as a disjuncture between the goals of the organization and the incentives of individuals making up the bureaucracy. Thus, bureaucracies are another example of a collective action problem, a major theme of this book. It is important to note, however, that these collective action problems are not equally present or debilitating in all bureaucracies. To date, there exists no blueprint for fixing all the problems facing bureaucracies. This does not mean, however, that under the proper circumstances, the problems of bureaucracy cannot be decreased or controlled.

As we will see below, private bureaucracies, such as business corporations, are able to solve many (though not all) of the collective action problems that face them. Government bureaucracies, by contrast, face problems that can range from the benign to the severe. The extent to which the internal collective action problems of government bureaucracies can be solved varies depending on both the type of goods and services that the bureaucracy is responsible for providing and whether the particular bureaucracy is embedded in a polycentric system or is the sole provider of a set of public goods or services.

PUBLIC BUREAUCRACIES

One of the differences between government bureaucracies and market bureaucracies, such as IBM, Sears, Microsoft, and thousands of other business corporations, is that the goods and services produced by government bureaucracies are often difficult to measure or evaluate. This is because the production processes that government bureaucracies utilize make it difficult or even impossible to assess the appropriate number or quality of inputs needed. Other times, it is because the outputs of government bureaucracies are difficult to quantify or adjudge. These difficulties often make it difficult for managers of government bureaucracies to monitor the inputs and outputs of their organizations.

These difficulties have been captured by political scientist James Q. Wilson, who argues that there are four basic types of public organizations. In Table 10.1, we have rearranged his categories to form a two-by-two typology based on how easily the inputs and outputs of government bureaucracies can be monitored.[2]

TABLE 10.1 Organization Types as a Function of Ease of Monitoring Inputs and Outputs

	Inputs	
	Hard	Easy
Outputs Hard	Coping organizations	Procedural organizations
Outputs Easy	Craft organizations	Production organizations

Source: James Q. Wilson, *Bureaucracy: What Government Agencies Do and Why They Do it* (New York: Basic Books, 1989).

DILBERT reprinted by permission of United Feature Syndicate, Inc.

The easiest organization to manage is what Wilson refers to as a **production organization.** In production organizations, managers will find it easy to monitor both the labor input of individuals and policy outcomes. Thus, tried and true managerial techniques employed by conventional economic organizations can be used to ensure that shirking is minimized. An example of such an organization is the Social Security Administration. Employees have straightforward tasks that can be monitored, and the speed of the service can be, and is, monitored. If significant shirking by employees occurs, managers will know.

Managers in **craft organizations** find monitoring of inputs to be more challenging. In this type of organization, employees usually work in the field, away from an office. Managers find it difficult to monitor whether employees are putting in the required time on the job. However, outputs can be monitored, so employees are at least partially accountable. What managers cannot establish is whether the outputs the employee is producing are optimal for that particular task. An example is the Army Corps of Engineers. Managers will know if dams are designed and built, if dikes that prevent rivers from flooding are erected, and if lock systems on navigable rivers are repaired and improved; however, they cannot know whether, given the hours each worker is supposed to work, more dams, dikes, and locks might have been built, maintained, or improved. How can a manager tell if an engineer is thinking hard about how to solve a tricky engineering problem or sitting at her desk daydreaming? Evaluating appropriate levels of inputs in this type of organization is a nearly impossible task.

In **procedural organizations,** managers can observe inputs, but outputs are difficult to measure. This is a very common type of organization. The National Weather Service is a good example of such an organization. All employees can easily be accounted for, but how well should they predict the weather? If a hurricane is barreling down on the coast of Texas and the weather service predicts it will hit Galveston, was the "output" wrong when the hurricane veered and leveled Corpus Christi? In many policy areas, outcomes are a combination of predictable factors and exogenous ones, such as acts of nature. Managers can yell and scream, but hurricanes will be only somewhat predictable. How predictable will remain unknown in the near future.

Finally, **coping organizations** are quite difficult to manage, because both inputs and outputs are difficult to monitor. Thus, managers must cope with a difficult situation where there exists much uncertainty about how an organization is performing. A very good example of a coping organization, one with which you are very familiar, is a university. The goal of a typical large university is best understood in regard to the expectations of faculty. Faculty members are supposed to teach, do research, and provide service to the university, their discipline, and the community. Thus, a university does more than simply provide an educational experience to students, although that is its primary goal.

How, then, do managers (chairs and deans) get faculty members to do their jobs to promote the goals of the university? Teaching inputs are difficult to judge. How much time does a faculty member spend on preparation? The outputs are easily measured by student evaluations, but how good are these evaluations? Someone could obtain good evaluations but shirk teaching responsibilities. Thus, teaching is notoriously difficult to evaluate. Research inputs are also difficult to assess. Is someone who travels to do research actually doing the research or merely vacationing? Research outputs are the easiest to observe, because ultimately faculty members are expected to publish. But how good is the research? Who judges?

When either inputs or outputs cannot be monitored effectively, managers must do more than simply try to monitor more thoroughly, because this will fail. Gary Miller argues that managers in a successful organization must do more than simply monitor and sanction.[3] Managers must do their best to provide a trusting organization—one in which employees will care enough about their jobs that they will limit shirking. Shirking cannot be eliminated, but a good manager can minimize the effects of shirking on organizational outputs by instilling a sense of trust and responsibility in employees. Many of us have had jobs we liked and jobs we hated. We probably shirked more in the latter. The manager needs to create a job environment that the employee enjoys.

In sum, government bureaucracies differ dramatically in the ease in which policy inputs and outputs can be successfully monitored. Solving problems associated with the oversight of government bureaucracies is in large part dependent on how well political and administrative managers adopt strategies to cope with the problems of monitoring inputs and outputs.

Delegation

An intrinsic problem of all bureaucracies is that in bureaucracies, the goals of one set of people are necessarily delegated to others to be carried out. Unfortunately, the employees of bureaucracies have an interest in and often, depending on the measurability of inputs and outputs, the ability to pursue their own preferences instead of the preferences of those to whom the bureaucracy is presumed to be accountable. That is, bureaucracies have an inherent problem of inefficiency, as agency employees seek to shirk (avoid carrying out assigned tasks) or to increase the agency's budget above what is necessary for it to carry out its stated objectives. This happens because the individual bureaucrats have individual desires that are not consistent with the objectives of the principals to whom the bureau is supposed to be responsible.

This problem of bureaucracy is known as the **principal-agent problem:** employees and even managers of bureaucracies have an interest in pursuing their own preferences, and often the ability to do so, at the expense of the goals of the organization. For example, employees may seek increased leisure time. Managers may try to obtain larger budgets from the legislature than they really need to achieve the organization's goals. Or they may seek policy goals that are different from (or even antithetical to) those of the public.

While inefficiency is a universal problem in bureaucratic agencies, it is a particularly common problem in government bureaucracies that are sole providers of public goods or services. It is less of a problem in market-based bureaucracies, such as business corporations, or in government bureaucracies that are embedded in polycentric systems. Why is this true? In part, it is true because of the discipline that derives from the marketplace and from polycentric systems, both of which operate to identify inefficient, unresponsive bureaucracies; and in part, it relates to the lack of incentives for the public and its elected representatives to spend time and effort in monitoring what government agents do. Let's look at each of these factors.

We'll begin with a look at market-based bureaucracies. One of the classic functions of markets is to impose discipline on business enterprises to seek out efficient ways of organizing business practices. Market-based bureaucracies in which managers and/or employees pursue their own preferences instead of customer preferences often begin to perform poorly on the bottom line. If managers seek bigger budgets to buy expensive items for their offices, these resources are skimmed directly from the profit of the business or corporation. Likewise, when employees spend long hours on cigarette breaks while customers wait for hamburgers and fries, the company's bottom line is soon harmed. These customers will begin to shop elsewhere, where the service is faster. Employees selling nothing soon become unemployed people earning nothing. The market can be an effective motivator, both for managers who oversee employees and for employees themselves, because managers will seek ways to monitor employees closely when a market is poised to discipline the business.

In short, customers may begin to turn elsewhere to obtain the goods and services that they want. Some customers may refuse to pay for things that are too divergent from their preferences. Other customers may simply choose to buy fewer of the things produced by the company. Eventually the company may find itself unable to pay its bills and be forced either to close its doors or to reorganize itself to better respond to customers. This is the discipline of the marketplace.

Government bureaucracies sometimes experience a form of external discipline that is analogous to the market discipline faced by business organizations. This type of discipline is often present when government bureaucracies are embedded in a polycentric structure of governance, and it is generally absent when a bureaucracy is the sole provider of a set of goods or services within society. Why? In a polycentric system, multiple governments collectively have jurisdiction over a circumscribed geographic area, such as a metropolitan area, much as multiple restaurants, grocery stores, dry-cleaners, gas stations, and so on are found in a typical American metropolis. The multiplicity of vendors of goods and services offers consumers information about the costs of each different bundle of goods and services that they are potentially interested in purchasing. Likewise, the presence of multiple governments in close proximity that are offering similar goods and services provides information about prices for the goods and services produced by government bureaucracies. As we saw in Chapter 5, the information about public goods and services produced in a polycentric political system creates a powerful mechanism in two ways.

In Chapter 5, we discussed how the availability of information about public goods and services that stems from polycentricity is directly connected to conceptions of democracy. In that chapter, we saw how it encourages democratic expressions of preferences in that it gives citizens the opportunity to vote with their feet. Although moving isn't costless, it also isn't unusual; from one year to the next, 16 to 20 percent of the American population typically moves at least once.[4] When people are moving—for example, from a dormitory room to an apartment or from an apartment to a house—they often take into consideration the value of the government services most important to them (for example, the quality of the schools that their children will attend or crime rates) relative to how much they must pay in taxes to live in one jurisdiction compared with other nearby jurisdictions. This dynamic puts pressure on the government agencies in an area to improve the quality of their services and to find more cost-effective ways of delivering them.[5] Otherwise, government agencies risk losing residents, and thus tax revenues. This dynamic works best, of course, when there are many government jurisdictions in close proximity, as is the case when citizen mobility is greatest.

Notice, however, that bureaucratic agencies that are embedded in a polycentric system are subject to external discipline in a second way. Public officials who act as the principals with authority to oversee bureaucratic agents gain a great deal of leverage when there are multiple bureaucracies in a geographic area delivering similar goods or services. Information about the performance of agencies in nearby jurisdictions can be used by public officials as standards by which to judge the quality of service offerings and operating costs of agencies in their own jurisdiction. In a polycentric system, public officials have the opportunity to act decisively to counter shirking by agents.

When agency inefficiency is suspected, public officials can use **outsourcing,** obtaining the production of services in their own communities by **contracting out** (contracting with nearby agencies or private firms to deliver services at lower costs). That is, public officials can contract with outside sources for services in much the same way you or your parents make decisions about, say, lawn service (you can do it yourself or hire someone else to do it for you for a specified price). Scholars of local public services find that municipal governments that are located in close proximity to many other governmental jurisdictions contract out to other governments, and to a lesser extent to private companies, for a large array of services. Services that are often contracted out include police patrols, crime scene investigations, short- and long-term incarceration, snow removal, water treatment, electricity production and distribution, low-income housing, management of sports arenas, zoning, restaurant inspections, and more.[6] When public officials can readily contract out for services, they are able to reduce the opportunities for employees of public bureaucracies in those areas to get away with shirking, because employees must worry that, if they shirk, their jobs will be contracted out. In so doing, these bureaucracies will be more efficient.

Contrast this with the situation in which public bureaus are the sole providers of a set of goods or services in society as a whole (which we refer to as **public monopolists**). There is little that the public can do about shirking in this situation. You may remember when the Department of Defense got away with paying $900 for toilets and $500 for hammers. Why was this possible?

The answer is that the incentives for monitoring the behavior of public monopolists are fairly weak. Why monitor, if there is little you can do to respond to problems? Unlike the situation in the polycentric case, when faced with a public monopolist, the public is unable to seek equivalent services from a more efficient bureaucracy in a different jurisdiction. Voting with the feet is not a readily accessible alternative if it requires moving across state boundaries or from one nation to another. Thus, even if there is evidence of gross inefficiency, individuals can do little about it except at the ballot box or through public protests. Notice, however, that even the public's elected representatives find it difficult to determine the magnitude of inefficiency by public monopolists. Without the frame of reference offered by multiple agencies providing similar bundles of services, elected officials are unable to make unambiguous comparisons about the performance and efficiency of bureaucracies that operate as public monopolists.

Elected representatives also possess few tools for countering inefficiency when it is detected. While elected officials can resort to slashing the agency budgets, these officials cannot know whether budget cuts are appropriately sized or will succeed in rooting out the sources of inefficiency within the agency. An agency that is targeted by elected officials for cuts may respond by slashing essential services rather than eliminating waste and fat. For example, the state license bureau may choose to reduce hours that its branch offices are open to the public rather than lay off unneeded employees. Or the Immigration and Naturalization Service may slow the rate that it processes requests to immigrate into this country rather than eliminate perks available to senior officials. Public monopolists are able to perform in ways that are inconsistent with public preferences.

Rent Seeking

Another cost of government bureaucracies is the phenomenon known as rent seeking, which we first encountered in Chapter 3 in the discussion of representative democracy. Rent seeking occurs when organized groups colonize a government bureau so that the bureau promotes the specific interests of the organized groups at the expense of the public as a whole. This phenomenon is directly related to the inability of the public to effectively monitor the behavior of bureaucratic agents. Individual citizens usually pay little attention to specific policy choices, both because monitoring is costly and because the benefits that any individual citizen generally derives from such monitoring are minuscule. The general public, as discussed above, has little incentive to closely monitor the behavior of agencies. The same is not true for businesses and groups whose livelihoods are directly influenced by the decisions of an agency. For these organizations, there is a strong incentive to pay close attention to the day-to-day actions of bureaucratic agencies.

To summarize what we discussed in Chapter 3, the logic of rent seeking is as follows. Businesses try to derive profits from doing business. Competition among businesses reduces profits. Governments, having the power to regulate businesses, can determine the rules of the game for competition. A business can try to get the government to make it more difficult for its competitors to do business. If successful, the rent-seeking interest group will reap extra benefits, called rents, from the action of the government.

Typically, bureaucratic measures involve some sort of governmental restriction on freely competitive market exchanges. These restrictions include licensing to restrict entry into an industry, such as requiring special schooling for beauticians or barbers. Another such restriction is the granting of monopolies, such as rights of way for power lines or television cables or rights to use a portion of the radio frequency spectrum for cellular telephone companies or radio stations. Another restriction is controls on price and/or quantity, such as existed in agriculture for many years and continues to exist for dairy and sugar. Barriers to entry can include municipal fees imposed on taxicab drivers. Many other regulatory rules discriminate in favor of some businesses and against others.

All this sounds abstract, but the principle is simple. In Chicago, for many years plumbing regulations banned the use of plastic pipes, although the entire industry had moved from metal to plastic. The plumbers' union in Chicago dug in their heels when developers were clamoring to be able to use the cheaper and safer plastics. (Metal requires soldering, which can introduce lead into drinking water.) Essentially, plastic pipes require less labor, and for a long time the plumbers had been successful in keeping on the books requirements that pipes be metal. Why would regulators not surrender this policy, even if it were in the interests of the public? The answer is that plumbers contributed many dollars to city politicians who did not want to lose that support.

Why would a government do this? Government can reap its own rents by extracting payments in the form of bribes or campaign contributions from business interests. Bureaucrats want to play this game because if an agency provides rent-seeking measures, the legislators who also benefit will likely support the agency.[7] Rent-seeking payoffs to government officials can take a variety of forms. They include offers of high-paying jobs in the private sector for agency personnel, lobbying in the legislature on behalf of programs and initiatives that are dear to the agency, and contributions of campaign funds to elected officials who are close supporters of the agency or on the agency's oversight committees. In return for these favors, businesses and groups with a direct stake in the agency may obtain programmatic initiatives, regulatory rulings, or financial subsidies that advance their economic interests.

All rent-seeking activity represents transfers of wealth, via the machinery of government, that advantage some businesses and groups at the expense of taxpayers and the consumers of certain products or services. Furthermore, this activity, by its very nature, alters economic activity and produces what economists call **dead weight losses.** These losses are above and beyond the losses of certain groups in society that are gained by others.

To understand the concept of dead weight losses, suppose there exist two groups in society, cotton farmers and consumers. Imagine that it were possible to sum up the wealth of farmers and of consumers before and after the rent seeking by farmers produced protective government measures. If the combined wealth of farmers and consumers before and after the rent seeking were exactly equal, then the effect of the rent seeking would be simply a transfer of wealth from consumers to farmers. The rent-seeking farmers would have exactly the amount of additional wealth represented by the loss of wealth of consumers. This would be regrettable and arguably unfair. Much of the time, however, rent seeking leads to dead weight losses. When dead weight losses exist, the combined total of the wealth of farmers and consumers is smaller after rent seeking than before. The reason this happens is that the economy becomes distorted, and farmers produce less after rent seeking, even though their profits are greater.

Thus, the ability of businesses and groups to exploit bureaucracies through rent seeking comes at a social cost. Rent seeking causes harm to society as a whole in the form of a reduction in total economic output. Prices are artificially increased for some goods and services. This distorts the flow of economic resources into the activities where the resources could most efficiently be used. The economy becomes increasingly weighted down by inefficiencies that were created by the coercive power of government. Firms learn that providing better products and lower prices isn't the only way to compete, or even the best way to compete. Throughout the economy, firms find that a more secure way of obtaining wealth is by obtaining favorable dispensations from government that allow them to charge prices in excess of what would be possible in a competitive market with a level playing field. In the end, consumers lose, but so does society at large in a world of many rent seekers.

How can rent seeking be contained? As this discussion indicates, rent seeking is the exchange of resources between a seeker of private benefits and government agents. Thus, the way to contain rent seeking is to stem the flow of resources from businesses and organized groups that accrue to the private benefit of government officials. At a minimum, this means enforcement of laws against corruption. In a country such as the United States, where outright bribes are now relatively uncommon, anticorruption laws serve to inhibit many forms of rent seeking. In many less developed countries, a business or individual cannot do business without resorting to outright bribery. Dead weight losses can be severe in these countries. Laws against such behavior are almost always on the books, but the norms of behavior or corruption make these laws unenforceable.

In the American context, the resources provided by business and organized groups to government officials take the form of campaign contributions. Campaign finance laws are an area of legal uncertainty. Columnist George Will has argued over the years that campaign contributions are a form of free speech protected by the Constitution. While not a legal scholar, Will makes a spirited—if not overwhelming—argument that regulations concerning campaign contributions violate First Amendment guarantees of free speech. It is also possible, however, to view campaign contributions as forms of legalized bribery, insofar as they are often intended to bring about actions by government that reward private interests at the expense of the public. While overt influence peddling is illegal in the United States, legalized corruption, where interest groups provide money to members of Congress to receive favors, may be prevalent.

One way to determine whether campaign contributions are forms of "speech" analogous to the votes cast in the voting booth or attempts to bribe officials for private gain is to de-link campaign contributions from specific appeals to government officials. In Chapter 3 we discussed the idea of a campaign contribution system that would be analogous to the so-called Australian ballot that is used in this country. This reform would involve a blind account into which all campaign contributions would be put. Contributors would be permitted to designate any candidate or party they wished to help fund. Candidates would receive any contributions designated to benefit their campaigns, but without any identifying information that might permit them to determine what individuals, groups, or businesses provided those funds. In this way, campaign funds would express the preferences of contributors as to their preferred candidates or parties, but elected officials and challengers would not know from whom contributions were collected. Contributions would be of little use in currying favor with government officials. They would no longer be available as legalized bribes used by businesses and organized groups for rent seeking; they would function only as a form of political speech.

Policy Subsystems

An additional cost of bureaucracies stems from the formation of **policy subsystems**. Policy subsystems are the product of the bonds that are forged between members of a bureaucracy, interest groups, recipients of the bureau's services, and legislators with ties to the interest groups and recipients. What are policy subsystems, and how do they work? Policy subsystems are networks of relationships among different actors, all of whom have a stake in a policy arena. At the heart of most policy subsystems is a set of government programs. In a policy subsystem, each set of actors

> attempts to pursue their goals, but doing so requires the cooperation of other actors in the subsystem. The functional relationship between legislators, agencies, interest groups and program recipients is symbiotic. Each actor in the subsystem relies on other actors in the policy subsystem. Legislators depend on interest groups to provide them with campaign funds and other types of electoral resources. Interest groups depend on agencies to provide federal moneys and other forms of assistance to their members. Beneficiaries of programs depend on interest groups to voice their concerns both to the agency and to the legislators. And agencies depend on legislators to provide funding and programmatic authority. These circular flows of dependency and influence define the policy subsystems that populate the federal government.[8]

One of the strengths of policy subsystems is the development of expertise. Through policy subsystems, people who specialize in particular policy areas are able to interact on an ongoing basis. These specialists spend much of their professional careers thinking about how policies operate and how those policies might be altered. These professionals tend to develop common world views with respect to their particular policy areas through their regular interactions, conferences, specialized journals, and the like. This expertise can play a valuable role when political actors need advice on difficult policy problems or are confronted with the need to respond to public demands for new policy initiatives.

What problems, then, are caused by the existence of policy subsystems? One problem is that the linkages that underpin policy subsystems allow bureaucracies to live long after the problems that caused the bureaucracy to be created in the first place have been eliminated. Policy subsystems are often somewhat insulated from the rest of the political system because the bureaucracies and legislators that support them owe an important part of their longevity to interest groups and to each other, rather than to voters.

A second problem is that voters' preferences may have little correlation with subsystem outputs. The argument here is the same as in the rent-seeking discussion above. Subsystems benefit from the inability of the public to effectively monitor the actions of government agents. When the public cannot monitor government agents, organized interests can exploit the agencies and legislative overseers for their own narrow purposes at the expense of society as a whole.

One of the ways that subsystems can obscure the correlation between voter preferences and bureaucratic outputs is through their impact on the election of representatives. The problem is not merely that incumbents obtain campaign contributions from the interest groups involved in subsystems. The problem is bigger than that. Subsystems may negatively influence the likelihood that highly qualified challengers will choose to run against incumbents. Facing well-funded incumbents who have used their connections with bureaucratic agencies to forge close ties with powerful institutions and organizations in local districts, potential challengers, especially those already holding a local office, may decide to forgo a race against incumbents. This diminishes the range of good choices that voters have when they go to the ballot box. Policy subsystems undermine the ability of voters to choose between qualified candidates by suppressing the likelihood that quality challengers will enter electoral contests.

The problem of policy subsystems stems from the organization of a society's political system. As already noted, subsystems in American national governments thrive on campaign contributions. Thus, one of the ways to limit the influence of policy subsystems is to change campaign finance laws. Another way to limit their influence is to take advantage of the underlying polycentricity in the American political system by devolving policies to the lowest level of government that is feasible. This approach utilizes the multiplicity of governmental jurisdictions in a polycentric political system to make it much more costly to sustain policies based on narrow special interests.

As we have emphasized throughout this text, part of the genius of the American political system is that it permits citizens to vote with their feet, not just at the ballot box. Businesses and groups of individuals who are most disadvantaged by special interest policies resulting from subsystems have the option of relocating to another jurisdiction when policies are the responsibility of lower levels of government. Individuals rarely move from one country to another (although the increasing liberalization of the world economy is making it easier for businesses to move across national borders). But moving across state borders or from one municipality to another is not particularly difficult. The devolution approach relies on a mechanism that disciplines irresponsible jurisdictions through a marketlike mechanism.[9]

To the extent that state and local governments care about their own economic conditions and the tax revenues resulting from economic activity, they have little incentive to produce narrowly self-interested policies at the behest of policy subsystems. Notice, however, that this approach does not eliminate policy subsystems. On the contrary, it takes advantage of the expertise that they provide. Well-reasoned policy proposals that do not raise the prospect of inducing other organized groups and members of the public to flee a jurisdiction are likely to be welcomed. Devolution of policy responsibilities to the lowest feasible level of government merely limits the ability of policy subsystems to pursue policies that are harmful to the public.

CONCLUSION

Bureaucracies play an important role in modern societies. Indeed, we could scarcely live without them. Yet bureaucracies have worrisome tendencies, especially the national bureaucracies that are responsible for providing many of the goods and services on which the country relies. These tendencies include inefficiencies that stem from the delegation of tasks to agency employees, such as shirking and oversized budgets; rent seeking, which permits bureaucracies to promote the interests of organized groups at the expense of the public; and policy subsystems, which allow bureaucracies to achieve a level of insularity in relation to the rest of the political system and obscure the correlation between voter preferences and bureaucratic outputs.

These problems do not equally affect the performance of all public bureaucracies. Both the types of policies that are being produced by a particular bureaucracy and the degree to which the bureaucracy is embedded in a polycentric system have an impact on the severity of these problems. As we saw, the worst-case scenario exists in government agencies that are the sole producers of a set of goods and services. These agencies take on the characteristics of public monopolists.

One of the most encouraging things about the problems of bureaucracies in the United States, however, is that the system of governance often serves to attenuate bureaucratic failures. The multitude of governmental jurisdictions and their frequent proximity—features characteristic of a polycentric political system—create conditions in which public bureaucracies are prone to marketlike discipline. In short, the very complexity of the American political system, with its tens of thousands of governments, its overlapping jurisdictions, and its dynamism, suppresses many of the problems of bureaucracy that too often afflict countries in which power is concentrated in a centralized state apparatus.

Key Terms

bureaucracy *p. 183*
hierarchy *p. 186*
command and control *p. 186*
impersonality *p. 186*
continuity *p. 186*
expertise *p. 186*
division of labor *p. 186*
production organization *p. 189*
craft organization *p. 189*

procedural organization *p. 189*
coping organization *p. 190*
principal-agent problem *p. 191*
outsourcing *p. 192*
contracting out *p. 192*
public monopolist *p. 193*
dead weight losses *p. 195*
policy subsystem *p. 196*

Suggested Readings

Arnold, Douglas. 1979. *Congress and the Bureaucracy.* New Haven, Conn.: Yale University Press.

Borcherding, Thomas E. 1977. *Budgets and Bureaucrats*. Durham, N.C.: Duke University Press.

Buchanan, James M. 1975. *The Limits of Liberty: Between Anarchy and the Leviathan*. Chicago: University of Chicago Press.

Downs, Anthony. 1966. *Inside Bureaucracy*. Boston: Little, Brown.

Haider, Donald. 1974. *When Governments Come to Washington*. New York: Free Press.

Miller, Gary. 1992. *Managerial Dilemmas: The Political Economy of Hierarchy*. Cambridge, England: Cambridge University Press.

Niskanen, William A. 1971. *Bureaucracy and Representative Government*. Chicago: Aldine and Atherton.

Stein, Robert M., and Kenneth N. Bickers. 1995. *Perpetuating the Pork Barrel*. New York: Cambridge University Press.

Tullock, Gordon. 1965. *The Politics of Bureaucracy*. Washington, D.C.: Public Affairs Press.

Weber, Max. 1958. *From Max Weber: Essays in Sociology*. Translated and edited by H. H. Gerth and C. Wright Mills. New York: Oxford University Press.

Weingast, Barry. 1995. "The Economic Role of Political Institutions: Federalism, Markets, and Economic Development." *Journal of Law, Economics, and Organization* 11: 1–31.

Will, George F. 1994. *Restoration: Congress, Term Limits and the Recovery of Deliberative Democracy*. New York: Free Press.

Wilson, James Q. 1989. *Bureaucracy: What Government Agencies Do and Why They Do It*. New York: Basic Books.

Notes

1. Max Weber, *From Max Weber: Essays in Sociology*, trans. and ed. H. H. Gerth and C. Wright Mills (New York: Oxford University Press, 1958).

2. James Q. Wilson, *Bureaucracy: What Government Agencies Do and Why They Do It* (New York: Basic Books, 1989).

3. Gary Miller, *Managerial Dilemmas: The Political Economy of Hierarchy* (Cambridge, England: Cambridge University Press, 1992).

4. U.S. Bureau of the Census, "Annual Geographical Mobility Rates, by Type of Movement: 1947–1997," in *Current Population Survey* (Washington, D.C.: U.S. Government Printing Office, 1998).

5. See, once again, Charles M. Tiebout, "A Pure Theory of Local Expenditure," *Journal of Political Economy* 44 (1956): 416–424.

6. See, for example, Robert M. Stein, *Urban Alternatives* (Pittsburgh: University of Pittsburgh Press, 1991).

7. Anne Krueger, "The Political Economy of the Rent-Seeking Society," *American Economic Review* 64 (1974): 291–303.

8. Robert M. Stein and Kenneth N. Bickers, *Perpetuating the Pork Barrel* (New York: Cambridge University Press, 1995), p. 6.

9. Barry Weingast, "The Economic Role of Political Institutions: Federalism, Markets, and Economic Development," *Journal of Law, Economics, and Organization* 11 (1995): 1–31.

11

Analyzing Proposed Policies

INTRODUCTION

We have focused on many processes and institutions throughout this book. We now turn to specific techniques of policy analysis and their role in solving policy problems. Policy analysis is designed to guide the choice of policy options. In recent years, policy analysts have moved from doing ad hoc analyses to more systematic analyses. These analyses are typically grouped into two broad categories: *ex ante* **analyses** and *ex post* **analyses,** or what are commonly thought of, respectively, as forward-looking analyses that guide future policy choices and backward-looking analyses that assess the relative success or failure of past policy choices. In this chapter, we concentrate on *ex ante* policy analyses. In the next chapter, we introduce methods for engaging in *ex post* analyses.

Policy analysis is the effort to think carefully about policy problems and potential solutions. In so doing, it is important to examine the underlying characteristics of policy problems and to think carefully about how policy alternatives are influenced by and, in turn, influence the institutions within which individuals live and work. That is, the political economy approach to policy analysis, as described in this book, is premised on a thoughtful examination of the institutional conditions under which a policy will be implemented. This entails a careful consideration of the type of policy good that is at stake, the advantages of bottom-up versus top-down approaches to policy-making with regard to the particular policy issue, the strengths and weaknesses of utilizing market incentives for addressing the problem, the potential efficacy and risks of utilizing forms of government coercion, and an awareness of the likelihood of bureaucratic failures.

EX ANTE ANALYSIS

The purpose of *ex ante* analysis is to guide future policy choices. One of the major tools of forward-looking, or *ex ante*, policy analysis is **cost-benefit analysis.** Simply put, cost-benefit analysis is the systematic analysis of the net benefits and costs of proposed policy choices. The idea behind cost-benefit analysis is simple: those projects with the highest net benefits should be enacted. When the choice is about how large a project should be or the extent of regulation required for solving some problem, the choice should be the policy that maximizes benefits minus costs. Of course, if faced with just a single policy choice, any project that provides more benefits than costs should be funded. But in the real world, governments consider many policy proposals, so a basic decision criterion must allow for comparison among proposals.

Sometimes actually calculating the benefits of a policy proposal can become difficult or controversial. For example, if a safety regulation is being considered, there are problems associated with trying to value human life. Techniques have been developed by economists for estimating values of life, which we will explore below when discussing the estimation of costs and benefits in monetary terms. But these techniques remain controversial when applied to valuing individual lives. For how much money would you be willing to sacrifice your life? The vast majority of people would say that there is no amount of money that would be worth this sacrifice. In such cases, analysts sometimes use a methodology called **cost-effectiveness analysis.** This is a variant of cost-benefit analysis in which the effects of a policy are quantified in terms of the number of lives saved or lost, but without attempting to value lives in monetary terms. The policy proposal that saves the most lives per dollar would then be the one decided on by this approach.

Much critical evaluation of cost-benefit analysis has produced many developments in the methodology. The most controversial aspects of cost-benefit analysis involve what to count as costs and benefits and how to assign monetary values to them, a process called **monetization.** There are both practical and conceptual difficulties associated with monetizing costs and benefits, and any two cost-benefit analyses of the same project often give wildly conflicting results.

Even though placing a value on costs and benefits has its problems, cost-benefit analysis has been most successful at ensuring a thorough analysis of policy alternatives. Interest groups and bureaucrats converse in the language of cost-benefit analysis, and this shared language improves political debate. It is important to understand, however, that cost-benefit analyses are political. They are never fully objective. However, they have great utility, as we will see below.

COST-BENEFIT ANALYSIS

Cost-benefit analyses involve a number of steps.[1] These steps include problem identification, solution development, data collection and analysis, estimation of costs and benefits, choice of decision criteria, and policy recommendation. A good policy analyst will keep in mind who will ultimately use the cost-benefit analysis in selecting a policy. This means the analyst is part of the political process, not merely a technically skilled bureaucrat immune from politics. That said, a good policy analyst will try diligently to make sure that the analysis is not biased in some systematic fashion.

A good example of the rigor, the uncertainties, and the politics associated with cost-benefit analysis can be found in Case 11.1, which describes the competing cost-benefit studies that have been conducted on the proposal by the U.S. Department of Transportation to build a new interstate highway across the southern half of the state of Indiana. You may find it helpful to read this case prior to working through the components of cost-benefit analysis that we discuss below. Sometimes, having a specific case in mind helps bring to life the myriad tasks involved in trying to evaluate policy proposals.

Problem and Objective Identification

The first part of cost-benefit analysis requires understanding what the policy problem is. What are the goals of the policy? Who will be affected? What are the potential costs and benefits? This stage requires the policy analyst to understand, in basic terms, the nature of the policy problem. We will have more to say about this below. In general, however, the analyst must determine the basic problems that need addressing and from where the costs and benefits likely will come.

Once these very general questions are answered, the policy analyst must begin to translate them into more specific (or operational) guidelines for doing policy analysis. For example, if the general aim is to reduce congestion on freeways, how does congestion get measured? If the goal is to reduce pollution in major cities, what objective condition can be identified to know that pollution is being contained? These objectives are very important, because if they cannot be identified easily, then the cost-benefit analysis will be difficult, and perhaps even impossible, to perform and justify.

Of course, this stage is also one of the most controversial. When problems are identified, assumptions must be made about individual preferences for these problems to be legitimated. Individual preferences must be guessed at, because in general, individuals will not be willing or able to freely express their true preferences. To cope with this problem, policy analysts typically impute preferences by attributing common goals to individuals. This is an area where policy analysts, as elites, may impute preferences that are more likely to be a bureaucrat's preferences than the preferences of typical citizens.

What Are the Potential Solutions?

Once a problem is defined in operational terms, potential solutions can be identified. It is hoped that the policy analyst will determine these potential solutions based upon a thoughtful consideration of the institutional factors within which the policy will be implemented. Sometimes a policy problem has been studied by a number of different scholars, with various policy prescriptions offered. The analyst may be able to select a range of policy options from these. Still other times, or perhaps most of the time, interest groups may be advocating policy options that they feel best cope with the underlying problem. Thus, group-advocated policy options are often the focus of cost-benefit analyses.

Therefore, the identification of potential solutions will largely be done before a cost-benefit analysis is performed. The purpose of the policy analysis is to determine potential solutions and to recommend the best available alternative. This means that the analyst has an obligation to consider options that go beyond those of special interests or political officials, who may ignore solutions that do not serve their narrow purposes. The analyst, of course, also has the obligation to explain why a recommended alternative is more viable or is to be preferred over the proposals made by special interests and political officials.

Suppose, as an example, that the policy objective is to increase student reading abilities in educational institutions serving kindergarten through twelfth grade. Many may propose the introduction of phonics to achieve this purpose. Others may offer a less traditional educational tool. The role of the policy analyst is to consider a range of potentially viable tools to achieve this goal. Thus, an analyst may introduce a multipurpose tool for increasing reading abilities. A good policy analyst does not simply accept the policy choices provided by political actors. This crucial component of policy analysis helps move beyond political debates that too often simply mirror the simplistic, dualistic political arguments generated as a function of the two-party system in the United States.

Data Collection and Analysis

The moving parts of cost-benefit analysis begin with data collection and analysis. What needs to be determined? For example, what data need to be collected and analyzed to determine the impact of a school voucher program on the education of children? Essentially, **policy forecasts** must be produced. Policy forecasts ask, if Policy A is implemented, what will happen? If Policy B is implemented instead, what else will happen? In other words, policy forecasts attempt to project the likely consequences of a policy action. Based upon these forecasts, the analyst begins to assemble relevant data.

The production of policy forecasts is a tricky endeavor. The determination of the effect of a school voucher system, for example, is controversial, even though there are cases where vouchers are used in public schools. When there are no precedents, producing policy forecasts is very difficult. For example, early research on the effects of privatizing public schools was controversial, because the studies were based on schools where parents and students had self-selected into private schools.[2] Because education is co-produced (something we discussed in Chapter 4), it is very possible that students attending private schools might do better not because the schools were better but because the students worked harder to educate themselves. That is, the positive results that private schools did a better job of educating students may have been due to the differences in the preferences of the parents whose children attended private schools as compared with the preferences of the parents with children in public schools. The authors assume that parents and students do not differentially select public versus private schools as a function of their demands for education. It is, of course, plausible that parents do differentially select public schools versus private schools based upon how much they value education. It is difficult in nonexperimental research to determine cause and effect. Consequently, analysts usually try to be explicit about the assumptions they are making about the causal processes they are trying to understand so as to alert consumers of their research to the possible limitations of its generalizability.

The problem with producing policy forecasts is not limited to school vouchers. Indeed, the rule is that the production of policy forecasts is very difficult. The reason is that usually no experimental evidence is available to guide analysts in the production of forecasts. Policy experiments are sometimes done, but often they are poorly designed. Often policy experiments are thought to be unethical, because they require choosing individuals randomly to get one policy treatment or another. For example, a school voucher experiment that could be designed to overcome the problems with the above study would require students to be randomly assigned into the voucher group. As a student, would it be fair that someone else, based on randomization, received an opportunity you did not?

Estimation of Costs and Benefits

The most important data, and the most difficult to generate, measure the demand for a project. Why are these data difficult to produce? You might assume that the policy analyst could simply ask individuals what policies they want and then extrapolate from the individuals to determine the demand for a policy. The problem is that we cannot simply ask what policies people want to obtain truly useful information to guide our policy choices.

Recall the discussion of democratic decision making in Chapter 3, where we saw that no democratic decision-making process is immune from manipulation. This means that how we ask people what policies they want, or the order in which the questions are asked, can determine what answers we get. But the problem is even bigger than that.

The problem is that individuals are unlikely to reveal sincerely what they want when projects or regulations are not explicitly tied to individual preferences. How much will this project benefit you? If you are asked this question, you are likely to exaggerate the benefits (or costs) of the project in order to have maximum influence on the enactment of a policy proposal. This problem occurs because a single individual pays only a small cost of a single policy, so benefits (or costs) are not tied directly to the taxes or subsidies required for the policy. You may exaggerate how much you will benefit from a project so that you can offset those who will have small or negative benefits. Moreover, if you are asked, without regard to cost, how much you like such a project, you may very well overstate the benefit to you. After all, in the absence of costs, why not support a project that provides at least some modicum of benefits? Thus, asking people how much they want a project is always problematical.

What analysts must do is figure out, given data and policy forecasts, the likelihood that individuals with certain demographics will benefit (or lose) from certain projects or regulations. This determination requires assumptions about individuals who will be affected by a project or regulation.

For example, suppose a project is proposed to dredge a river for sediment. This appears to be a good use of resources. But what is the impact? Suppose the river is used to allow transportation of goods to a certain area. This dredging will make such transportation easier than before, but it will also make more costly, relative to shipping, transit using trucks and trains. Is the cost of such a project justified given alternative methods of transportation? What is the environmental cost of dredging a river? Who cares about the loss of a species of fish or frog? How do we compare the loss of trucking, railroad, and maritime jobs? What about other individuals who are affected by the consequences of additional highway, rail, or maritime traffic? Imputing costs and benefits to individuals is very difficult. Indeed, as we describe below, it is here that politics has its most important role.

Monetization

Costs and benefits must be translated into a common measure that allows all the costs and all the benefits to be added up and compared with one another. This measure is money. The act of assigning dollar values to costs and benefits is called monetization or monetizing. This is clearly another step that requires assumptions to be made. The goal is to determine how much net value a project provides to individuals as a whole.

The actual economics of monetization is beyond the scope of this chapter. One of the problems that must be overcome is **substitution effects.** Substitution effects occur when people appear to be benefiting from a new project, but are in fact shifting their activities from a similar project that already exists. Building a reservoir may clearly result in people boating, swimming, and fishing, but how many of these individuals would instead use another lake nearby? What must be measured is the number of new boaters, swimmers, and fishers resulting from the building of the reservoir, because some of the users of the new reservoir would otherwise use an existing reservoir.

Because most projects and regulations will affect individuals for a long time, the monetary benefits of a project must be discounted over time. **Discounting** is a method for calculating how much something will be worth to us at some time in the future, if we are able to have it in the present instead. All individuals discount the future over the present. So too must governments. How much is $10 worth to you now versus five years from now? The way to think about this is how much someone could pay you today so that you would pay the person $10 five years from now. Of course, this is connected to the concept of interest. Thus, we must discount future benefits relative to present benefits to be consistent with the idea that individuals discount the future relative to the present.

Valuing Human Lives

As we indicated above, one of the most difficult and controversial aspects of estimating costs and benefits of policy proposals is assigning dollar values to lives that are likely to be saved or lost if a policy option is adopted. People naturally and appropriately recoil from the prospect of assigning a dollar value to a particular person's life. Indeed, society is quite willing to spend enormous sums of money to save individuals whose lives, if not rescued soon, are certain to be lost. Watching the nightly news will provide proof of the great risks taken by firefighters to rescue a child, without regard to that child's likely future earnings or financial value to society. Likewise, the Coast Guard spends large sums each year rescuing fishers and boaters from harm that is all too often self-inflicted, again without regard to the value to society of the particular people involved.

The assignment of values to lives in cost-benefit analyses, however, is undertaken to assess how societal resources can be used most efficiently so those resources can be used, if desired, to preserve as many lives as possible. Moreover, the issue is never about individual lives that are at certain risk of survival or death but rather about saving "statistical" lives at differing levels of relatively low risk. That is, the question is not what a particular person is "worth." The question is how much risk to human lives should be reduced (or incurred) in pursuing a policy option. The goal is to decide how to allocate scarce resources to reduce risk by some amount while accomplishing as much of the policy goal as is possible, given the available funds.

Perhaps you would like to assert, instead, that no value can be placed on human life. But this does not free you from the underlying dilemma. To understand why this is the case, consider the following hypothetical situation. A proposed new interstate-type highway segment is expected to cost $1 billion and would replace an existing two-lane highway. For simplicity, let us say the benefits of the new highway would include some new jobs, because some companies in the road corridor would expand their businesses to take advantage of decreased transportation costs, decreased travel time for people using the new road, and a net decrease in highway fatalities by five persons per year. This decrease in fatalities would be due primarily to three factors: multilane roads, which permit motorists to avoid the need to move into oncoming lanes to pass slower vehicles; controlled access, which means that vehicles need not stop in the middle of the road to make left-hand turns and traffic entering the roadway need not cross through oncoming traffic; and grading and straightening of the roadway, which reduces the likelihood that cars will inadvertently swerve or slide off the road into oncoming cars or obstructions.

Let us assume, first, that the benefits from increased jobs and reduced travel time would exceed $1 billion. With these benefits, we can safely recommend that the highway be built, regardless of the value that is placed on the five statistical lives saved. But let us make the situation more difficult, as well as more realistic, by assuming that the highway would provide $900 million in benefits

Road and bridge construction projects are often controversial because some people see projects such as this one as examples of the "pork barrel" and others see them as valuable investments. *Tony Freeman/PhotoEdit.*

from new jobs and reduced travel time. Now the question of whether the highway will be built hinges entirely on how much society values the five lives per year that would be saved. If you say that no value can be put on a human life and refuse to factor this variable into the cost-benefit calculation, then you are, in effect, sending five persons per year to their graves—clearly not the outcome you intended.

In contrast, perhaps you want to assert that the value of each life saved is infinite. On this basis, the road should be built, since after all, infinity beats 1 billion by a lot. But notice that this would mean that every two-lane road should be turned into a multilane, interstate-type highway. Since lives would always be saved when shifting from a two-lane to a multilane interstate, it follows that building these roads would always be justified. This would justify spending all of society's resources on new roads so long as risk was reduced by some amount, no matter how small, and regardless of the other ways that these resources might be spent. The basic problem is that in the real world resources are scarce, public and private needs are many, and risks are always present to one degree or another. Thus, we are forced to ask about the basis for making sensitive decisions among competing goals.

Risk Assessment

The question, thus, is how values should be assigned to statistical lives to incorporate information about the costs and benefits of reducing risks to humans when evaluating a proposed policy option. Several methods have been used to determine such values.

One of the oldest methods is based on measures of income that an individual might have been expected to earn had he or she lived a normal lifetime. This method continues to be used by the court system in the United States to assess damages in personal injury cases, but it is rife with flaws, not the least of which is that it perpetuates disparities in earning power that are due to racial, gender, socioeconomic, and age bias.

A second and better accepted methodology among social scientists for making value-of-life determinations was pioneered by Kip Viscusi.[3] In this methodology, the analyst bases values of lives on the imputed value that people themselves assign to the reduction or increase of risks in their daily lives—the **imputed value of life.** The risks that this method analyzes are relatively small risks of death that are incurred in the course of everyday life. The question is how ordinary people value the reduction or increase of fairly common risks, including everything from eating fatty meats, to driving small, fuel-efficient cars, to swimming at unprotected beaches, to driving on two-lane highways.

Underlying this method is the idea that people expect to be compensated for engaging in an activity with greater hazards. This is known as their **willingness to accept,** because it is the wage premium that people demand in order to accept a riskier job (for example, to be an emergency medical technician in a helicopter rather than in a ground-based vehicle). The same idea, but from the opposite point of view, is that people are willing to pay (through forgone wages or higher prices) for an added measure of safety. This is known as their **willingness to pay.** This is the amount, for example, that you give up during the summer to work at a clerical job rather than an outdoor construction job, or to work in a sales job at the mall rather than on a road construction crew.

With this seemingly simple insight, Viscusi and others have used this methodology to try to discover how much individuals assess the value of reducing different kinds of risks. By using labor market information on differences in the riskiness and earnings across a host of different occupations, these analysts have been able to determine the amounts that people act as if their lives are worth when they are faced with differing levels of very small risks of death on the job. In these studies, it appears that workers act as if their lives are worth between $3.6 million and $5.4 million, in 1990 dollars.

Notice, however, that the underlying point of these studies is not to determine the value of a life for its own sake. The underlying goal is the development of a yardstick so that society's resources can be most efficiently used to reduce different kinds of risks. With imputed values of life, it becomes possible to assess the relative value of safety-enhancing policy proposals. This is done by multiplying the number of statistical lives saved under each policy proposal by the average value attached to lives by members of society. These values can then be used in cost-benefit studies to help determine the most efficient ways of using scarce resources to accomplish needed social objectives and at the same time reduce risks faced by individuals.

An example of how policymakers use cost-benefit analysis to grapple with these issues of life and death can be drawn from the debate in 1994 over the universal health care plan proposed by First Lady Hillary Clinton.[4] In designing the proposal, one of the key issues to be resolved concerned the medical treatments that a federally financed health care plan should cover. The methodology adopted by the proponents of the plan was to use cost-benefit analysis to determine the procedures and treatments that would be covered by the government. For each procedure or treatment, the question was by how much the risk of death would be reduced if the procedure or treatment were covered, and how much it would cost to cover the procedure or treatment. By multiplying the reduction in risk of death times the cost of the procedure or treatment that would produce that reduction in risk, it was possible to estimate the cost for saving a statistical life.

The commission that formulated the Clinton health care plan used as its decision rule a figure of approximately $100,000 per life saved from a procedure or treatment in order for the procedure or treatment to be covered by the government health care plan. It was on this basis that the proposed health care plan included coverage for women in their 50s to receive annual mammograms.

The estimated cost per year of life saved for women receiving mammograms in their 50s was $108,401. The proposed health care plan, however, did not include coverage for mammograms for women in their 40s. The reason was that the reduction in risk from annual mammograms was not sufficiently large to justify the cost of this procedure. The estimated cost per year of life saved from mammograms for women in their 40s was $186,635—a figure that was too great for such a procedure to be recommended for coverage by the government. The decision to set $100,000 per year of life saved as the standard for whether to include a procedure or treatment in the health care plan is, of course, open to question. Why only $100,000? Why not $200,000? Or why not $50,000? This issue is never simple or uncontroversial. The bigger point, however, is that by being explicit about the costs associated with achieving a benefit, it becomes possible to ask how to achieve the most benefits with a limited budget. Isn't it better to save as many life-years as possible with the nation's limited health care budget than to use the available dollars on high-cost procedures and treatments that promise to save fewer lives?

Decision Criteria

How should we judge whether any activity is good or bad for society? One answer is provided by Harold Lasswell.[5] In his view, a policy is good for society when it is the product of a political process that produces a settled distribution of benefits and costs among contending groups. That is, Lasswell's position is that any politically acceptable outcome is also an acceptable policy. This means that the acceptable policy may simply be what the best organized and most well heeled interest groups want. Notice, however, that what is politically acceptable at a given point in time may bear little or no relationship to what is most safety enhancing or what provides the greatest benefits to all members of society.

Another answer is offered by philosopher Vilfredo Pareto.[6] The criterion he offers for deciding whether a policy is acceptable states that one allocation of resources, by which he means a policy alternative, is better for society than another if that allocation makes no person worse off, and at least one person better off, than the original allocation. This criterion is known as the **Pareto principle.** To illustrate the Pareto principle, suppose three individuals have $100 each. A policy is referred to as Pareto superior if, after the policy is enacted, no person has less than $100, and at least one person has more than that. As a principle of efficiency, as economists refer to this outcome, the principle cannot be refuted. Who would think the original society of three individuals was better off than the society after the policy was enacted? Unfortunately, few policies in the real world result in a Pareto superior outcome. In most cases, some individuals gain while others lose.

Lasswell and Pareto represent two extremes of normative judgment. Lasswell is concerned only with the distribution of pains and gains. But as a society, we must try to go beyond the question of who can win politically. Pareto, in contrast, justifies outcomes that maximize the improvement in benefits but is unconcerned about the distribution of outcomes. Somewhere in the middle ought to be a happy medium.

The **Kaldor-Hicks criterion** attempts to make the Pareto principle useful for policy analysis and gives us the possibility of incorporating distributional concerns in a way that may also be consistent with Lasswell.[7] The Kaldor-Hicks criterion specifies that a policy is efficient if, in relation to an initial allocation of resources, some individuals who gain from the policy could compensate those who are disadvantaged by the policy. Thus, if the initial allocation of resources were $100 for three people, and two ended up with $200 and the third with $99, then the distribution of resources would be Kaldor-Hicks efficient, because the two winners could easily compensate the loser to create a Pareto superior allocation. The idea is that even though such compensation might not take place, the outcome for society is still better than if no policy change takes place.

Of course, the Kaldor-Hicks definition of efficiency introduces distributional issues to the equation. Why should one person shoulder the costs for society at large? The idea behind the Kaldor-Hicks criterion is to provide a justification for taxation and spending so that society can be made better off. From a normative perspective, the Kaldor-Hicks criterion appears justifiable; for any policy problem, some individuals often suffer the brunt of the costs, and it should be possible under any policy to provide compensation to offset those costs.

Note that the use of the Kaldor-Hicks criterion violates one of Kenneth Arrow's conditions, as presented in Chapter 3. Recall that one of Arrow's conditions was that each person's preferences must be weighted equally. The Kaldor-Hicks criterion implicitly requires that individuals' preferences receive different weights. For example, in the above three-person example, the individual who begins with $100 but ends with $99 receives less weight in the social choice function than do the winners.

Is this democratic? At first, it may seem that it is not. But democratic choice rarely requires that votes be unanimous. Ordinarily, we expect that choices in democracies will be made according to majority rule, which means that each individual democratic choice often, if not always, leaves a minority of voters worse off. In essence, democracies declare that the preferences of voters on the losing side of issues should count less than the preferences of voters on the winning side of issues, because the losers are in the numerical minority. Thus, the Kaldor-Hicks criterion operates in a manner that is somewhat analogous to the majority rule criterion utilized in most democratic decision-making processes.

While a decision criterion based on Kaldor-Hicks may promote efficiency, policies have effects above and beyond simple efficiency. These, too, should be accounted for in any cost-benefit analysis. The most important criterion beyond simple efficiency is the distributional impact of projects and regulations. The Kaldor-Hicks criterion ignores who gains and who loses. But the Kaldor-Hicks criterion explicitly requires that a policy produce benefits sufficiently large that losers could be compensated by winners. Thus, it offers a way to incorporate Lasswell's concern with who wins and who loses. Policies that increase the benefits for wealthy individuals at the expense of poor individuals may not be very desirable, unless actual compensation is forthcoming. While such compensation is not required by the Kaldor-Hicks criterion, it may be necessary politically to realize the efficiency gains potentially achievable in the Kaldor-Hicks selected policy option. Any sound cost-benefit analysis needs to determine the distributional impact of policies on various social, economic, and ethnic groups in society. The Kaldor-Hicks criterion offers a tool for ensuring that distributional impacts can be accommodated under a selected policy.

Policy Recommendation

A good cost-benefit analysis will offer a policy recommendation. Several recommendations may be necessary to accommodate possible political calculations about the distribution of pains and gains. The analyst must realize that a single recommendation may be ignored, but one that offers some flexibility for policymakers is more likely to be influential in final decisions. For example, a school voucher system may be so politically controversial that any cost-benefit analysis recommending one will be ignored. However, if a second recommendation offering a more modest system is proposed, policymakers may be able politically to adopt a policy change that is still an improvement over the status quo.

Cost-benefit analysts need to understand that as a general rule, policy is made on an incremental basis in the United States. While occasionally a cost-benefit analysis recommending sweeping change will have deep consequences in reforming a policy area, more often these types of analyses are deemed too revolutionary for political officials who are understandably worried about moving too quickly or too far from the status quo for fear of causing unanticipated negative reactions within the public.

POLITICS AND COST-BENEFIT ANALYSIS

Cost-benefit analysis can best be thought of as a language spoken by bureaucrats and special interests alike. As a language, cost-benefit analysis is a way to communicate arguments about policies. But just as orators can overstate a case on the Senate floor, so can cost-benefit analysis be used to exaggerate a case for a specific policy proposal. Thus, cost-benefit analyses, within a political context, can take on the role of political argument, not scientific evidence. Ironically, the use of cost-benefit analysis to justify preexisting policy opinion has proliferated with the growth in the use of cost-benefit analyses. There is a correlation over time between the increasing legitimation of cost-benefit analysis as a policy tool and its use as a mere rhetorical device.

A good cost-benefit analyst will strive for objectivity so that future studies will be viewed as credible. However, due to all the uncertainties about policy prediction and measuring costs and benefits, different views of the world, which get built into the assumptions of an analysis, often result in cost-benefit analyses that are slanted in certain ideological directions. An analyst working for a special interest group will almost always have this slant, because the group has a certain worldview.

For example, suppose you are a cost-benefit analyst working for the Sierra Club. There is a policy proposal to allow additional logging in a national forest in California. The Sierra Club is almost always against logging in national forests, so the expectation is that you would produce a cost-benefit analysis of this policy that would have high costs relative to benefits. Your worldview no doubt is more or less the same as that of the Sierra Club leadership. If not, you would not have been hired. Thus, the assumptions you make about policy forecasts (erosion, regrowth, and so forth), benefits (logging jobs, revenue from logging sales), and costs (global warming, negative impact on wildlife) will necessarily make your report the strongest statement against this new logging in California.

Of course, policymakers and the public know what to expect from a Sierra Club cost-benefit analysis on this policy, so the actual report becomes a political argument. It is not useless, but it is predictable. It is useful in making the most rational argument available for the policy position of the Sierra Club. A policy analyst in this position has no alternative to producing the report that makes the strongest case for the Sierra Club's position. A report coming out of the Sierra Club that gives even lukewarm support for logging this forest in California would have a strong impact, because it would be unexpected. Thus, as a policy analyst, your job within this context is to provide the most rational support for existing Sierra Club policies.

To create a credible cost-benefit analysis, an analyst should make sure to include a number of sensitivity analyses. In a **sensitivity analysis,** different assumptions are made to find out how sensitive the results are to assumptions made during the analysis. The resulting recommendation from such an analysis leaves it to political officials to decide which assumptions appear most likely to be correct. In addition, analyses providing a variety of potential outcomes provide political officials with more information than simply ones that offer a single policy recommendation.

Case 11.1

Cost-Benefit Analysis of an Interstate 69 Extension

FOLLOWING THE passage of the North American Free Trade Agreement in 1992, the federal government stated that a high priority existed for interstate highways that would simultaneously connect the United States to Canada and Mexico. One such highway was Interstate 69 (I-69), which would provide a "mid-continent highway" between Port Huron, on Michigan's border with Canada, and Laredo, Texas, on the border with Mexico. One key link in this road would be a new highway between Indianapolis and Evansville, Indiana.

Controversy has surrounded this proposal to complete I-69 through the southern half of Indiana almost since its announcement. Indiana government and business leaders argued that the benefits of the I-69 extension would outweigh the costs. Opponents claimed the costs would outstrip the benefits. Before such an enormous and controversial undertaking could be undertaken, all costs and benefits would have to be considered. This highlights an important fact: multiple cost-benefit analyses of the same project can conflict due to very different considerations included in the studies.

One of the most frequently cited statistics concerning the extension of I-69 from Indianapolis to Evansville is that for every dollar spent on the project, $1.39 would be returned in travel benefits.[1] This seems so simple: after boiling everything down, the benefits are greater than the costs. The core of the cost-benefit analyses of the highway was two related studies provided by the Indiana Department of Transportation: the 1990 *Southwest Indiana Highway Feasibility Study* and the 1996 *Southwest Indiana Highway Corridor: Draft Environmental Impact Study* (EIS).[2]

The feasibility study concluded that the extension would provide a relatively low benefit-to-cost ratio over 30 years, at a ratio of 1.23. The EIS considered the positive aspects of economic development, linking highways, and safety and traffic improvements in relation to the possible negative impact of the highway on mines, wells, wetlands, endangered plants and animals, nature areas, historic sites, schools, hazardous waste sites, and peoples' homes. The EIS claimed that there would be 4,000 of these "environmental avoidance areas" but that the economic, travel, and safety benefits would still outweigh these negatives. Furthermore, the study showed that following the highway's construction, there would be 9,456 fewer accidents and 61 fewer deaths over 30 years. In the final analysis, the EIS relied on the positive benefit-to-cost ratio provided by the 1990 feasibility study as evidence that the highway should be built.

Opponents disagreed with the findings of these studies, however. First, although the 1990 feasibility study had a positive benefit-to-costs ratio, the report itself recommended that the highway not be built because the projected benefits only marginally outweighed the costs, and the expensive price tag on construction made the risk too great.[3] The claimed benefit-to-cost ratio of 1.23 did not include costs associated with the environment or maintenance—a point that, remarkably, was not raised in the EIS. Critics funded a separate "independent" economic analysis that found that costs would actually trump benefits by $115 million. The critics admitted that the number of Indiana jobs created by the highway seemed impressive, but that over thirty years the average number of jobs created would be four per county per year. For the price of the highway, each of these jobs would cost $1.5 million.[4]

Furthermore, a coalition of farmers, taxpayer-rights groups, and environmentalists banded together to argue that instead of building a new highway, the improvement of existing highways could achieve the same goal for much less money. Two national television network news shows focused on the I-69 extension as a waste of money. An American Broadcasting Company news show claimed that the project would cost $1.2 billion and would save only 10 minutes' driving time over the current route. The cost of improving the existing route would be only $500 million—less than half the price of the extension.[5] A National Broadcasting Company news report stated that 41 rivers and streams would have to be crossed, 1,000 acres of forests and 3,000 acres of farmland would be lost, and the highway would cut through an Amish community "like the Berlin Wall."[6]

Proponents of the I-69 extension complain that the opposition to the extension comes from business groups and politicians living in areas holding the current routes between Indianapolis and Evansville. These extension proponents argue that rather than being concerned with the actual cost of the project, critics are intentionally misconstruing the cost-benefit conclusions to protect their own business interests. Opponents retort that the I-69 extension is pork barrel politics at its worst. What are the real costs and benefits? Clearly, the example of the I-69 extension shows that there are multiple ways to skin a cat. Considerations of costs and benefits depend greatly upon what factors are included in the calculations.

1. Rep. John Hostettler, "I-69 to Provide $1.39 for Every $1 Spent Says Feasibility Study" [press release] (Sept. 24, 1995), available at *http://www.house.gov/hostettler/i69/9-2469.htm*.
2. Donohue & Associates, Cambridge Systematics, Congdon Engineering Associates, *Southwest Indiana Highway Feasibility Study* (Indianapolis: Indiana Department of Transportation, 1990); U.S. Department of Transportation, Federal Highway Administration, Indiana Department of Transportation, *Southwest Indiana Highway Corridor: Draft Environmental Impact Study* (Indianapolis: Indiana Department of Transportation, 1996).
3. Donohue & Associates, *Southwest Indiana*, pp. 10–20.
4. Taxpayers for Common Sense and Friends of the Earth, "Road to Ruin: I-69 Highway Extension, Southwest Indiana, $600 Million," available at *http://www.taxpayer.net/TCS/RoadRuin/i-69in.htm*.
5. James Walker and Charles Gibson, "Your Money: The Politics of Highways," *ABC News World News Tonight with Peter Jennings* (July 30, 1998).
6. Bob Kur and Tom Brokaw, "Proposed Multi-State Interstate Would Spend a Billion Taxpayer Dollars While an Existing Road Could Be Improved at Much Lower Cost," *NBC Nightly News* (April 29, 1998).

CONCLUSION

Ultimately, decisions are political. It is the job of the cost-benefit analyst to provide as objective an analysis as possible given the policy problem and the context. Many think that science is about providing answers to puzzles about the physical and social world. This is true, in part. But science is also about providing an estimate of the uncertainty we have about how the world works. A responsible analyst does this.

One of the virtues of cost-benefit analysis, in particular, is that it obligates policy analysts to consider the implications of policy for the plight of ordinary citizens and workers. There is an unfortunate tendency among policy analysts to forget that policies have very real consequences for very real people. Caught up in spreadsheets, budgetary categories, and abstract indicators of policy performance, analysts and technical bureaucrats sometimes become elitist, focusing on the objectives of policy specialists and career politicians. Of course, the definitions of costs and benefits can easily reflect these elitist leanings, but the very nature of having to document costs and benefits induces analysts to search for costs and benefits that they might otherwise fail to consider.

Key Terms

ex ante analysis *p. 202*
ex post analysis *p. 202*
cost-benefit analysis *p. 203*
cost-effectiveness analysis *p. 203*
monetization *p. 203*
policy forecast *p. 205*
substitution effect *p. 207*

discounting *p. 208*
imputed value of life *p. 210*
willingness to accept *p. 210*
willingness to pay *p. 211*
Pareto principle *p. 212*
Kaldor-Hicks criterion *p. 213*
sensitivity analysis *p. 215*

Suggested Readings

Boardman, Anthony, David Greenberg, Aiden Vining, and David Weimer. 1996. *Cost-Benefit Analysis: Concepts and Practice*. Upper Saddle River, N.J.: Prentice-Hall.

Haveman, Robert H. 1972. *The Economic Performance of Public Investments: An Ex Post Evaluation of Water Resources Investments*. Baltimore: Resources for the Future, Johns Hopkins Press.

Haveman, Robert H. 1987. *Poverty Policy and Poverty Research: The Great Society and the Social Sciences*. Madison: University of Wisconsin Press.

Lipsey, Mark W. 1990. *Design Sensitivity: Statistical Power for Experimental Research*. Newbury Park, Calif.: Sage Publications.

Mikesell, John L. 1994. *Fiscal Administration: Analysis and Applications for the Public Sector*. 4th ed. Belmont, Calif.: Wadsworth.

Musgrave, Richard A., and Peggy B. Musgrave. 1984. *Public Finance in Theory and Practice.* 4th ed. New York: McGraw-Hill.

Viscusi, W. Kip. 1992. *Fatal Tradeoffs: Public and Private Responsibilities for Risk.* New York: Oxford University Press.

Notes

1. For a much more thorough treatment of the subject, see Anthony Boardman, David Greenberg, Aiden Vining, and David Weimer, *Cost-Benefit Analysis: Concepts and Practice* (Upper Saddle River, N.J.: Prentice-Hall, 1996).

2. John Chubb and Terry Moe, *Politics, Markets, and America's Schools* (Washington, D.C.: Brookings Institute, 1990).

3. See, for example, W. Kip Viscusi, *Fatal Tradeoffs: Public and Private Responsibilities for Risk* (New York: Oxford University Press, 1992).

4. National Center for Policy Analysis, "Guide to Regulatory Reform: The Cost-Benefit Rule," Brief Analysis, no. 150 (January 31, 1995), available at http://www.ncpa.org/ba/ba150.html.

5. Harold Lasswell, *Politics: Who Gets What, When, How* (New York: McGraw-Hill, 1936).

6. Vilfredo Pareto (1906), *Manual of Political Economy* (New York: A. M. Kelly, 1971).

7. Lasswell, *Politics.*

12

Evaluating Existing Policies

INTRODUCTION

In the previous chapter, we looked at one of the major approaches for analyzing future policy choices. In that chapter, our goal was to help you think systematically about whether a government should adopt a particular public policy. In this chapter, our concern is with the evaluation of existing policies. This type of evaluation is known as *ex post* policy analysis, which simply means that it is "backward looking." Studies of this type are designed to evaluate past policy performance and are typically called **policy impact studies** or policy impact evaluations.

As we will see, the high degree of polycentricity in the United States permits analysts to engage in what we call sideways analyses, which blur the lines between *ex ante* and *ex post* policy analyses in beneficial ways. This is because the rich variety of government jurisdictions in the United States affords us the opportunity to evaluate policy choices that have been adopted in other jurisdictions to gain information that can be used in recommending the adoption of a similar measure in our own community or state. Notice, however, that the goal of all types of policy analysis, whether *ex ante, ex post,* or this hybrid type of sideways analysis, is to improve future policy performance.

SUMMATIVE VERSUS FORMATIVE STUDIES

Not all policy impact studies are equally capable of ferreting out information on the operation of the component parts of a policy on a target population.

Some studies are designed to answer the question of whether a policy has worked or not but are not capable of determining the specific factors that are responsible for its success or failure; other studies are designed to identify the specific factors that are responsible for policy success or failure. Studies that are designed to do the former are called **summative studies;** the latter are called **formative studies.**[1] These terms take their meaning from the root of each word. Much as a news report might conclude a discussion of an event with the words *in sum,* summative studies give a summary indication that a policy either has or has not had an intended impact. By ferreting out the factors that contribute to the success or failure of policies, formative studies enable policymakers to reform policies. In other words, formative studies are designed to permit policy formulation that builds on factors contributing to success and minimizes factors contributing to failure.

Formative studies are clearly superior to summative studies. The former provide much more precise guidance to policymakers. In this type of study, individual components of a policy can be identified as working in specific sorts of ways. By contrast, summative studies, at best, can answer the question about a policy impact with only a yes or no—that is, that a policy did or did not have an impact. So why aren't all policy impact studies designed to be formative? There are basically two answers to this question: one practical and one ethical.

The practical reason is that analysts often do not have sufficient control over the implementation of a policy to design a study that is able to do more than say whether the policy had an effect or not. To draw formative conclusions, it is generally necessary to observe the "state of the world" prior to the implementation of the policy in question. This preimplementation observation—often called a pretest—is compared with a postimplementation observation (called the post-test) to see what specific kinds of changes in the state of the world have occurred as a result of the policy. Having both pretest and post-test observations is not the only study attribute that is necessary in formative analyses, but as we will see below, it is typically required. As a practical matter, it is often beyond the reach of analysts to draw pretest observations, particularly when a policy is already being implemented at the time the analyst is asked to undertake a policy impact study. Sometimes it is simply too late to turn the clock backward to observe the state of the world that existed before a policy was implemented.

The ethical issue is that when human lives and well-being are involved (which often is the case in public policy research), the demands of formative analyses sometimes impose unnecessary hazards on individuals. In such cases, summative analyses are preferred over formative analyses.

Consider the following example. In the mid-1980s a research hospital in Houston adopted a protocol for the treatment of extremely premature babies—that is, babies born between 20 and 28 weeks' gestation (out of the normal 40-week gestational period). Such babies often weigh between 500 and 1,000 grams at birth, which is roughly equivalent to a birth weight of 1 to 2 pounds. These babies, if they survive, are at high risk of experiencing one or more types of **morbidity,** which in this case is defined as any type of physical or mental damage sustained by a baby that persists for more than a year after birth. The treatment protocol involved a combination of chemical sedatives that had already been approved for use with infants, physical restraints, and minimization of handling by health care providers and family members, all of which were intended to minimize the movements of the premature baby for a period of a week after birth, with the idea that this would reduce the likelihood of bleeding in the brain and resulting morbidity.

Using this experimental treatment protocol, the research hospital was able to reduce the morbidity level among the babies receiving the treatment to a level substantially below that experienced by similar premature babies in that hospital prior to the adoption of this protocol, as well as in other hospitals treating similar premature babies in the Houston area and elsewhere. The evaluation of this protocol by the hospital was what we have described here as summative. Thus, the researchers at the hospital concluded that something about the combination of drugs, restraints, and minimal handling was succeeding in reducing morbidity levels, but they could not tell, nor did they try to tell, what specific elements of the protocol were most responsible for the benefits.

The question is, would it have been ethical for the research staff to do a formative study to identify the specific factors that were most responsible for the protocol's effectiveness? In a formative study, the researchers would be trying to identify how much, if at all, each part of the treatment protocol was contributing to the overall effectiveness of the protocol. Such a study would have exposed additional babies to the likelihood of lifelong damage that might include anything from blindness, to a loss of part or all of their small intestines, to mental retardation, to cerebral palsy, and on and on. Surely the gains from such a study are hardly worth the costs in terms of impaired lives. In this situation, it is better to conclude that the protocol adopted in this hospital should be adopted broadly for extremely premature babies, even though the specific factors that were responsible for its effectiveness were not well understood.

ANALYSIS OF SUBOBJECTIVES

In cases where it is both feasible and ethical to conduct formative studies, the policy analyst should give considerable thought to analyzing the impacts of each of the component activities that collectively make up a particular policy. In one of the best texts on impact analysis available, Lawrence Mohr argues that policy implementation is comprised of a chain of activities that must each occur in order for the overall goal of a policy to be realized.[2]

For example, consider the case of the new welfare system that you read about in Chapter 8. The new policy is intended to move recipients off welfare assistance into self-sufficiency through full-time participation in the work force. For the new policy to work, a series of activities must occur. Potential clients must have, or be able to obtain, the necessary employment skills and qualifications; they must have the opportunity to work, in the sense that they must not have insurmountable barriers to work such as a lack of child care or lack of transportation; they must be offered employment for which they are qualified; employers must offer compensation superior to the benefits available in the welfare program; and clients must actually want to engage in sustained work force participation. The new welfare policy will fail if one or more of these objectives is not achieved. Mohr refers to these chains of intermediary outcomes as the **subobjectives** of a policy. He makes a compelling case that "measurement and analysis of subobjectives and activities . . . operates to suggest actions to change the program in certain ways to make it more successful."[3]

The analysis of subobjectives in policy impact evaluations can be described in general terms as a sequence of policy impact evaluations of each of the pairs of intermediary activities and subobjectives in a causal chain. The goal is to determine the strength of each link. Just as in the welfare case above, every policy comprises some sort of a causal chain. Some causal chains are quite long and complex; others are fairly short and simple. Sometimes the successful attainment of policy objectives is undermined because the causal chain that makes up the underlying theory behind the policy has one or more weak links. Let us see why this is so.

Assume for the moment that a policy intervention involves a very simple chain with two linkages: A is expected to produce B, and B is expected to produce C, so that A leads ultimately to C. If A fails to produce B, then the policy fails (regardless of the linkage between B and C). Likewise, if B does not produce C, the policy again fails (again regardless of the linkage between A and B). Only if both subobjectives are achieved will the policy succeed. That is, only if A is successful in producing B and B is successful in producing C will A have had the desired impact and lead to C. The reason for analyzing subobjectives is to identify where in this causal chain the policy is compromised. If the problem is between B and C, then the policy should be reformed at that linkage— not at the linkage between A and B. It is possible that a policy such as this, which has a single weak link, may be reformed. In contrast, if all the links in a causal chain are shown to be weak, then the entire theory behind the policy is probably fatally flawed and should be discarded.

TYPES OF POLICY IMPACT STUDIES

Several methods have been devised for carrying out the analysis of policy impacts. Of these methods, the most powerful is the true **policy experiment.** True policy experiments permit us to draw firm conclusions about the impact of a policy on one or more variables of interest that we can know are valid with a very high degree of confidence. As we will explain below, true policy experiments require that the researcher have an unusually high degree of control over the implementation of a policy—control that, for good reasons, is often not forthcoming. In practice it is often necessary to rely on studies of policy impacts that utilize elements of true experiments but lack some of the key attributes that make experiments so powerful. This type of study is called a quasi-experimental study (quasi-experiment). These studies vary in their power to permit valid assessments of the true impacts of policies, for reasons that we will discuss later.

Policy Experiments

Ideally, before a new program is adopted on a society-wide basis, a policy experiment would first be conducted to demonstrate that the program is likely to be successful in achieving the desired goals. True policy experiments are extremely powerful because they are designed intentionally to eliminate factors from consideration that might mistakenly be credited with producing a policy impact. How do experiments accomplish this goal?

The secret to true policy experiments is the **random assignment** of subjects to the groups that will receive or not receive a given policy action—often called the treatment. In other words, individuals are randomly put into the group that will receive the treatment (the **treatment group**), as well as into the group that does not receive the treatment (the **control group**). Why is random assignment effective in eliminating the problem of noncausal factors being misidentified as causal factors? The answer is that when random assignment is used to allocate individuals to treatment and control groups, any factors that might be correlated with the outcome of interest, other than the treatment itself, will also be randomly assigned to the two groups. If the treatment and control groups are sufficiently large, any spurious factors that might be associated with the outcome of interest will be found in both groups in approximately equal numbers. Consequently, such factors will "wash out" when the two groups are later compared to see if outcomes are different between the treatment and control groups.

The simplest type of true policy experiment involves the random assignment of individuals to two groups, with one to receive the policy treatment; both are observed at some point at time after the treatment to determine if the treatment group shows a difference from the control group on measures of outcomes of interest. This type of simple experimental design is depicted in Table 12.1 as design TE.1, "Random Assignment, with Comparative Post-test." Interpreting the schematic depiction of this design is straightforward. The letter R indicates random assignment of subjects to the treatment and control groups. The X indicates the policy activities of interest to which the treatment group is exposed.

TABLE 12.1 Types of Policy Impact Studies[1]

True Experimental Designs

TE.1   Random Assignment, with Comparative Post-test

$$\frac{R \qquad X\ O}{R \qquad\quad O}$$

TE.2   Random Assignment, with Comparative Post-test and Within-Group Comparison

$$\frac{R \quad O \quad X \quad O}{R \quad O \qquad\quad O}$$

Nonexperimental Designs

NE.1   Comparative Post-test

$$\frac{X \quad O}{O}$$

NE.2   Within-Group Comparison (Treatment Group Only)

$$O \quad X \quad O$$

Quasi-experimental Designs

QE.1   Comparative Post-test with Within-Group Comparison

$$\frac{O \quad X \quad O}{O \qquad\quad O}$$

QE.2   Interrupted Time Series

$$O\ O\ O\ O\ O\ O\ O \ldots O\ X\ O\ O\ O\ O\ O\ O \ldots O$$

QE.3   Interrupted Time Series, with Comparison Group

$$\frac{O\ O\ O\ O\ O\ O\ O \ldots O\ X\ O\ O\ O\ O\ O\ O \ldots O}{O\ O\ O\ O\ O\ O\ O \ldots O \qquad O\ O\ O\ O\ O\ O \ldots O}$$

QE.4   Multiple Comparative Post-tests and Within-Group Comparisons

$$\frac{O \quad X \quad O}{}$$
$$\cdots$$
$$\frac{O \quad X \quad O}{}$$
$$\frac{O \quad X \quad O}{O \qquad\quad O}$$
$$\cdots$$
$$\frac{O \qquad\quad O}{O \qquad\quad O}$$

QE.5   Multiple Interrupted Time Series, with Multiple Comparison Groups

$$\frac{O\ O\ O\ O\ O\ O\ O \ldots O\ X\ O\ O\ O\ O\ O\ O \ldots O}{O\ O\ O\ O\ O\ O\ O \ldots O\ X\ O\ O\ O\ O\ O\ O \ldots O}$$
$$\cdots$$
$$\frac{O\ O\ O\ O\ O\ O\ O \ldots O\ X\ O\ O\ O\ O\ O\ O \ldots O}{}$$
$$\frac{O\ O\ O\ O\ O\ O\ O \ldots O\ X\ O\ O\ O\ O\ O\ O \ldots O}{O\ O\ O\ O\ O\ O\ O \ldots O \qquad O\ O\ O\ O\ O\ O \ldots O}$$
$$\cdots$$
$$\frac{O\ O\ O\ O\ O\ O\ O \ldots O \qquad O\ O\ O\ O\ O\ O \ldots O}{O\ O\ O\ O\ O\ O\ O \ldots O \qquad O\ O\ O\ O\ O\ O \ldots O}$$

1. Adapted from Cook, Thomas D. and Donald T. Campbell. 1979. *Quasi-experimentation: Design and Analysis Issues for Field Settings.* Boston: Houghton Mifflin.

The O indicates observation of a group on a set of variables that the researcher wishes to measure in order to make comparative statements about changes within or across groups, typically because these measures are expected potentially to vary, in some way, as a result of the policy activity X. Finally, the line separating the two rows of Rs, Xs, and Os indicates that the two groups are to be compared with each other.

Notice that in design TE.1, only one set of observations is taken, which occurs after the treatment group has been exposed to the policy of interest. It is the exact design used in the study discussed above involving the new treatment protocol for extremely premature babies. This type of design lends itself to the summative type of analysis, insofar as it permits conclusions about whether the treatment is effective in producing a different outcome in the treatment group versus the control group. But notice that information about intermediary activities that together make up the policy intervention and about subobjectives cannot be easily extracted from this design. About the only way that this design can be used to disaggregate subobjectives is to have, in addition to a control group, multiple treatment groups to which subjects are randomly assigned, so that each treatment group might be assigned a different intermediary activity. In other words, rather than compare the control group to one treatment group that is exposed to the entire package of activities that make up the policy of interest, each treatment group would receive an individual portion of the policy and be compared with the control group.

Case 12.1 contains a description of the Milwaukee school voucher program, which utilized an experimental design. In this study, the design was more complicated than the one that we have been discussing. The voucher study used a design akin to TE.2 in Table 12.1, "Random Assignment, with Comparative Post-test and Within-Group Comparison." This design adds a set of observations taken prior to the commencement of the experimental treatment.

There are two main reasons for incorporating pretest observations, both of which turn out to be important in the voucher study. The first is to engage in formative evaluations. Given the high stakes in the school voucher debate, it is important to know not just whether the voucher students are performing better or worse than public school students but by how much and in what areas. Likewise, it is important to know whether families are more or less satisfied, and again by how much and in what ways. With scores from a variety of survey questions and records indicating scores on standardized tests, it was possible to ascertain both specific changes within the voucher student population after several years of exposure to private schooling and differences between the voucher student population and the public school population over this same period. Some of the same kind of comparisons could also be drawn in regard to parental satisfaction.

The second reason for incorporating pretest observations turns out to have been even more important in the case of the voucher study. One of the great difficulties in conducting true experiments on policies that deal with human beings is that humans interact with one another, engage in learning, and adopt a variety of adaptive behaviors—often as a direct result of their knowledge of the experiments. This knowledge can, and often will, contaminate the results of experiments. It is a phenomenon known as **reactivity.** Reactivity is the reason that it is common in medical studies to give subjects assigned to the control group a **placebo,** which is simply a "treatment" that the individuals believe to be real but is not. Sometimes this can take the form of sugar tablets or plain saline solution. Other times it is a theatrical performance intended to deceive the patient or family members into believing that the patient has received the actual treatment. Indeed, in many cases, the prospect of reactivity is so great that a **double-blind procedure** is employed, in which neither the patient nor the caregivers that will attend to the patient during the study are aware of whether the patient has been given the true treatment or not. The staff that actually administers the treatment or placebo is a special team that is never permitted to interact with the patient from that point forward and that is sworn to secrecy when discussing patients in the study with other staff members. The reason for this is to avoid the very real possibility that caregivers will treat patients differently based on their expectation that the treatment ought to work and that the placebo ought not to work.

Why was the pretest important in the voucher study in dealing with reactivity? Because the voucher study incorporated pretest observations, it was possible for researchers to identify the characteristics of students, both in the voucher group and in the control group, at the beginning of the study and as the study unfolded. The original design in the voucher study involved the random assignment of students to private schools and back into the Milwaukee public school system, which was possible because there were far more applicants for the program than slots available in the participating private schools. However, it is interesting (and perhaps not surprising) to note that many of the parents who had tried unsuccessfully to get their children into the voucher program did not quietly accept having them enrolled in the public school system that they had tried to escape. Many moved away from Milwaukee; others utilized an alternative program that allowed their children to be enrolled in suburban school districts. As the study progressed, a shrinking number of students who had been randomly assigned to stay in the public school system remained in the study and thus were available for post-test observations. Of these, several did not take or complete the standardized tests from which a comparison to the voucher students could be made.

Based on these pretest observations, it is apparent that most of the differences that at first blush appeared to be due to participation in the voucher program were instead due to the selective withdrawal of children in the control group. Many of the more ambitious and more capable students who were assigned to the control group fled the Milwaukee public school system, leaving behind a collection of students that was no longer representative of the population of students who originally had been assigned to the control group. Despite the best efforts of the researchers, in the end the actions of the parents meant that the control group could not be considered equivalent to the treatment group in all respects; it was equivalent only in exposure to the treatment itself.

The lesson here is that true policy experiments require that researchers have enormous control over individuals prior to the commencement of the policy of interest. Furthermore, even when well crafted, true policy experiments are difficult to sustain, given the self-knowledge and adaptive behaviors of human beings. Thus, the question is, is there a viable alternative to experiments?

Quasi-experiments

True policy experiments always involve the random assignment of subjects to one or more treatment groups, as well as to a control group. What happens if random assignment is eliminated? Consider for a moment the design NE.1, "Comparative Post-test," in Table 12.1. In every respect it is identical to the experimental design TE.1, except that subjects are not randomly assigned to the treatment and control groups. Let us imagine that the experimental treatment, whatever that may be, has concluded, and both groups are measured to see how they score on some variables of interest. To what can differences between the two groups be attributed? One possibility is that the treatment has produced differences between the groups. But it is also possible that the groups were already different. The two groups may have been selected for study precisely because they were already conveniently organized to serve as treatment and control groups. Post-test differences between the two groups may be the result of differences in the preferences and histories of the people who have to be in one group or the other. This type of difference is known as a **selection bias,** and it is common whenever people are able to choose for themselves the groups to which they belong or in which they participate. Because of the high possibility of selection bias and the total inability of analysts to eliminate it as a possibility when using this design, no firm conclusion can ever be drawn about the impact of a policy. The comparative post-test design is considered a nonexperimental design. Although unfortunately not uncommon, it is almost useless.

A better design, often called a **quasi-experimental design** because it shares attributes with true experimental designs but lacks random assignment, is the comparative post-test design with the addition of a pretest for both the treatment and control groups. This design in Table 12.1 is QE.1, "Comparative Post-test with Within-Group Comparison." Why is this a better design? With the inclusion of a pretest, the analyst has the opportunity to check to see how comparable the treatment group is to the control group. This presumes, of course, that the analyst can anticipate and measure every type of factor, other than the treatment itself, that could cause the two groups to differ. In many cases, this will not be possible—and if it is not, the design is only marginally more powerful than the nonexperimental design discussed above.

In situations where the control group is comparable to the treatment group, this quasi-experimental design is capable of providing valid conclusions about the impact of a policy. Case 12.2 provides a good example of studies that employed the comparative post-test with within-group comparison design. These studies assessed differences in perceptions of crime rates and citizen satisfaction with policing services in metropolitan areas with large, consolidated police forces versus metropolitan areas with small, community-based police forces. Obviously, the researchers could not control the assignment of policing services to different communities. Consequently, they could not randomly assign consolidated police services to some communities in metropolitan areas and more traditional, community-based policing to others. Instead, the analysts used preexisting data to match communities as closely as possible in order to remove factors, other than the organization of policing services, that might account for differences in citizen perceptions and satisfaction levels. To be sure, there may be some factors of importance that the analysts were unable to eliminate as alternative explanations of their findings. But by replicating their studies in multiple metropolitan areas, the analysts attempted to alleviate this concern insofar as possible.

Another commonly used quasi-experimental design is the "Interrupted Time Series," QE.2 in Table 12.1. At first glance, this design looks a great deal like the nonexperimental design NE.2, "Within-Group Comparison (Treatment Group Only)." In both cases, there is only a treatment group, where the experimental treatment is bracketed by pretest and post-test observations. In the interrupted time series design, there are multiple pretest and post-test observations. The strength of this design lies in the repetition of observations both before and after the introduction of the policy of interest. With repetition of observations, the analyst can eliminate a number of the most frequent threats that make drawing conclusions about policy impacts difficult.

For example, you may be interested in determining whether the adoption of the death penalty in a state is responsible for lowering the murder rate. If all you have is a single observation of the murder rate before and after the death penalty is passed by the state legislature, what can you conclude? Perhaps the new penalty is responsible for lowering the murder rate. But there are many other possibilities as well. One is that things in the outside world might be responsible for producing the change. Unemployment may have increased or decreased, leading to more or less criminality. Or perhaps drug use has increased or decreased. These kinds of factors are often called **history threats** to drawing valid conclusions. They are phenomena that have occurred in the outside society that, rather than the policy itself, may account for a change in the outcome of interest. Another type of threat is known as **maturation,** which is a change within the treatment group itself. For example, the population of males aged fourteen to twenty-five may have increased or decreased. This type of change could account for a change in the murder rate.

With a single pretest and post-test observation, you cannot separate out these factors from the impact of the policy that you are interested in evaluating. But with many pre-test and post-test observations, you can be fairly confident in eliminating these other factors. A variety of statistical techniques exist for removing or controlling for the influence of factors that may account for the trends in time series data. Some of these statistical techniques are quite sophisticated and powerful. What they have in common is the goal of clarifying the pattern in time series data that is due to factors other than the policy impact of interest, so that the amount of change that is due to the policy can be measured and tested for significance.

One of the limitations of the simple time series design is that it is possible that something could have intervened in the time series at about the same time as the policy of interest. This is particularly likely in cases like the death penalty, where politicians are responding to an increased level of public demands that something be done about crime. There may be something else going on in society at the same time as the demands for public action to pass a death penalty. A quasi-experimental design that is particularly adept at dealing with this possibility is the "Interrupted Time Series, with Comparison Group," listed in Table 12.1 as QE.3. This design adds a control group to the "Interrupted Time Series" design, which is observed on all the same occasions as the treatment group but is not exposed to the policy of interest. The control group allows the analyst to test for a shift in the trend line that might happen to coincide with the adoption of the policy. If the comparison group fails to show a shift during the same period the policy is adopted, but such a shift is visible in the treatment group, then the analyst can be reasonably confident in concluding that the policy is producing the impact.

A variety of permutations of these basic quasi-experimental designs have been utilized. They all share one or more of the basic features that we have discussed here. Policies may be introduced at one point in time in one time series and at another point in time in another series. Policies may be introduced at one point in time and then ended at a later point in time. What these designs share is an effort to control for factors, other than a policy itself, that might account for an outcome of interest. True experiments do this through random assignment. Quasi-experiments must do this through repetition of observations, the addition of comparison groups, and statistical controls.

SIDEWAYS ANALYSIS

The American political system offers a rich set of possibilities for analyzing policies that blur the lines between *ex ante* and *ex post* analyses. The reason for this feature is the high degree of polycentrism in the United States. To this point, we have been implicitly taking advantage of this feature in our discussion of methods of policy analysis. Polycentrism allows analyses of policies not only by speculating about a jurisdiction's future policy performance or by looking at past policy performance but also by **sideways analysis**—looking sideways at the current and past policy performance of other jurisdictions. At numerous points in this text we have pointed to the opportunities for policy learning afforded by the polycentrism in the United States. This is the thesis that we are now explicitly presenting.

Recall that one of the first stages in a cost-benefit analysis is the identification of potential solutions. Where does an analyst obtain information on potential solutions? Out of thin air? No, analysts arrive at potential solutions through a thoughtful appraisal of policies that are already being utilized elsewhere in society. The wide variety of multiple, overlapping, and proximate jurisdictions in the United States means that there are almost always similar institutional settings from which an analyst is able to draw up a list of possible policy options.

Likewise, cost-benefit analysis demands that analysts arrive at estimates of costs and benefits, in monetary terms, associated with the adoption of a particular policy option. In the absence of the multitude of governmental jurisdictions in the United States, such estimates would be almost purely speculative. But in practice, many of these estimates are relatively easy to produce, precisely because other jurisdictions have already implemented a similar policy. In other words, while cost-benefit studies are future oriented, current and past policy actions in other jurisdictions typically provide the factual bases for these studies.

Policy impact studies can be made far more powerful in a polycentric political system. Consider again the issue of how policing should be organized, which is discussed in Case 12.2. While the design used by the research team was the comparative post-test with within-group comparison, an even more powerful extension of this design is shown in Table 12.1 as QE.4, "Multiple Comparative Post-tests and Within-Group Comparisons." This design adds a large number of additional study settings in which some receive the policy in question and others do not. In the issue of police organization, the advantage of this study design is that powerful statistical techniques can be employed to help rule out any differences across communities, other than the organization of police services, that might be responsible for differences in perceptions of safety and satisfaction with policing. The inherent difficulty of matching communities, which requires trying to find nearly identical settings, is thereby eliminated. Such a design is feasible only in a political system that offers a very large number of jurisdictions of varying sizes and characteristics. Indeed, the larger the number of jurisdictions, the better from the point of view of policy analysis.

Or consider the quasi-experimental design QE.5 of Table 12.1, "Multiple Interrupted Time Series, with Multiple Comparison Groups." This design is similar to QE.3, "Interrupted Time Series, with Comparison Group," but it has multiple treatment groups and multiple control groups, all observed repetitively

Case 12.1

Impact Analysis of Milwaukee School Choice Program

ONE OF the greatest arguments for the pick-yourself-up-by-the-bootstraps American ethos is that poorer Americans can climb the socioeconomic ladder through education. Indeed, the U.S. public education and university systems provide a far greater possibility of upward mobility than exists in any major European country. Nevertheless, Americans increasingly perceive that U.S. schools fail their children—especially poorer, inner-city children.

Numerous theories of how to remedy the failings of American schools have sprung forth. These theories provide ideological combatants with an arena for their battle. One such theory was first advanced by Milton Friedman in the 1960s. Friedman called for the government to provide vouchers to families so that parents could spend educational dollars anywhere they chose rather than having either to send their children to taxpayer-funded public schools or pay both educational taxes and tuition at a private school.[1]

Friedman's proposal has been hotly debated.

Proponents argue that the infusion of money to private schools would improve their ability to pay quality teachers while also forcing public schools to improve themselves through competition for students and the students' vouchers.[2] Following Friedman's argument, the market mechanism provides an excellent means to regulate society, and this is another example of where the infusion of consumer choice would demand a better supply by producers. Opponents counter that such programs would allow private schools to segregate their enrollment by admitting selectively on achievement, class, and race. Further, opponents contend that such vouchers would merely provide a tax break to families who would have sent their children to private schools anyway.[3]

A number of school systems have introduced school choice where parents can choose from a number of public schools, but few have experimented with providing vouchers to spend at private schools. With a failing school system, Milwaukee, Wisconsin, implemented a limited school voucher program in 1990, called the Milwaukee Parental Choice Program, for low-income students to attend nonsectarian private schools of their choice.[4]

After four years of the program, different reports suggested differing interpretations of the Milwaukee program's success. All agreed that private schools expanded their curricula to include programs such as foreign languages, as well as improved the physical status of their buildings with the increased capital. Additionally, all sides found that parents of children who took advantage of the vouchers (choice students) were much happier with their children's schooling than nonvoucher parents (nonchoice students). Both the schools' environment and the discipline were seen much more positively by parents of choice students.[5]

The point of contention, however, stemmed from students' achievement during the program. One group of researchers found that in math test scores, the students admitted to the choice program greatly outperformed those who had been rejected by the program. The release of the report attempted to promote the continuance of the program, as well as to receive attention at the 1996 Republican National Convention, whose audience would support such findings.[6]

John Witte of the University of Wisconsin, who had been selected by the state as the independent evaluator of the program, obtained results that differed from those above. His disagreement with the other findings centered on the comparison between those accepted and those rejected from the choice program and on statistical findings of the report. Witte argued that comparing those accepted to those rejected would not be appropriate, because there was no random mechanism for deciding rejection. Thus, a comparison was being drawn between students who were unlikely to have been as academically capable as those accepted. Additionally, some of the rejected students were likely to have had disabilities that private schools could not deal with but that might lower the test scores of the rejected students.[7]

The second criticism, the statistical challenge, centered on the fact that there was no improvement in reading for choice students compared with rejected students during the program, but that there was a significant improvement in math scores of the choice students over the rejected students. This is curious, because standardized test scores in the two subjects typically are highly related to one another. A significant increase in one as opposed to the other should not happen. When studying the actual test results, Witte found that five rejected students had math scores that reflected the fact that they had not completed that portion of the test, and thus had received scores of zero. These students had had normal math scores on the previous year's test, so there was little reason to think they had gotten the wrong answer on all of the problems. When these five students were removed from the comparison, the results showed that there was no improvement over time for choice students in comparison with rejected students. Further, when comparing the choice students' test scores with those of lower-income Milwaukee public school students, Witte did not find evidence that students from the choice program performed any better than comparable students in the Milwaukee public schools. Further, despite the general improvement of private schools affected by the plan, three private schools went bankrupt, leaving students scrambling to enter other schools in mid-year.

The Milwaukee Parental Choice Program was an important laboratory to test the hotly debated policy innovation of allowing parents to use public funds to pay for private education. The debate shows a number of things about such policy debates. First, changes in education involve political groups such as community school districts, teachers' unions, religious schools, nonsectarian schools, and others who believe this debate is a microcosm of a much larger, politically charged public policy debate. Second, achievement is not an easy phenomenon to measure. Was the Milwaukee program successful because parents felt happier with their children's education? Or do the results that show no actual improvement in student performance mean that the program should be shelved? Third, is it reasonable to place enormous requirements on public schools, such as educating students with disabilities and those who need special attention, while allowing private schools to receive public funding without any such

continued

requirements? Finally, would a program with broader social-class application provide greater competition and perhaps a better comparison? Or has the lack of success in Milwaukee shown that such a broader application would merely underwrite the private education of middle- and upper-income students?

1. Carol Ascher, Norm Fruchter, and Robert Berne, *Hard Lessons: Public Schools and Privatization* (New York: Twentieth Century Fund Press, 1996).
2. John F. Witte, *The Market Approach to Education: An Analysis of America's First Voucher Program* (Princeton, N.J.: Princeton University Press, 2000).
3. *Ibid.*
4. Ascher, Fruchter, and Berne, *Hard Lessons.*
5. *Ibid.*
6. Witte, *Market Approach.*
7. *Ibid.*

before and after the imposition of a policy in the treatment groups. This is an extremely powerful design. Implicit in it, however, is the presumption that the political system permits variability in the adoption of policies by subnational governments. If all jurisdictions were required to adopt identical policies at the same time, then the opportunity for policy learning would be seriously compromised. By allowing a degree of autonomy in subnational jurisdictions, it is possible to monitor the performance of groups of jurisdictions to ascertain what sorts of impacts policies are having.

Polycentrism encourages—and undergirds—formative policy analysis. Polycentrism allows jurisdictions to look sideways at other jurisdictions to learn from both their policy successes and policy failures. It permits this sideways-looking analysis to be conducted using highly powerful and sophisticated research methods. In short, it gives policymakers the opportunity to adopt policies with reasonable expectations about how the policies will operate in the future, because those expectations can be founded upon a careful analysis of policy performance in other communities.

CONCLUSION

Why is systematic policy analysis useful? As stated at the outset of this chapter, policy analysis forces policy proponents and opponents to quantify and verify their policy positions. The result is that decisions are more likely to be made in a systematic, rather than in an *ad hoc,* way. Of course, each special interest will attempt to sway policymaking in a direction that is consistent with its position, but this is politics and is hardly bad. It forces those who are interested in the outcome of a policy debate to make their positions clearly known and exposes the merits of their analyses to scrutiny.

Prior to embarking on systematic policy analyses, analysts must construct a mental image of how a set of policy options might fit within an institutional context in which individuals and groups are seeking to act on their preferences and shared understandings. This means that policy analysis must be located within the context of a thoughtful examination of the institutional conditions in which policies will be implemented.

To be sure, there is no cookbook or how-to book that can adequately guide policy analysis. There are simply too many variables, too many assumptions, and too many preferences to permit the use of a simple, one-size-fits-all technique for selecting the best policies that should be adopted in societies. Nevertheless, it is possible to move in the direction of more systematic policy analysis. The strengths of policy analysis lie not merely in its rigor. Its strengths are due partly to the adoption of a common language that is shared by policymakers and policy advocates. Its strengths are also due to the impetus policy analysis gives to all participants in policy debates to recognize the broader social implications of policy.

Perhaps this is the most important virtue of systematic policy analysis: it compels all participants in policy debates to recognize the broader social implications of policy. If politics were only about who wins and who loses, society would find it difficult to try to solve problems. If politics were only about solving problems, groups of citizens that end up bearing costs disproportionately might begin to view themselves as permanent minorities or resort to violence to seek redress for their grievances. In the end, policy analysis is about how society operates, its failures, and the opportunities for altering it. Thus, the tools and techniques of policy analysis must be thought of in the context of the existing political system, the institutions and incentives that underpin markets, and government coerciveness and bureaucratic agencies through which that coercion is applied.

Key Terms

policy impact study *p. 220*	reactivity *p. 227*
summative study *p. 221*	placebo *p. 227*
formative study *p. 221*	double-blind procedure *p. 227*
morbidity *p. 222*	selection bias *p. 228*
subobjective *p. 223*	quasi-experimental design *p. 228*
policy experiment *p. 223*	history threat *p. 229*
random assignment *p. 224*	maturation *p. 229*
treatment group *p. 224*	sideways analysis *p. 231*
control group *p. 224*	

Suggested Readings

Allison, Paul D. 1984. *Event History Analysis: Regression for Longitudinal Event Data*. Newbury Park, Calif.: Sage Publications.

Cook, Thomas D., and Donald T. Campbell. 1979. *Quasi-experimentation: Design and Analysis Issues for Field Settings*. Boston: Houghton Mifflin.

Hedrick, Terry E., Leonard Bickman, and Debra J. Rog. 1993. *Applied Research Design: A Practical Guide*. Newbury Park, Calif.: Sage Publications.

Impact Analysis of Community-Based versus Consolidated Policing

O VER THE past quarter-century, law and order has been a salient policy issue in the United States, especially in the country's large metropolitan areas. This focus on crime was nowhere more apparent than in the Hollywood television and movie industry, which shifted from highlighting the honesty of small-town sheriff Andy Taylor of Mayberry and the quaint determination of Sgt. Joe Friday of the Los Angeles Police Department to featuring the breakdown of law and order in New York City, San Francisco, Miami, and elsewhere. The shift in image followed skyrocketing crime rates and increasing violence. Scholars of urban affairs and public policy began to debate how best to structure modern urban police departments to reduce crime. The question was how to organize policing efforts to best reduce crime rates.

Local and state police provide an important service, but police need help from communities in order to reduce crime. *Steve Frischling.*

One of the most popular approaches for reducing crime rates called for a consolidation of numerous urban police forces into a larger, more specialized and technically expert police department.[1] Many argued that larger departments would offer specialization of services in urban areas and enhanced professionalization within police departments. Taking police control away from specific communities was thought by those arguing for consolidation to guard against graft and amateur policing. In contrast, those supportive of community policing argued that larger departments would destroy the social conditions that deter crime: "The degree of safety enjoyed by a community results primarily from the activities of many individuals interacting with one another within a broad set of institutional arrangements which includes, but is not limited to, the police."[2] One set of studies undertaken in the early 1970s attempted to test whether consolidated police forces performed better than community-based policing. The coexistence of multiple, proximate jurisdictions employing different models of policing permitted a perfect laboratory in which to assess whether community-based policing should be replaced by consolidated police departments.

In the late 1960s and early 1970s, Indianapolis attempted a new form of government called "Unigov," where the city incorporated other cities within its surrounding county. These newly incorporated portions of Indianapolis would be policed from the downtown headquarters. Three smaller communities remained separate from this incorporation into Indianapolis, however, and kept their local police forces. Because these smaller communities (none larger than 20,000 people) are adjacent to Indianapolis neighborhoods that are similar in demographics and other characteristics, they provide an excellent comparison. The researchers interviewed residents of the neighboring areas of Indianapolis and the three smaller communities about their attitudes concerning police performance.

The Indianapolis Police Department comprised 1,100 officers and was broken into seven sectors. This force was regarded as modern and professional in comparison with other major U.S. urban police departments. The smaller community police departments had between 18 and 25 officers and, on average, spent only 60 percent of what Indianapolis police spent per capita. Some money was saved by using specialty services, such as the state crime laboratory in Indianapolis, when needed, whereas the Indianapolis Police Department had its own specialty services.

But how did citizens feel about their police services? Performance was judged on the following criteria: rapid response by police, perception that crime was increasing or decreasing, quality of the police-citizen relationship, whether police accepted bribes, and overall performance judgments by citizens. Despite having similarities to their Indianapolis neighbors, the citizens of the smaller communities were victimized by household crimes 7 percent less than their Indianapolis counterparts and tended to report crimes to police 8 percent more frequently. The perception of increasing crime held for only 23 percent of the smaller-town residents, while 39 percent of the abutting Indianapolis residents feared that crime was increasing. Also, the small-town police responded to emergency calls within five minutes 80 percent of the time, whereas Indianapolis police did so in only 60 percent of cases. There was no real difference between the groups on whether police accepted bribes (a significant finding, considering that those arguing for consolidation did so partially due to the fear that smaller departments

continued

have higher rates of graft and cronyism). However, a significant distinction presented itself concerning overall judgment of police performance. Seventy-five percent of small-town residents thought "the police in this neighborhood are doing an outstanding" or "good job." This compared with 54 percent of the adjoining Indianapolis locales.

These findings suggest that consolidation of police agencies has not led to positive reactions by citizens. Both public opinion and victimization favor the community-based approach to policing. While these findings were present in these largely white areas, would they also exist in predominately minority communities? A similar study done by the same researchers that compared the predominantly black communities of Phoenix, Illinois, and East Chicago Heights, Illinois, with adjacent Chicago neighborhoods found little difference in perception of performance between the small minority community police performance and big-city police forces. What was noteworthy, however, was that the resources spent within the adjacent Chicago neighborhoods were fourteen times greater than the resources spent within Phoenix and East Chicago Heights. Yet the communities had similar experiences with policing.

Clearly, the findings of this research exhibit the importance of trust that local communities have in their police forces, which appears to be missing when police efforts are centralized in urban areas. This research also shows the advantages of being able to make "sideways" comparisons to inform policy choices. The presence of multiple, similar communities that differed primarily in the policy variable in question makes it possible to draw useful conclusions about what kinds of policies work, and under what circumstances.

1. This case draws from the following monograph: Elinor Ostrom, William Baugh, Richard Guarasci, Roger Parks, and Gordon Whitaker, *Community Organization and the Provision of Police Services*, ed. George H. Frederickson, Administrative and Policy Studies Series (Beverly Hills, Calif.: Sage Publications, 1973).
2. *Ibid.*, p.16.

Miller, Delbert Charles. 1991. *Handbook of Research Design and Social Measurement*. 5th ed. Newbury Park, Calif.: Sage Publications.

Mohr, Lawrence B. 1988. *Impact Analysis for Program Evaluation*. Chicago: Dorsey Press.

Patton, Carl V., and David S. Sawicki. 1993. *Basic Methods of Policy Analysis and Planning*. 2nd ed. Englewood Cliffs, N.J.: Prentice-Hall.

Rossi, Peter H., Howard E. Freeman, and Mark W. Lipsey. 1999. *Evaluation: A Systematic Approach*. 6th ed. Thousand Oaks, Calif.: Sage Publications.

Weiss, Carol H. 1972. *Evaluating Action Programs*. Boston: Allyn & Bacon.

Notes

1. Michael Scriven, "The Methodology of Evaluation," in Carol H. Weiss, ed., *Evaluating Action Programs* (Boston: Allyn & Bacon, 1972), pp. 123–136.

2. Lawrence B. Mohr, *Impact Analysis for Program Evaluation* (Chicago: Dorsey Press, 1988).

3. *Ibid.*, p. 27.

V

Conclusion

13

Reform of Public Policy

INTRODUCTION

We hope that students have taken many things from this book. First and fore-most, we want students to have gained an appreciation of the vast complexi-ties and opportunities underlying modern governance. Furthermore, we hope that students now realize the multiple impediments to good governance that collections of people seek to overcome in making good public policy.

We have emphasized three fundamental concepts and problems we face in analyzing public policy. First, public policy ultimately can be boiled down to an interplay between individual desires and group outcomes. Most public poli-cies try to change the way individuals behave. Deciding how to do so is tricky, because democracy involves aggregating individual values into a collective choice. What results from this complexity is something called collective action problems. Individual incentives lead individuals to do what is best for them, but when everyone behaves this way, the group or society is worse off than if everyone provided for the collective good. The conception of government is to solve these collective action problems by coercing or cajoling people into providing for the collective good.

Second, difficulties arise whenever we demand collective solutions to the problems we face. In a democracy, policy is supposed to be a function of indi-vidual preferences. However, there is no single way to aggregate individual pref-erences into a group preference without sacrificing democratic fairness or logical completeness. Although Arrow's theorem is very abstract, in practice what it tells us is that there can be no perfect democracy. Thus, by their very nature, democratic institutions are not entirely democratic. This means that the deci-sion about what policy to pursue will be as much a function of the institutional structures that make up a democracy as it will be of public preferences. The idea is to design institutions in a way that balances the tradeoff between fairness and coherence.

Third, democratic institutions are varied and rich. The traditional political economy model of public policy usually posits the existence of a government that will coerce individuals into providing for the common good. In reality, and especially in the American context, there are many governments. This polycentricity was once thought to be a problem because it was inefficient. However, more analysts now realize that such a rich set of institutions is likely to be beneficial. The benefits are especially obvious when we consider the nature of government failures; a strong centralized government may have a greater capability to fail than would a polycentric system.

Indeed, it is on this last point that we end the book. Much of this book is about failures—both failures of the market and failures of government. That is, much of the book discussed what goes wrong when we rely on either markets or governments to solve problems. Theories about market and government failures abound. Such failures are the focus of most work on the political economy of public policy. It is unfortunate, perhaps, that we know less about what works well than about what does not work. Yet it is possible to offer some suggestions about which institutions work better than others.

The irony embodied in the political economy approach to public policy is that the 1990s witnessed the United States in its most successful period in decades, if not in all time. The United States won the Cold War with the former Soviet Union. Most of the 1990s was a time of an unheard-of combination of economic prosperity and near-zero inflation. By the end of the century, consumer confidence was as high as it had been since the 1960s, and it was almost at an all-time high.

Donald Wittman, in a compelling book, argues that democratic institutions work well, and he dares to argue that these institutions are efficient.[1] His argument is that the give and take of democratic politics, especially interest group politics, balances the interests of individuals against the need to solve problems in a way that produces good public policies. He argues that policy analysts accentuate the negatives when applying theory to government. In the real world, things get messy, but democracies work much better than any alternatives, especially a hands-off (laissez-faire) approach.

CRITICAL INSTITUTIONS

Providing you with tools to think systematically about policies within varying institutional conditions is the purpose of the political economy approach to policy analysis described in this book. Without unduly repeating the previous chapters, we suggest that there are at least five major sets of institutional factors that you should consider in doing policy analysis before ever attempting to undertake a systematic study: (1) the characteristics of the policy good that is at stake, (2) the relative merits of a bottom-up versus top-down approach with regard to a particular policy issue, (3) the strengths and weakness of utilizing market incentives for addressing the problem, (4) the type and amount of government coercion that may be necessary, and (5) the likelihood of bureaucratic failures.

Characteristics of the Policy Good

There are many ways to conceptualize policy problems. Most policy problems are, in fact, collections of smaller problems that may each have different characteristics and require different types of policy solutions. Consider education. Most forms of education are experience or postexperience goods, because consumers of education may not be able to evaluate the quality of the policy good that they have received until after—and sometimes long after—they have consumed it. Education creates positive externalities. Society as a whole derives benefits from having a well-educated citizenry and work force. Education is also a co-produced good. The efforts of education providers, as well as efforts by consumers of education services, are needed for the policy good to be effectively produced. That is, you must be in class and attentive, be willing to discuss concepts and ideas from class with other students in the class, do assignments outside of class, and prepare papers and study for tests. At the same time, your instructor must be prepared, explain concepts clearly and carefully, hold your attention, and give you assignments that are pedagogically sound. All of this must occur if you are to receive much value from a class. And you may not come to appreciate some of that value until you're out in the "real world," thinking about issues that affect your job or your family.

Notice that each of these aspects of education may require different kinds of policies. This is often the case. In the real world, problems are usually clusters of different policies. It is thus important to analyze carefully the characteristics of the particular aspect of a situation that appears broken in order to identify solutions that do not fix the wrong thing, especially something that wasn't previously in need of fixing. The earlier chapters of the text offer ways of thinking about different aspects of specific policy problems.

Bottom-Up Versus Top-Down Policy Approaches

The United States is a big country, with lots of states and local jurisdictions. This means that we have both large and small policy problems. We have policy problems that are the same everywhere and problems that vary geographically. Problems vary enormously in the scope of their consequences. One of the implications of this variability is that the country comprises numerous overlapping publics, based upon how the consequences of issues are distributed across the population. The country is not composed of a single public across all issues.

Consequently, it is important to think through the advantages of encouraging bottom-up innovation and experimentation either instead of, or in addition to, top-down policies in which the federal government plays the key role in inducing policy change. As discussed in Chapter 8, some of the key criteria in sorting out the level or levels of government at which policy solutions should be cast include the geographic scope of problems, the technical and social complexity of problems, sensitivity to policy failure (that is, the extent to which the public can tolerate mistakes when trying to solve a public problem), and the goal of promoting democratic control over policy alternatives.

Consider, for example, how a mismatch in the selection of the level of government can lead to later problems in trying to recommend a policy alternative using cost-benefit analysis. Suppose that a federal grant is required to support a transportation project in a small city with a population of less than 100,000. Only those living in or frequently visiting this city will benefit. Perhaps the nonbenefactors-to-benefactors ratio is something like 2,000 to 1. How can a project of such scale be justified on the basis of willingness to compensate? The Kaldor-Hicks criterion appears to be wildly implausible in this circumstance, because the scope of the proposed project does not match the geographic boundaries of the jurisdiction implementing the policy. This sort of mismatch occurs when a project benefits a small geographic area, such as a single city in the United States, but the entire nation pays for the project. The problem for the Kaldor-Hicks principle is that the mismatch between the boundaries of the benefiting public and the boundaries of the public bearing the costs makes it unlikely, or even impossible, that the beneficiaries will be able to compensate the losers under the policy. Of course, the problem is not with cost-benefit analysis per se. The problem stems from the original choice to use a top-down policy approach that encourages a distributive policy that intentionally spreads costs in a diffuse manner over the country, while providing concentrated benefits to a public located in a local jurisdiction.

Market Incentives

Markets are powerful mechanisms for coordinating human interactions. They permit voluntary transactions in which individuals are able to match their preferences with the goods and services that they consume. In this sense, markets promote the goals of a democratic society. Markets, however, are not panaceas. They do not just appear. As we saw in Chapter 6, they exist within institutional frameworks that are created and sustained by governments.

Moreover, markets—or more specifically, market failures—are the source of many of the policy problems that policy analysts find themselves trying to solve. This means that when trying to determine the precise characteristics of a policy problem, it is often necessary to think hard about how market incentives may be creating or contributing to the underlying policy problem. Thus, a determination of the market forces at work in a particular situation is often an important first step in the process of policy analysis, and it should occur long before cost-benefit analysis.

It is also true, however, that market forces often can be harnessed to try to solve a problem. That is, it may be possible to alleviate a problem by implementing policies that alter market institutions. Thus, the particular policy options that are to be examined in a policy analysis may be identified by thinking creatively about how market incentives may be put to public purposes.

Government Coercion

As we discussed in earlier chapters, public policies virtually always involve the application of some form and degree of government coercion. While this is inevitable, it is also problematical in a democratic society. The use of coercion means that individuals are being compelled to act in ways that are contrary to their preferences. The application of coercion may be for the betterment of society, but it always ought to be strongly justified and never excessively utilized.

In policy analysis, it is thus important to consider carefully policy options based upon the extent and type of coerciveness that may be required. As a policy analyst, this will lead you to examine a policy instrument on the basis of the intrusiveness and government coercion that is involved in the implementation of that policy instrument. Why is this important? As a policy analyst, you have an obligation to consider the implications of your work, not just for particular clients or employers but for society more generally. When you select policy options to subject to a cost-benefit study or to a policy impact study, you should be attuned to the potential implications of the study for the individuals who may be affected by a policy change that you recommend.

Bureaucratic Failure

Government policies often involve government bureaucracies. For this reason, it is necessary to consider the likelihood that the implementation of policies may not be as smooth or trouble-free as advocates of the policies may assume. As we saw in Chapter 10, bureaucracy is a double-edged sword: on the one hand, it is necessary in a modern, complex society; on the other hand, it is rife with opportunities for members of the bureaucracy to pursue goals other than those formally assigned to the organization. The costs of bureaucratic shirking, rent seeking, and goal diversion are the overhead costs of utilizing government bureaucracies.

Too often, studies ignore the above institutional issues. Notice, however, that these issues should be dealt with when the lists of potential costs are being drawn up and monetized and prior to the initiation of the formal policy analysis. These issues should also be considered in impact studies inasmuch as one of the goals of a thoughtful policy analyst should be to identify, in advance, the unintended consequences of the implementation of a policy change so that these consequences can be measured and assessed. Bureaucratic failures are among the most common unintended consequences of public policies, because policies almost always, in some way, rely on bureaucracies for their implementation. This means that careful consideration should be given to minimizing bureaucratic failures. While such failures may be impossible to eliminate, it may be possible to reduce them through creative thinking about the design of policies. Sometimes the solution lies not in trying to eliminate bureaucracies altogether but in relying on bureaucracies that are embedded within polycentric arrangements. In this way, innovation, experimentation, and learning are encouraged.

CONCLUSION

In the end, we are optimistic about the ability of people living in democracies to construct policy solutions that address, if not perfectly, the problems that they encounter in their daily lives. In a society with complex overlays of market institutions, governmental jurisdictions that are small and large and every size in between, and nonprofit organizations, there are numerous possibilities for people to devise solutions to public problems. Indeed, this is one of the things that makes being a student of public policies so interesting. In every community, as in the country as a whole, there are opportunities aplenty for making a difference. The key is a sober mind and an openness to learn from the experiments in public policy that are under way all around us every day.

Note

1. Donald Wittman, *The Myth of Democratic Failure: Why Political Institutions Are Efficient* (Chicago: University of Chicago Press, 1996).

Index

Boldface page numbers indicate pages on which key terms are introduced.